Ella Deloria's *The Buffalo People*

Ella Deloria's
THE BUFFALO PEOPLE

Julian Rice

University of New Mexico Press
Albuquerque

Library of Congress Cataloging-in-Publication Data
Deloria, Ella Cara.
[Buffalo People.   English and Lakota]
Ella Deloria's The Buffalo People / [edited by] Julian Rice.—
1st ed.
p.   cm.
Narrative in both Lakota and English with critical essays by
Julian Rice.
Includes bibliographical references and index.
ISBN 0–8263–1506-2.—ISBN 0–8263–1507-0)pbk.)
1. Dakota Indians—Legends.   2. Dakota Indians—Women.   3. Teton
Indians—Legends.   4. Teton Indians—Women.   5. Lakota dialect—
Texts.   I. Rice, Julian, 1940–   II. Title.
E99.D1D3913   1994
398.2'089975—dc20   93-33519
                                                              CIP
                                                              r94

For Noah

Contents

Preface

This book is the third in a series about a unique and relatively unknown literary figure. Ella Deloria's thousands of manuscript pages in both Lakota and English comprise a remarkable achievement in the creation of a Lakota language literature and provide a model for other bilingual Native American literatures. For information on the circumstances and extent of Deloria's writing, readers should consult the introductions to the first two books: *Deer Women and Elk Men: The Lakota Narratives of Ella Deloria* (Albuquerque: U of New Mexico P, 1992), and *Ella Deloria's Iron Hawk* (Albuquerque: U of New Mexico P, 1993).

In addition, brief biographies by Agnes Picotte appear as an afterword to Deloria's novel *Waterlily* (Lincoln: U of Nebraska P, 1988) and, with Paul N. Pavich, in the introductions to Deloria's *Speaking of Indians* (Vermillion, South Dakota: State Publishing, 1983) and *Dakota Texts* (Vermillion, South Dakota: Dakota Press, 1978). The most complete biography is Janette K. Murray's "Ella Deloria: A Biographical Sketch and Literary Analysis" (doctoral dissertation, University of North Dakota, 1974).

Acknowledgments

Vine Deloria, Jr. granted permission to quote from several unpublished manuscripts by Ella Deloria. From the Boas Collection at the American Philosophical Society in Philadelphia: "Dakota Tales," "Dakota Tales in Colloquial Style," "Dakota Texts from the Minnesota Manuscript," "Dakota Texts from the Sword Manuscript," "Ethnographic and Conversational Texts," "Old Dakota Legends," "Teton Myths" (The George Bushotter Collection). From the Deloria Family Collection at the Dakota Indian Foundation in Chamberlain, South Dakota: "Generation Story" ("The Buffalo People").

Agnes Picotte, Director of the Ella C. Deloria Research Project, at the Dakota Indian Foundation in Chamberlain, South Dakota, assisted my examination of manuscripts from the Deloria Family Collection.

Tapes and transcripts from The South Dakota Oral History Center at the University of South Dakota in Vermillion were obtained with the assistance of its directors, Herbert Hoover and Leonard Brughier.

The South Dakota Historical Society granted permission to quote from the unpublished book, "Camp Circle Society" by Ella Deloria.

Marvene Riis, archivist, facilitated access to the manuscript.

Albert White Hat, Sr. allowed me to see a draft of his Lakota language version of *The Buffalo Woman* by Paul Goble. As mentioned here in chapter 4, Goble and White Hat, Sr. are preparing a bilingual edition of that book.

Ella Deloria's *The Buffalo People*

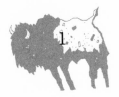

The Many Voices of Ella Deloria

As an ethnologist and a linguist, Ella Deloria collected many stories from the Lakota reservations throughout the 1930s. Unlike even the most prestigious of mythographers, however, she was a native speaker of the language her informants spoke. And unlike other writers of oral narratives from Boas and Benedict through Hymes and Tedlock, Deloria used neither notebook, tape recorder, nor previously transcribed texts to produce her story versions. "The Prairie Dogs" and "The Buffalo People" were synthesized from several tellers but primarily from the noted Makula (Breast, also known as Left Heron, see Walker, *Lakota Myth* 19–21, 101–33). Deloria placed the stories in a manuscript folder entitled "Dakota Tales in Colloquial Style" (see Works Cited). With this term Deloria defined her deliberately unscientific method of foregoing dictation and writing from memory:

> As a sample of colloquial Dakota, this is far from satisfactory, because the tonal inflections, and the facial expressions, the laughter at certain places are not recorded satisfactorily. Obviously too, I can't stand with pencil and paper and record this; the spontaneity would disappear; I must just depend on my

memory, and write it as I remember it, immediately after. That is what I am doing all the time, but that method allows for many slip-ups, and does not give time to finish one paper, with translations, notes and glossary, before something else comes up to be recorded.
("Colloquial Dakota" in "Dakota Ethnographic and Conversational Texts" 8:1, 90–91)

These "slip-ups" suggest that Deloria should be viewed as a literary creator rather than a scrupulous recorder in the Boasian sense. Of the hundreds of stories, autobiographies, speeches, conversations, and proverbs that Deloria set down, all finally come to the page through her memory, imagination, and voice. All of this written material exists in both Lakota and English versions, although in almost every instance Deloria's informants spoke exclusively in Lakota. The stories are therefore as much Deloria's creation as those of Makula or any storyteller who produced "original" versions based on rearranging elements of the tradition—plots of whole stories, interchangeable episodes of character or phrases of different stories, even conventions of pause or pronunciation.

By listening to hundreds of stories, and by reworking them in transcription and translation, Deloria became as imbued with the narrative tradition as any of its oral practitioners. She spent an apprenticeship polishing and translating the thousand-page George Bushotter manuscript and other writings by George Sword in Lakota, as well as Santee texts in Dakota collected by the Pond brothers and Stephen R. Riggs (see Works Cited). But the stories she produced in "colloquial style," first in relatively short form for her collection *Dakota Texts*, and later in longer, elaborate versions, such as those published here and in the previous volume in this series, *Ella Deloria's Iron Hawk*, represent her unique achievement as a gifted storyteller adapting her art to written form.

Deloria's translations convey most of a story's meaning and structure, but of course the Lakota versions supply additional nuances of tone and cultural significance. The "colloquial style" method suggests that Deloria's own voice and vision necessarily shaped and unified the stories. If so, her literary personality does not conform to the "unequivocally negative stance toward warfare" or the "exceptional adherence . . . to the spirit and letter of kinship law" referred to by Raymond J. DeMallie in his afterword to Deloria's novel *Waterlily* (242). Written in the 1940s for an assumed non-Indian, non-scholarly audience, *Waterlily* may have lessened the societal prestige arising from war, though this is a matter of interpretation, (see *Waterlily* 85–91), but few would agree that Deloria exaggerated the importance of kinship in Lakota life. As for violence, one has only to randomly examine the hundreds of unpublished manuscripts to observe her unedited inclusion of every kind of human experience. By way of introduction to this volume, and with the hope that other scholars will bring out more of the work Deloria meant to publish, I will discuss three stories that defer neither to Christian moral strictures nor to romantic sensibilities. (Complete texts appear in Chapter 2.)

These stories illustrate Deloria's remarkable ability to subordinate her own voice to that of different narrators. All three concern women in dangerous situations, but the three narrative *personae* are so distinct that the actual narrator, Deloria herself, seems to disappear. "The Prairie Dogs" and "The Buffalo People" represent the myth genre of Lakota narratives, tales of "a remote past" and "a different age" (see Deloria, *Dakota Texts* ix). These stories, called *ohunkakan,* include culture hero stories, trickster tales, and, as in the examples printed here, tales of origin in the early days of the world. Stories in the other major genre, *wicowoyake,* tell of events that actually occurred. Some *wicowoyake* take place in the distant past and include supernatural events, while others occur in historial time. "A Sioux Captive Rescued by his Wife," "Stake Carriers," and "A Woman Captive and her Baby" report incidents that an eighty-five year-old narrator like Makula might have personally remembered (see Rice, *Ella Deloria's Iron Hawk* 3). Deloria does not name the original narrators of these stories, however, and the variations on the first two suggest that in each case the narrator adapts a plot line to reflect on cultural values. In this kind of story history often becomes myth, but not necessarily the same myth each time it is told. In "Sioux Captive" the heroic woman becomes a perfect balance of love and courage. In "Stake Carriers" she becomes an epitome of efficient and merciless action. In "A Woman Captive and Her Baby" she personifies the will to live in the face of hopelessness.

The frame of each story immediately establishes the teller's tone. "Sioux Captive" comes from a man who calls Deloria "Tanḱśi" 'Younger Sister,' because he had married the widow of a man that called her brother, Vine Deloria, Sr., "Misun" 'Younger Brother' in the complex Lakota way of determining relationships. He presents the story as a gift for a relative rather than as information for an investigator:

> Tanḱśi, woyaḱapi iyagnin s'a keyapi canḱe lecala Blo-oketa wai k'un el heca anuġoptan waun yunkan le oyaḱapi nawaḣ'un ca eya tanyan enaḣtakamic'ila le wagli ye lo.

> My younger sister, they tell me you are on the lookout for stories right along, so this last time I was at Potato Creek I kept my ears open and heard this legend which I think I have done a good job of stamping on my mind; and I have returned. (unit 1)

The frame also initiates the narrator's emotional style, when he makes the Lakota captive's suffering palpable rather than stoic. He describes him vertically spread-eagled on crossed beams of wood with the comment, "ihanblaṕśice s'e kuwapi" 'they treated him as in a nightmare' (unit 3). In a footnote Deloria adds that the torture consisted of depriving the victim of food and drink and exposing him to the ridicule of the crowd (note c). The narrator's attitude toward this act is far from the fatalistic acceptance of the fortunes of war implied in "Stake Carriers." Such behavior appears to horrify him, and he does not want Deloria to think that he condones it: "tunweni miye iśta un heca wanżi wanblakeśni" 'I myself have never seen such a thing' (unit 4). The note of repulsion continues as he mentions that the Crow captors danced around the Lakota man incessantly, stopping only when they "watuḱa it'api" 'were dead tired' (unit 7). Six old men, presumably more prone to sleep on watch, are left to guard him, thus setting the stage for the story's central act, the rescue by his wife.

Throughout, the narrator emphasizes the loyalty between relatives that began when he presented the story to his "younger sister" (unit 1). He introduces the story's heroine as a wife who "tokeḣci tehila" 'must have thought everything of' her husband (unit 8). Beyond this explicit statement of her deep love, the woman's personal qualities begin to emerge in the mention of her taking two war horses with her to the Crow camp (unit 9). Careful, precise, and prepared in everything she does, she takes few chances, but her selection of the swift war horses that women rarely rode suggests her firm resolve to risk her life for her husband.

This combination of intense feeling and controlled, careful action emerges in every move she makes. Upon arriving at the enemy camp, she ties her horses "oškokpa mahel wanyankaukteśni" 'in a depression where they would not be seen,' and then "tokeśke ecun kinhan hocoka kin itimahel iyayinkta hecinhan he iyukcan" 'thought of a way of entering the enemy camp' undetected (unit 10). She goes in at twilight, a time of minimal visibility but still enough for her to discern her husband's whereabouts. Her disguise as a woman carrying a piece of rotting wood like a baby under her blanket again reveals her attention to technique, as well as the disparity between a woman's usual protected security and this woman's seemingly fragile power to protect her husband and herself. In the context of this telling their mortality seems imminent in the "canpunpun" 'rotting wood' body of the child (unit 11). But the narrator gradually uses the woman's self-admitted vulnerability to indicate her powers of concentration and will. She starts to search the camp in the precise manner of a mother soothing her child to sleep (unit 12). In addition to describing her as "iwayupiya ecun" 'managing skillfully' to do this so that "atayaś ablezapiśni" 'she was not noticed at all,' the narrator interjects his own emotional response to her action: "Lila ohitika nacece" 'How brave she must have been' (unit 13).

He goes on to describe how she learns where her husband lies by walking around the whole circle of tipis without stopping until she returns to her starting point (units 14–15). On this circuit she had passed the large tipi in the center where her emaciated husband was tied. She had seen enough to thoroughly test her self-control. The narrator's details again evoke the woman's feelings and suggest his condemnation of the torture. The husband wore only a breech cloth, and around his "nige oh'ap" 'caved-in stomach' his ribs "yugwezap s'e" 'stood out like ridges' (unit 19). His condition implies that it will be difficult for him to move, even if she succeeds in freeing him.

The narrator also refers again to this particular woman's impelling energy of love, effectively directed by precise thought: "unśikila un ceya iyaya tka ca tokecela oigluspe" 'she almost cried out for pity, but she restrained herself' (unit 20). Her problem-solving mind consistently quells panic and directs her effectively to the task at hand, regardless of the circumstances: "Inahma s'e tokeske yuwipi kin ko ables nazin" 'Unnoticed she stood observing just how he was tied on' (unit 21). Then she returns to the horses, prepares them for flight, and obtains a knife "wikan kin hena wakicipsakinkta" 'suitable for cutting the ropes' (unit 22).

Once again her disguise effectively brings her to the prisoner's tipi, while narratively reiterating the extraordinary courage of one raised to soothe children now enacting a warrior's role of rescue. She is said to exemplify "wacin tanka" 'patience' and "cante t'inze" 'bravery' (unit 25), literally "great mind" and "strong heart," that is, she draws upon all of her resources to preserve her husband's life. But the narrator does not assert that she was without fear. He emphasizes her control of fear more than her lack of it:

> Tuwa aiyoka yunkanś hecinkte: "Le tuwehci ungna wimayunga eśa kinhan Kangi wicaśa iwayeśni kin slolyinkte," ecin, na un canl-wankakte'.
> Ho, eyaś winyan kin le hecin naceca tka iyowinyeśni iyute'. Na hehanl wacin tanka kepe kin he lecel wake': Ito inahni keś takunl ciścila eśa iyukcanśni ecun kinhan un oyuspaunkta tka'.

> Anyone less might have feared, "If anyone should happen to run into me and question me, they will know I am not a Crow, and then—" and such a thought might have frightened one.
> But if this woman entertained such fears, she did not give way to them; trying anyway.
> And by patience I mean this. Had she been in too much haste she might have blundered in some small detail, and thus been apprehended. (units 26–28)

"Anyone less" might not have feared more but would have been unable to look past the fears to the actions she had to perform.

The narrator praises her concentration with the detail that she did not get tired (unit 29), as she waited for absolute quiet in the sleeping camp. When she finally enters the tipi, the elderly guards are asleep. Her first whispered word to her husband has the tenderness of the relational term. The message that follows expresses a tone of command not usually taken by a wife but appropriate again to the unusual qualities that have been shown in this particular wife: "Wicahca, le miye ca cihiyowahi ye. Wacinksap kic'un na hotaninic'iyeśni, eya'" 'Husband, it is I who am come for you. Keep your wits about you. Don't make any sound' (unit 31). The narrator's next words express the full emergence of the masculine side of her character, a temporary metamorphosis, fully justified by the situation:

Heyin na hena yankau kin cokaya miwakan wan maka pahli owotanlahcin han canke yuslotin na un wicahcala śakpepi k'un iyuhahcin pa-wicakakse'. Na wawicaśpa ca wicapehin śakpe ataya aki śke'.

Then she took up a sword which stood upright there, with the point planted deep into the earth, and with it she cut off the heads of all the old men there. Then she scalped them, all six of them, and took their scalps home. (units 32–33)

After this ultimately unaccustomed but absolutely essential act of ensuring their escape, the narrator allows her control to slip slightly, as she cuts the ropes around her husband "cancan s'e" 'in mad haste' (unit 34). Almost immediately, however, she again assumes her deliberate rhythm, as she half drags her weakened husband to the horses, puts him on one, and sends him off for home. But she herself, playing the invasion game as if she were an accomplished spy, returns to make one more round of the camp with the rotting wood baby to make sure that everyone, as Deloria deftly puts it, is "atayaś t'api" 'dead in sleep' before she finally turns to catch up with her husband.

The narrator then frames the story's conclusion with a correction: the woman did not scalp the guards until her final return to check the camp: "he icimagnuni" 'I was confused on that point' (unit 37). This detail helps to connect the narrator to his protagonist as one who attends precisely to an act of restoration. It also adds another level of emotion to the intensely controlled heroine. When her husband's life is all but assured, she finally gives way to rage against those who have harmed him. While the woman's feeling is natural under the circumstances, the narrator's final reflection returns to his unifying theme. The woman's strength and that of the Lakota kinship system depends on absolute love and mutual sacrifice: "Ho, he winyan kin ihaṅkeya hingnaku teḣila na wica iyecel oḣ'an śke'" 'That woman, because of the deed she accomplished, which was the kind that only men are able to do, takes first place as loving her husband' (unit 38).

The second story, "Stake Carriers," praises the woman more for her bravery than for the balance between bravery and love idealized in "Sioux Captive." The voice that comes through Deloria this time is more formal, perhaps because it is not that of an older brother. This narrator's primary purpose is to define and praise the bravery of the Lakota people. His first line also initiates a degree of underlying anger: "Lakota oyate, le waśicu kin Su eyapi kin heca eya zuya aya ke'" 'Some Indians, this kind the white men call Sioux, were on the warpath' (unit 1). Speaking in the early reservation period, when it was difficult for the Lakota to attain honor, the narrator presents a description of the stake carrier, an especially prestigious rank in each warrior society. If a war party had to retreat, the stake carrier stood and fought tied to a stake planted in the ground, until the rest had escaped (see Wissler, "Societies" 43–45). Although Deloria mentions that the narrator was too young to have fought in this way, he probably derived his technical details from someone who had seen the battle action and the implements he describes (see 42n). The rope spans four times the length of a man's outstretched arms; the stake measures about a foot, and it is sharpened and painted red; when the enemy attack begins, the retreating stake carriers give some bear cries for courage (see Deloria, *Dakota Texts* 228n) before they turn to fight; during the fight they circle on a radius no longer than the rope that ties them (units 4–6).

This is the frame of the story. The narrator presents himself as professionally informed on war and interested on this occasion in reporting a deed of exceptional bravery. One of his two stake carriers is surrounded by the Crow and captured. Though the story will be primarily about his wife's act of rescue, the beginning makes much more of the husband's courage than "Sioux Captive." The stake carrier's words to his fellow warriors reflect the tradition of establishing reputation on the basis of witnessed reports: "Ho po, wanżiħcin ni tiyata yakipi kinhan owotanla woyaka po" 'Now, if at least one of you should get home alive, see to it that you report events accurately' (unit 9).

The husband is attentive to the people's need to have their confidence renewed by stories of courage. His wife, however, seems to need little inspiration. Her pragmatic efficiency differs from the emotional control of the woman in the first story. Instead of taking two swift war horses for the escape, she simply sets out on horseback for the Crow camp (unit 13). The narrator describes her attitude as being like that of an experienced warrior. She does not stop to plan her actions but confidently improvises as she goes along. She starts by going directly to the battleground. From there she tracks the Crow party to its camp. Once there she cleverly proceeds to seize every opportunity to deceive, as the occasion demands. Unlike the heroine of "Sioux Captive," the woman reveals little disparity between her disguise as a nurturing mother and her behavior as a warrior. At all times she is primarily an avenger. The narrator does not mention the fear she may have felt and takes her bravery for granted in line with the opening assumption of courage in "those Indians the White men call Sioux" (unit 1).

Before entering the tipi where her husband is guarded by the old men, the woman expresses virtual disdain for both the dangers of the situation and for any thought that a woman may not be suited for the job she is about to do: "Canke wana hokśicala-kaġapi un he tiyopa el owanżi eunpi na 'Lena owanżi ħpaya ye, niyate iwacukte,' eya ke'" 'So she carefully laid the doll at the doorway, and said, "Lie still here, while I take your father away"' (unit 22). After entering the tipi and cutting the ropes, she neither addresses him as husband, warns him to be alert, nor shows any concern for his condition. In "Sioux Captive" the woman had cut her husband's ropes "in mad haste." Here she is emotionless, seemingly intent only on preserving his honor as a warrior: "'Oyakihi hecinhan wicaśa kin le wanżiħcin waśpa ye,' eya" '"If you can possibly do so, scalp at least one of these," she said' (unit 24).

When he is too weak to try, she instantly kills the guards, not by cutting off their heads, as in the first story, but by cutting their throats in one unhesitating sweep down the line of sleeping men and without stopping to take scalps (unit 25). On the way out she stops to address her doll: "Lena cinkś lipaya ye, niyate tehanl ewegnakin na hehanl cigliyo-waukte" 'Lie right here where you are, son, while I take and leave your father far from here; and then I shall come after you' (unit 26). The narrator personally takes up this disdain of danger when, without attributing the thought to the woman, he has her "hektakiya hokśicala kin gliyoi" 'go back after her doll' (unit 27) once she has dragged her husband from the camp. The doll again accentuates the difference between a woman's conventional role and this woman's action. Instead of feeding the child, she takes the enemy's food and two of his horses for the return trip (unit 29). Since the horses are tethered when she comes upon them, they are war horses or buffalo runners kept apart from the tribal herd.

The woman's emotions are never articulated in all these actions. If anything, she seems to completely transcend emotion, unless she is thought to be bolstering her own courage by reassuring her doll. Presumably her feelings toward her husband are tender and protective, though they are not stated as such. Perhaps she refrains from taking scalps to avoid usurping her husband's honor. In any case her character and the voice that conveys it differ significantly from those in "Sioux Captive." The first narrator does not glorify war and emphasizes that he has never seen a captive tortured. The second narrator speaks of a stake carrier's implements as if he had seen or used them. In both stories Deloria projects herself into two male perceptions of a woman's response to danger. And she sustains the narrators' *personae* right through the concluding frames.

The first narrator speaks carefully and corrects his own memory lapse at the end. The second narrator has no second thoughts and presents a heroine who never hesitates. Every circumstance seems to play into her hands, because she creatively takes advantage of unanticipated situations. In the end she is celebrated not as one who took "first place in loving her husband" but as one who showed absolutely no fear in the Crow camp. Upon their arrival the people hold a victory dance "on a big scale" and name the woman "Canpunpun Hunku" 'Rotting Wood's Mother' (unit 32). They name the husband "Mnihuha-śina In" 'Wearer of a Cloth Blanket,' because his wife wrapped him in a shawl after she cut him loose (unit 33). The narrator adds two comments to frame the story. First he did not know exactly what kind of shawl she used (unit 34). This scrupulous attention to fact resembles *waktoglaka* (kill talks) that report battlefield exploits, thereby implying that he has reported the woman's deed accurately, as if she were a warrior. Then he adds that the husband's receiving a name from his wife's deed did not diminish his own prowess as a warrior: "ho, na hetanhan taopi k'un he ohakap ake lila okicize el wohitika keyapi'" 'It is said that after that, this one who was wounded, later took part again in many fights, and he was always fearful and brave' (unit 34). In the end the second story speaks to the invincibility of the Lakota people, misconceived as well as misnamed by those who call them "Sioux" (unit 1).

The Lakota language version of each story communicates Deloria's skill in literarily impersonating the voices she heard. The Lakota stories employ the quotative endings "śke'," "keyapi'," and "ke'," for 'they say' or 'it is said' (see Rice, *Deer Women and Elk Men* 52–54). Stories told as myths or as relatively formal versions of true stories use one or a combination of all three of the endings to mark every significant pause. The words also act as a verifying refrain. The narrator conventionally reports what "they say." He does not presume to speak independently. Deloria makes the pause conclusively definite with a final glottal stop, as in "keyapi'" 'they say'; the same word would not take the glottal stop if a group of characters within the story spoke of a fictional or historical event.

"Sioux Captive" begins informally with the narrator's presentation of the story to his younger sister. Since the story proper has not yet begun, his opening words are not followed by a quotative ending (unit 1). But then the narrator signals the beginning of his story with both "keyapi'" and "śke'" in close proximity: "He lecetu *keyapi'*: Wicaśa wan Kanġi-wicaśa wayaka yuzapi *śke'*" 'It was like this, they say. A man was captured by the Crow, and held prisoner [they say]' (unit 2). Thereafter he uses "śke'" only to indicate particular points of emphasis, such as the man's capture (unit 2), his being tied outstretched (unit 3), and his being tortured by the dancing enemy (unit 6). Otherwise the narrator pauses by concluding a sentence with the glottal stop alone, without "śke'," "ke'," or "keyapi'":

> K'eyaś wana hanhepi tonakel iwakcipi kin un ikiwinkcekcepe laka ecala s'eś wawanyaka kin akiyagle'. Tuktel tuweni kaiyap ihinkteśni iyecelya opiic'iyin na wana lila hantehan hanl ake canpunpun k'un he yuha na hokśikigna itutuya s'e omanihe'.

> But since this war dancing had been kept up now several nights, the spectators left comparatively early. She moved in such a way as not to bump anyone face to face, and when it was very late at night, she once more went about, aimlessly, as it were, singing to the "babe" of rotting wood (unit 23).

This irregular alternation of voiced pauses and pauses marked only by a glottal stop continues throughout the story. Deloria is not recording the pauses of any particular performance in the manner of Tedlock but simply pausing spontaneously in her own imagined rendition, as any writer supplies commas or periods. In Lakota glottal stops in storytelling are part of narrative technique. Deloria uses them in "Sioux Captive" wherever her "voice" naturally comes to rest. The narrator uses "śke'" conventionally to end the story proper when he says the woman and her husband set out for home (unit 36), but uses only the glottal stop when he parenthetically adds that the woman went back for the scalps rather than taking them after she killed the guards (unit 37). Then in his final summation, he strengthens his praise for the heroine by adding "śke'" for an emphatic close: "Ho, he winyan kin ihankeya hingnaku tehila na wica iyecel oh'an *śke'*" 'That woman, because of the deed she accomplished, which was the kind that only men are able to do, takes first place in loving her husband [they say]' (unit 38).

In a letter to Franz Boas of 29 August 1937, Deloria indicates that glottal stops alone should conclude narrative sentences only when the speaker recounts personal experience, and that in all other instances he or she should employ the quotatives *śke'*, *keyapi'*, or *ke'*. In "Stake Carriers" Deloria adheres strictly to this rule (see 44n). But she either wrote "Sioux Captive" before the letter to Boas, or she may have changed her mind after the letter and then written "Sioux Captive" as it appears here. Throughout her work she uses *ske'* in most instances to break a sequence of *ke'* endings. In "A Sioux Captive" the glottal stop replaces *ke'*, while *ske'*, as usual, provides emphasis (see Correspondence with Franz Boas, American Philosophical Society, B.B. 61).

The narrator of "Stake Carriers" is as consistent in his use of "*ke'*" as his male stake carrier is constant in his refusal to retreat and his female rescuer is even tempered in assuming a disguise, killing her husband's guards, and stealing horses for their escape. He begins the story with two strong "*ke'*" endings: "Lakota oyate, le wasicu kin Su eyapi kin heca eya zuya aya *ke'*. Ho, wana anpetu wikcemnawahecetuya heyata zuya unpi *ke'*" 'Some Indians, this kind that white men call Sioux, were on the warpath [they say]. By the time of this story, they had been out perhaps about ten days [they say]' (units 1–2). Then he drops the "*ke'*" endings but uses glottal stops to define the stake carrier (units 3–5). However, once he returns to the story proper every pause is spoken as "*ke'*." His relationship to Deloria is less personal, and he does not reveal emotion toward the events he describes.

The narrator of "Sioux Captive," on the other hand, felt compelled to say that he had personally never witnessed a captive being tortured. Perhaps he goes on to specify his female heroine's deep love for her husband because he wants to justify the killing of the guards. By using "*ske'*" for special emphasis, the first narrator indicates that the rescuer's behavior was unusual for a woman, as was her reincarnation as a warrior, riding a fast horse out of camp and leading another behind: "Hiyoya *ske'*. Sunk-luzahan, ikicize kin heca nunp iwicacu na unma akanyankin na unma is kaska yus ya *ske'*" 'She went after him [they say]. She took two war horses and rode one and led the other by a rope [they say]' (unit 9). These two uses of "*ske'*" in close proximity are preceded by three pauses where only the glottal stop is used (units 7–8), and followed by twenty-one pauses where again, with the exception of two "*ke'*" endings (units 11 and 12), only the glottal stop is used (units 10 and 13–32).

"*Ske'*" returns to underline the shock value of the woman's scalp-taking near the end. The narrator saves it only for this particularly unwomanly act, not even applying it to her beheading of the guards in the preceding sentence: "Na wawicaśpa ca wicapehin śakṗe ataya akin *śke'*" 'Then she scalped them, all six of them and took their scalps home [they say]' (unit 33). Thereafter, as mentioned, "śke'" concludes the story proper and finalizes the narrator's praise of marital devotion (unit 38). In "Stake Carriers" the other narrator also offers praise but directs it toward the whole Lakota people, confirming their reputation as a warrior nation. The consistency of "ke'" throughout provides an undertone of steady concentration that fits the woman's persistence, and the number of syllables between each pause is relatively uniform.

Like his emotions, the "Sioux Captive" narrator's sentences are more varied. He often uses short sentences for dramatic effect. After a long sentence detailing how the captive's arms and legs were bound spread-eagled with his feet just above the ground, the narrator drives home a succinct summation of the man's plight: "Hecunpi na ohomni iwakcipi na yuḱakiżapi śke'" 'Then the enemy stage a victory dance around it, and the captive is tortured [they say]' (unit 6). More longer sentences follow to match the sense of ordeal, as the enemies are said to dance until they are tired (unit 7). From here the sentences begin to shorten, building intensity and setting the stage for the entrance of the woman who "tokeḣci teḣila nacece" 'must have loved her husband very much' (unit 8). The narrator now implies the rarity of her act and the depth of her love by compressing its effect in a two word sentence: "Hiyoya śke'" 'She set out after him [they say]' (unit 9). The following image of her leading a second war horse (unit 9) carries through the sense of exceptionality. This image of departure would have been admirable but expected in a man. Here it creates special interest and excitement.

The "Stake Carriers" narrator, however, sees no unusual drama in a Lakota woman setting out to rescue her husband. The narrator simply describes the report of the stake carrier's capture, and without indicating explicitly how the woman felt, sets her on her way: "Yunkan le taopi k'un he tawicu wan oḱileya ke'. Śunkawakan wan aḱanyankin na" 'And behold, the wounded one had a wife who set out to look for him. She went on horseback' (unit 13). Almost every sentence is of approximately the same length. The only variation occurs naturally in differentiating dialogue from action and does not serve to intensify dramatic effect (see unit 24). Similarly, the woman's calm words to her doll on leaving the tipi after she has cut the throats of the four men, need little rhetorical flourish to be unforgettable (unit 12).

While the first narrator has the woman using her mind to control anger and fear, the second narrator implies that the Lakota have always considered enemies and suffering to be inevitable, and that it is their nature to do what is necessary to survive. Neither woman goes on to be a warrior. The first narrator tells us, wasn't this a wonderful woman? She "takes first place" in loving her husband. The second narrator says that this woman did only what many more will do. She and her husband took it in stride and went on with their lives. Her subsequent experience goes unrecorded. He later "took part in many fights" (unit 34). The story suggests that on occasion any woman might be as "fearful and brave" as this man constantly remained. Overall, the second narrator seems to be especially concerned to remind the listeners that Lakota men and women cannot be defeated.

Throughout both narratives, of course, we as readers hear only the interpretive voice of Ella Deloria. Unlike Tedlock she had no tape recorded original. Unlike Hymes she had no ur-text to rearrange. Ultimately, in both cases *she* is the storyteller in the same way a novelist might imagine characters speaking like real people he or she had known or overheard. In these and countless other stories Deloria's personality does not color the narratives she writes. These two stories are only a few of those that contradict generalized assumptions of her aversion to violence or overemphasis on kinship.

While ethnographic explanation enhances comprehension of "The Prairie Dogs" or "The Buffalo People," any sensitive reader should be able to grasp the import of the rescue stories. The narrator of "Stake Carriers" defines a stake carrier in order to introduce the idea of bravery, but otherwise little specific cultural knowledge is necessary. A third story, "A Woman Captive and Her Baby," also requires little background in the ethnography to be understood by modern readers. As I have suggested, "Stake Carriers" has a historical dimension in reasserting the virtues of the people "That white men call Sioux" (unit 1). "A Woman Captive" presents another image of tribal endurance in the arduous escape of a Lakota woman from her captivity "in the west" (unit 1). However, the narrator does not name the enemy or refer to the white man, as "Stake Carriers" does. The story may simply show that life can be hard for any nation or individual in any time or place. This introduction concludes with a discussion of "A Woman Captive" to exhibit still another of Ella Deloria's narrative voices, and to show as simply and untechnically as possible that reading a Deloria story in Lakota has certain aesthetic advantages over reading it in English.

"A Woman Captive" has no introduction, though it does have a brief conclusion outside of the story proper. It declares itself as a legend, rather than a historical account of recent memory, by ending its first three statements with the quotative "śke'" 'they say' (units 1–2). These sentences say that a woman captured by an enemy to the west married there; that after being treated badly by them for a long time she became obsessed with escape; that she had two children, one infant and one who, though older, was still too small to survive the journey, and so, crying and kissing him repeatedly she resolved to leave him behind. From this point on "śke'" reappears, as is common in Deloria, only to highlight emphatic points in the action (see Rice, *Deer Women and Elk Men* 53–56 and "Narrative Styles" 284–89). Pauses hereafter are usually signaled by a glottal stop after the concluding words of each section, as in "ikopeśniyan ena *ayuśtan'*" 'she was not worried to leave' (unit 3).

The opening sequence also introduces another aspect of verbal technique that the English translation does not preserve. This woman is distinctly characterized by her tendency to think everything out as thoroughly as she can. The narrator's description accordingly proceeds in sequences linked by various Lakota words of logical causation. The narrator says the woman suffered a great deal in captivity, "kin un" 'therefore' at last she grew tired of it and planned her escape (unit 1). In the next sentence, she has to admit that her older child is too small to make the journey, "kin un" 'therefore' she wept and kissed him goodbye (unit 2). Next, she makes herself feel better by remembering that her mother-in-law loves the child greatly, "canke" 'therefore' he will grow up in that tribe without abuse (unit 3), and "kin un" 'therefore' she had no qualms about leaving him behind (unit 3).

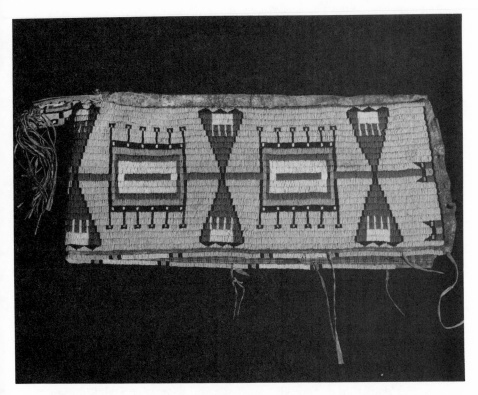

Baby Carrier. From *Vestiges of a Proud Nation: The Ogden B. Read Northern Plains Indian Collection*, ed. Glenn B. Markoe. Courtesy of the Rober Hull Fleming Museum (1881.3.30).

She proceeds to watch carefully for a chance to depart unnoticed, and "kin un" 'therefore' she made thorough preparations (unit 4). She put by food for herself, but her baby was still nursing, "canke" 'therefore' minimal provisions seemed sufficient (unit 5). All of these reasoned conclusions occur in Deloria's first five units. The word "kecin" 'she thought' is similarly repeated near the beginning to establish her character and to set up the unpredictable reversals that anyone's life holds in store. The woman "ognayan kecin" 'thinks about' the probable future of her son among his father's people (unit 3). She "kecin" 'thinks' about how to ready herself for her trip (unit 4). She also has a tendency to focus exclusively on certain thoughts. This is both a strength and a weakness. It does not prepare her for unexpected contradictions, but it is part of her innate perseverance and fortitude. When she contemplates escape, she thinks "ece" 'only' of that (unit 1), and when she actually begins to travel, she plans to go "wiohinyanpatakiya ece" 'only toward the east' (unit 6). "Ḱecin" and "ece" recur later at appropriate points.

The woman's movement then gradually slips away from certainty. Initially she had seen to everything, from mentally providing for the child she leaves behind to physically providing for herself and her baby. The narrator again bolsters security by employing terms of rational thought. He begins by making the woman's progress smooth and uncomplicated in a short direct statement, intensified by "ke'" 'they say,' a less emphatic form of "śke'": "Otohanyan makiyekiya *ke'*" 'For a time she knew the land [they say]' The next phrase suggests that there is no reason not to be optimistic, and that an intelligent plan is producing results: "hecel oyate kin iglaka-omanipi s'a *kin un*" 'She had travelled with the tribe all over that region on camping trips [and therefore that was why]' (unit 7).

As soon as the woman leaves the familiar landscape, however, words of cause and effect and demarcated endings disappear (units 7–9). First, she becomes entirely lost. At the end of the next day's walking, she comes upon the camp she had made the night before (unit 9). At this point rational expectation can produce only despair' "canke" 'therefore' she sits down and weeps (unit 9). But then without a break in the sentence the narrator illuminates the story's manifest virtue: "yankin na ceyhan na ake ya *ke'*" 'she sat down to weep before going on [they say]' (unit 9). This "going on" is the trait most worthy of notice in the woman, in the Lakota people, and in human nature. Appropriately then, the narrator stops the action momentarily with "ke'." "Śke'" would have been too strong at this point, since the forward momentum of the woman's spirit should also come through.

Gradually, the woman loses everything but this instinct to live. She runs out of food; she has no weapons; she has a baby to nurse and protect. She grows so weak she can only stagger, but she continues on, not even stopping at night (units 10–11). Neither "śke'" or "ke'" punctuates this steady weakening, and the relatively long sentences reflect a sense of interminable ordeal. A sudden change in phrasing forecasts imminent tragedy when she enters an ominous area of gigantic rocks and dark-leaved vegetation (unit 12). Now, for the first time since unit 2, the narrator signals a change, as if a new story were about to start with the short phrase: "Iǵuǵa tankinkinyan wan egna ku śke'" 'She came to a region where great rocks of brimstone abounded [they say]' (unit 12). "Śke'," used for the first time since the story's third sentence, suggests this new beginning. The immediate future does not promise to be happy for the woman, but then no "true story" can be second guessed. It can only be lived through. Logic, however, would certainly dictate despair in this setting. The rocks are huge and the leaves are dark, "canke wohankokipeya ececa" '[therefore they] looked most foreboding' (unit 12).

Once again the woman has no choice but to keep walking, to see what life brings her. As she comes around a rock, suddenly she is brought up short by the sight of a war party roasting buffalo ribs around a fire (unit 14). The narrator does not remind us that she is starving; nor does he need to reiterate that she is at the same time a very careful person. The detail that the men are enjoying the food accents the temptation she must have felt to simply announce herself. But the ordeal of starving for safety as well as for food will worsen before it improves. The narrator uses "ke'" rather than "śke'" to stop what little momentum she retains and to paralyze her with doubt: "kaiyap iwicahan ke'" 'she suddenly came upon them [they say]' (unit 13).

Accordingly, words of doubt temporarily torture and prevail: "wanyakapi kinhan" if they see her, and "hena tokapi hecinhan," if they think she is an enemy, they will kill her (unit 15). "Inahni nakipinkta," she would run away, but "haphap hingle kinhan" if she makes the leaves rustle, and "anawicaslata s'e wacinpi kinhan," if they think she is an enemy scout, they will shoot at her and kill her (unit 16). The "hecela" only probable outcome she can envision at this point is a return to captivity (unit 15). And so left with no escape and no defense, and enough strength only to keep down panic, the woman stands frozen (unit 17). Then suddenly, a naturally caused logical event seems to bring disaster. Because the woman is starving, her milk is bad. The narrator underlines the "of course" aspect of impending crisis with another "therefore" word: "ohinni locinla canke t'ehowaya iyaye'" 'the infant in her arms let out a great cry, because the poor thing was hungry [he was always hungry, therefore he cried]' (unit 17).

The result of this shock, however, is not only improbable, it is deliciously comic in light of the expected behavior of Plains warriors, and in its drastic reversal of the story's heretofore grim tone. The six men, "seca ohitiya yankapi" 'looking so formidable as they sat,' answer the baby with "Haṅtapo!" 'Run!' and vanish in a second, never to return. But true to form the woman does not count her blessings too soon. And the narrator does not allow his voice to come to rest with "ṡke'" until the woman has waited long enough to feel that the men will not return. Then after she has availed herself of the food they dropped while they fled, and is comfortably seated at their fire, the language of certainty returns: "*canke* ena wih'an *ṡke'*" 'so [therefore] now she found herself having her fill of good things [they say]' (unit 19).

This "ṡke'" marks both the end of the woman's long ordeal and the beginning of the narrative's final resolution. The last five units suggest alternate outcomes, reminding the reader that in the end one must live courageously within the limits of one's own story. The woman eventually learns that the men were Lakota, but "oyate etanhanpi *hecinhan* slolyeṡni," she did not know of *what* band (unit 20). "Hecapi slolya yunkanṡ el wicaikta *tka'*" *if* she had known they were her tribesmen, she would have gone directly to them (unit 19). Even later she never found out exactly who they were: "Iṡtecapi *sece*" '*Perhaps* they were ashamed' (unit 20).

The narrator then imagines the uncertainty of the men, while refraining from judging their fears. "Ṫunweya ca hokṡicala kunṡ ceye *seca* ḱecinpi *nacece*" '*Perhaps* it was a spy, crying like a baby, they *might* have thought' (unit 21). "*Naiṡ* wanaġi ḱecinpi *sece*" '*Or else* a ghost [probably]' (unit 21). "*K'eyaṡ tohunweni* ek'eṡ he awicakeya wakaneża ca hel makoṡkanl ceya ḱecinpiṡni" 'but *never probably* did they think it was a real baby in that deserted place' (unit 21). The narrator reintroduces a word of rational control, "ḱecinpi" 'they thought,' only to overwhelm it with a greater number of words that link the indefinite to fear, "hecinhan" 'if then,' "sece" 'maybe, possibly, probably' (three times), "nacece" 'perhaps' (units 20–21).

The inappropriate questions of the men sum up the comic effect of the story and its message. Courage has to do with enduring the indefinite. The woman has this courage. The men do not. The narrator had not begun outside the story in a framing statement of his deeper purpose. Now at the end his few remaining comments do not provide closure. Briefly, however, the woman's path and the narrator's words are unambiguously marked, both by the metaphor of footprints and the story's final "śke'": "Pilayapika wiohinyanpatakiya oye otawicapin na ecel He-Sapa kin el glihunni *śke'*" 'They did her this kindness; by leaving tracks she could follow eastward always till she reached the Black Hills [they say]' (unit 22). Nevertheless, by this time in the story the sense of approaching conclusion can only suggest that any particular safe arrival can only precede further ordeal.

The significance of this happily-and-unhappily-ever-after ending may lie in the number of moccasins the woman wore out (unit 23). Four suggests that her journey has universal application as a complete cycle. Like a ceremony involving sacrifice and conducted in patterns of four, the woman's deprivation ends only to be suffered again by someone else. In his final words the narrator clarifies the place of stories in the oral tradition and of individual persons in the group. Although the woman's specific identity is indefinite, her Lakota identity is clear. While any person's individual life may be unpredictable, the collective virtue of the tribe, perhaps of humanity in general, remains constant. At the beginning the woman had thought *only* of how she could bring happiness to herself and her children (units 1–6). At the end the storyteller reflects only on the courage that endures unhappiness, and on the tragicomic unpredictability of individual fate. The heroine here has no supernatural guides, and no heroic relatives come to her rescue. She exemplifies quiet fortitude rather than the aggressive courage of the warrior women in "Sioux Captive" and "Stake Carriers." But she is equally admirable, and her determination may be more frequently emulated in everyday life.

These three stories begin in part to demonstrate the versatility of Ella Deloria. The stories to follow, "The Prairie Dogs" and "The Buffalo People" (chapters 2, 3, and 4) resemble each other in style, perhaps because they both come from the same storyteller, Makula. In these stories Deloria acts as an ethnographer as well as an artist, informing the readers of specific aspects of nineteenth-century Lakota culture. Nevertheless, readers will have to familiarize themselves further with the Lakota ethnography to deepen their appreciation and to contribute the critical readings that these stories merit and evoke. The critical chapters included here suggest one method, though many are possible. "Sioux Captive," "Stake Carriers," and "A Woman Captive," as well as some of the stories in *Dakota Texts* and the unpublished manuscripts, are accessible to readers with only a general knowledge of Plains Indian history and culture. And while they are good stories in Deloria's translations, they are better in Lakota. Many more remain unread and entombed in the Boas Collection of the American Philosophical Society in Philadelphia and at the Dakota Indian Foundation in Chamberlain, South Dakota. While archives are a repository, they may also be a graveyard. Once the scholars have brought Deloria's stories to light, careful and critical readers will have the privilege of bringing them to life.

The Stories

"A Sioux Captive Rescued by His Wife"

"Stake Carriers"

"A Woman Captive and Her Baby"

"The Prairie Dogs"

"The Buffalo People"

A Sioux Captive Rescued by His Wife

The Lakota Text

1. Tanksi, woyakapi iyagnin s'a keyapi canke lecala Blo-ok'eta wai k'un el heca anugoptan waun yunkan le oyakapi nawah'un ca eya tanyan nahtakya mic'ila le wagli ye lo.

2. He lecetu keyapi': Wicaśa wan Kangi-wicaśa wayaka yuzapi śke'.

3. Tukte ekta heca tipi wan el akipi na ihanblapśice s'e kuwapi na ehanni ikce-wicaśa kin "Yukagal Okatanpi" eyapi kin hecaki-cunpi śke'.

4. Yunkan he taku kapi owakahnige kin lecetu'; ecin tunweni miye iśta un heca wanzi wanblakeśni eyaś oyakapi eciyatanhan lecetu':

5. Isto nupin yukagal iyakaśkapi na ceca nupin nakun; na eya maka yela eyaś sipa ecela tokecela maka icahtakya he ogna eglepi'.

6. Hecunpi na ohomni iwakcipi na yukakizapi śke'.

7. Wana tonacan hecunpi na ake hanhepi yunkan lila tehan wacipi un watuka it'api canke iyuha iśtinmapi na wicahcala śakpela awanyakapi'. Eya hena ehani zuya wicaśa kin hecapi kin un wayaka kin awanyakapikta ic'ic'upi'.

8. Yunkan le wicaśa wan wayaka akipi un he tawicu kin tokehci tehila nacece'.

9. Hiyoya śke'. Śunk-luzahan, ikicize kin heca nunp iwicacu na unma akanyankin na unma iś kaśka yus ya śke'.

10. Wana toka yankau kin ikiyela i canke hena asnikiyin na śunkakan kin hena tanyan ośkokpa mahel wanyankaukteśni iya-cinyan wicakaśkin na hehanl tokeśke ecun kinhan hocoka kin itimahel iyayinkta hecinhan he iyukcan yanke'.

11. Wana wi mahel iyayin na eya nahanhcin ozanzan eyaś ahankpasyakel yunke un hececa hanl ungna Lakota winyan un hee

27

ca śina pamahe icomin nahan canpunpun wan hokśicala inskokeca ca mahel aloksohan yuha u ke'.

12. Tiwegna hiyu eyaś le winyan wanżi wakanheża wan wayazan naiś ceyinktehcin yuha canśna nunġelake ki el żiżikilowan kaiśtinme-wacin kahunhuns yuze un hecehcin canpunpun kin kilowan hiyaya ke'.

13. Lila ohitika nacece. Kin un tokehcin iwayupiya ecun canke atayaś ablezapiśni, iś he tuwa Kanġi-wicaśa winyan ca hokśiglaiśtinme-wacin kecinpi'.

14. Hecel howokawinh takuku ableswacinye eyaś takuni el ewacinśni kahya hokśikignapi ecela ecun'.

15. Howokawinh glihunni na wana hingnaku kin tuktel yanke kin slolye'. Hocokata he tiikceya tanka wan el taku lila ikik'opi canke wana oiyokpaza caś hehanl eś iyotan iyekiyanukteśni kin un atayela el yapi kin icignunniyan ye'.

16. Icipatitan wawanyakapi ca opeya inażin na he taku ca hecehcin wanyakapi hecinhan slolyewacin'.

17. Yunkan hingnaku un e ca unśiyakel cokata yukaġal okatanpi wanyanke'.

18. Wana tonacan hecel nażin kin un tamaheca na lila ite unśik'e. Hehunhunniyan woteśni caś atanin', ite ekta.

19. Mnihuha wan nitiyapehan cegnak-ya un na paiyuksa hacocola'. Niġe oh'ap iyayin na tucuhu kin yugwezap s'e tanin'.

20. Wanyakin na unśikila un ceya iyaya tka ca tokecela oigluspe'.

21. Inahma s'e tokeśke yuwipi kin ko ables nazin'; na eya watohanl heyap iyayin na maninl śunkakan wicakigle un heciya ki'.

22. Wana taku iyuha yuwiyeya na mila wan un wikan kin hena wakicipsakinkta iyecelya mignakin na ake hocokatakiya u'.

23. K'eyaś wana hanhepi tonakel iwakcipi kin un ikiwinkce-kcepe laka ecala s'eś wawanyaka kin akiyagle'. Tuktel tuweni kaiyap ihinkteśni iyecelya opiic'iyin na wana lila hantehan hanl ake canpunpun k'un he yuha na hokśikigna itutuya s'e omanihe'.

24. Tokeniś tuwa wanyakin na ektawapaya yinkta ape eyaś tukteni ye wacinśni, iśe wakanheża kin he kahunhuns yuha omani kte kin ecela un tankal un s'e lececa'.

25. Wacin tanka na cante t'inze kin henaos un hingnaku nikiya keyapi'.

26. Tuwa aiyoka yunkanś hecinkte': "Le tuwehcin ungna wimayunġa eśa kinhan na Kanġi-wicaśa iwayeśni kin slolyinkte," ecin na un canl-wankakte'.

27. Ho, eyaś winyan kin le hecin naceca tka iyowinyeśni iyute'.

28. Na hehanl wacin tanka kepe kin he lecel wake': Ito inahni keś takunl ciścila eśa iyukcanśni ecun kinhan un oyuspanukta tka'.

29. Ho, eyaś iwatukaśni tehan waape na wana ecaca wiciśtinma hanl ake tankal canpunpun wan kigna omani na hankeya hocokata hingnaku okatan nażin un heciya ihunni'.

30. Yunkan wana tehan hecunhanpi kin un wicahcala śakpe un hena iyuha watukapi hunśe iśtinmapi'.

31. Hingnaku kin ecela kikta nażin ca el ihunni na heye': "Wicahca, le miye ca cihiyowahi ye. Wacinksap kic'un na hotanin-ic'iyeśni," eya'.

32. Heyin na hena yankau kin cokaya miwakan wan maka pahli owotanlahcin han canke yuslotin na un wicahcala śakpepi k'un iyuhahcin pa-wicakakse'.

33. Na wawicaśpa ca wicapehin śakpe ataya aki śke'.

34. Hehanl cancan s'e hingnaku wikan un iyakaśkapi un hena wapsak hiyayin na wicaśa kin ikikcu na hecena glicupi'.

35. Hel tuktel oiyokpaze un hehanl kiyela ahiśunk-kaśka canke unma akanl iyotak kiyin na kigleye'.

36. Hecun na iye ehakela ake canpunpun yuha okawinh glihuni eyaś wicoti kin atayaś t'api canke hecena lila glicu śke'.

37. Tankśi, wanżi ewektunże lo. Toka k'un han wicahcala kin ikce pa wicakaksin na inunpa-i un hehanl nakeś wawicaśpe śan he icimagnunni'.

38. Ho, he winyan kin ihankeya hingnaku tehila na wica iyecel oh'an śke'.

A Sioux Captive Rescued by His Wife

The English Translation

1. My younger sister, they tell me you are on the lookout for stories right along, so this last time I was at Potato Creek I kept my ears open and heard this legend which I think I have done a good job of stamping (engraving, printing) on my mind; and I have returned.

2. It was like this, they say. A man was captured by the Crow, and held prisoner.

3. They took him to whatever place the Crow were living, and there they treated him as in a nightmare, and they did to him what was known in the old days as being tied outstretched.

4. According to my understanding of it, that means this, (of course you must understand I have never seen such a thing, but this is judging by descriptions of it):

5. Both arms are pulled into an outstretched position, and also the legs; and the toes barely touch the ground, and in that way they are set up.

6. Then the enemy stage a victory dance around it, and the captive is tortured.

7. They had been doing this for several nights, and they must have been dead tired of it, for they slept early, and only six old men were guarding. These were old time warriors who had volunteered their services as guards.

8. Now this captive had a wife who must have thought everything of him.

9. She went after him. She took two war horses and rode one and led the other by a rope.

10. When she neared the locality of the enemy's camp she stopped and tied her horses carefully in a depression where they

would not be seen; and then she thought out a way of entering the enemy camp undetected.

11. It was sunset but still light in the twilight when the Dakota woman approached carrying a piece of rotting wood for a baby, under her blanket which she wore tight about her, so that she appeared to have a child in her arms.

12. She came straight into camp, but she came in the precise manner of a woman who walks about rocking the sick or fretful child in her arms, while whispering a lullaby to soothe it to sleep.

13. How brave she must have been. On which account she must have managed so skillfully, for she was not noticed at all; they thought she was some tribeswoman putting her child to sleep.

14. She went in that manner, around the circle of tipis, trying to observe what she could, but she gave the appearance of one whose only concern was to sing to her baby.

15. She returned to her starting point, and by then she knew where her husband was. In the very center was a tipi, a large one, and the excitement around it was so high that she went to see, knowing that there was too much confusion for her to be detected.

16. People pushed each other to see, and she stood amidst them, trying to discover just what held their interest so.

17. She saw it was her husband, pitably hanging stretched apart, in the center.

18. He must have stood thus several days already, for he was very thin, and his face was poor. All that while he had not eaten, that was plain from his face.

19. He wore a breechcloth and binding around his hips, and from there upward he was bare; his stomach was caved-in and his ribs stood out like ridges.

20. She almost cried out for pity on seeing him, but she restrained herself.

21. Unnoticed she stood observing just how he was tied on; and when satisfied she left and went back to her horses.

22. There she put everything in readiness for flight, and brought a knife in her belt, suitable for cutting the ropes; and once more she returned to the center.

23. But since this war dancing had been kept up now several

nights, the spectators left comparatively early. She moved in such a way as not to bump anyone face to face, and when it was very late at night, she once more went about, aimlessly, as it were, singing to the "babe" of rotting wood.

24. Even if someone did see her and watch to see where she was heading, they would have been unsatisfied, for she appeared bound for nowhere; simply she was staying outside to keep her baby quiet by keeping him in motion.

25. It was through her patience and bravery that she saved her husband, it is said.

26. Anyone less might have feared, "If anyone should happen to run into me and question me, they will know I am not a Crow, and then . . ." and such a thought might have frightened one.

27. But if this woman entertained such fears, she did not give way to them—trying, anyway.

28. And by patience I mean this. Had she been in too much haste she might have blundered in some small detail, and thus been apprehended.

29. Now then, without getting tired she waited, and when there was absolute quiet, then she walked outside with the rotting wood for a baby, and gradually worked towards the place where her husband stood tied.

30. The old men were all asleep, tired from long exhaustive dancing.

31. Only her husband stood awake, so she stole up to him, saying "Husband, it is I who am come for you. Keep your wits about you. Don't make any sound."

32. Then she took up a sword which stood upright there, with the point planted deep into the earth, and with it she cut off the heads of all the old men there.

33. Then she scalped them, all six of them, and took their scalps home.

34. Then in mad haste she cut the ropes with which her husband was tied fast, and took her man and hurried off.

35. There somewhere in the dark she had placed her horses nearer the camp, and so she placed the man on one, and sent him off for home.

36. Then she made one more round of the camp with the rotting wood for a baby, but the tribe was dead in sleep, so then she started home also. (to catch up with her husband.)

37. My younger sister, I forgot one thing. At first the woman cut off the heads of the watchers. It was not until she went back, after rescuing her husband and sending him home that she scalped them, I was confused on that point.

38. That woman, because of the deed she accomplished, which was the kind that only men are able to do, takes first place in loving her husband.

Notes

unit 1. The man who told me this is "my elder brother." I never met him till this past summer. He had come from the farther end of the reservation to become the husband of the widow of a certain man who called Vine younger brother. That would make him my elder brother, but I never was near enough for him to call me by any kinship term, nor for me to call him *tiblo,* elder brother.
So when this new husband of the widow of our brother came on the scene, automatically he became my elder brother. He is from the canyon country on Pine Ridge, where the people are all Lakotas in their ways; and he took our kinship very seriously, and was always entirely correct in his attitudes. Of course he sat and told me this story, but that is quite permissible even in the strictest groups now. And in mixed blood communities, there are many cases in which brother and sister argue and have cross words without hesitancy; and without any severe criticism, except from the oldest members.

unit 1. *maza nahtakyapi,* is printing. Iron; they cause it to kick against it.

unit 3. This has appeared in several tales that have come in my hearing. It is a kind of crucifixion, though the arms and legs are only tied, but the torture consists in abuse, depriving the victim of food and drink, and exposing him to heat and the ridicule of the dancing crowds. This position, long sustained, meant a terrible punishment to the victim, a captive from another tribe. Always that, I am fairly sure.

unit 7. *ic'ic'upi, k'u,* to give; the reflexive usually means to volunteer one's services.

At a feast the other day, a man said, "*Wowaśi wanicap ca ito wakpamni mic'ic'ukte lo*". Workers, helpers in the feast/ they are lacking/ so/ well now/ to pass food around/ I will give myself. I will volunteer to pass food around, because there is a shortage of helpers; attendants, etc.

unit 8. This is what the narrator meant, that the man must have been greatly loved by his wife. But the order of words would seem to indicate that the man loved his wife. Standing alone, that is what it would mean; but from the context the real idea is clear. To clarify it, in Lakota, the usual way would be to say, "*Yunkan le wicaśa wan akipi un he tawicu kin tokehcin hingnaku tehila nacece'.*" By the insertion of that word *hingnaku*, her husband, the meaning is quite clear.

unit 11. *pa*, head; *mahel,* inside; out of sight; within. The *l* is usually omitted in this phrase, *pamahe icoma*, to wear the blanket over the head, with the head inside. *iwacoma, iyacoma,* (I think). But it is avoided in the first and second person.

unit 11. *na*, and, is often amplified by *nahan*, in colloquial Lakota. It adds nothing to the word, except it might in certain cases seem to give the idea of "next," or "then." She did this, and (then) that. But so many use *nahan* without any need of the *then*-idea. It comes to be a manner of speaking.

unit 12. *punpun* is applied to such things as bone and fabric that have been partly buried for a long time, and will fall apart on being touched. *Punpun* wood is rotting wood, at times; other times, such wood as is light and corky, from having floated in water a good while, is called that. This piece of wood the woman carried to give the illusion of a baby must have been of that light, corky wood, easily carried. I translate it rotting wood; but that isn't exactly correct.

unit 12. *nunge*, ear; *la*, very; *ka*, as it were. The whole might be rendered as "into its very ear, so to speak."

unit 20. *tka*, but, is often meant for "almost, all but." She *all but* cried out, in her sudden wave of pity for him, but restrained herself.

unit 23. *winkcekce*, adv. means aimlessly; without purpose; deliberately, etc. *ikce*, common; ordinary; plain; simple.

wa, thing; *ikcekce.*

i(ma)kiwinkcekce, the novelty has worn off (for me). To lose interest in a thing, from surfeit, usually.

 unit 23. *ecala,* soon; early; *tehan,* long time; *tehanyan,* far; *kiyela,* near. All such words, when followed by *s'e,* as if, mean, *comparatively* soon; late; far; near.

 unit 23. *canpunpun,* already discussed under unit 12.

 unit 26. *aiyoka* I can not analyse; it always goes with *tuwa,* someone. I use it quite carelessly, and in my mind it means, sometimes, "Had it been somebody more" [or less], or sometimes just "had it been somebody else."

Stake Carriers

The Lakota Text

1. Lakota-oyate, le wasicu kin Su eyapi kin heca eya zuya aya ke'.
2. Ho, wana anpetu wikcemna-wahecetuya heyata zuya unpi ke'.
3. Ho, le yapi kin etanhan koskalaka nunp "Okaska Nazin" ewicakiyapi kin hecapi ca opapi ke'. Hena koskalaka woimnake cin hecapi ca.
4. Okaska nazin ewicakiyapi kin hena kicizapi can el wikan akatinpi top wahehanyan, ihanke ekta can wan sayapi ca kapestopi ca, he hunpesni, cansakala ca okini lehankeca sece—siiyutapi wanzi hehanyan.
5. Ho, wana awicahiyupi cansna okaska nazin kin hena hnahna kawinh iyayapi na ena can kin paslal eglepi'.
6. Na hena wikan kin he tohanyan kin hehanyela okawinh unpi can toka kin el hihunnipi na kici ecunpi'. Kohan ohunkesni kin napapikta ca un hecunpi'.
7. Wana le Lakota kin hena Kangi-wicasa op kicizapi ca Kangi-wicasa kin Lakota kin kuwa awicaupi ke'.
8. Wana anpetu ataya op ecunpi yunkan hehanl le okaska nazin kin unma hnahna kawinh iyayin na hena can-sayapi k'un paslal ekigle canke hecela Kangi-wicasa kin nazinyanpi.
9. Yunkan he ena kinazin na unma kin kigle-wicaye unhan, "Ho po, wanzihcin ni tiyata yakipi kinhan owotanla woyaka po," eya ke'.
10. Heces le okaska nazin un he taopi canke wana enakiyapi k'unhan Kangi-wicasa kin icupi na iye tipi ekta yuha kiglapi ke'.
11. Heci tiyata akipi na wakeya wan tanka iticagapi na tima yuakagal otkeyapi na ohomni wakte-gli-wacipi ke'.

12. Ho, icunhan iś le Lakota-oyate k'un hena tiyata iś-eya kipi, na oyakapi ke': "Okaśka nażin k'un he taopi na akiyaglape lo," eyapi ke'.

13. Yunkan le taopi k'un he tawicu wan okileya ke'. Śunka-wakan wan akanyankin na.

14. Ho, makoce wan el okicize keyapi k'un hel i na hetanhan Kanġi-wicaśa kin hena oye otap awicaya ke'.

15. Watohantu wan wana Kanġi-wicaśa tipi kin ihunni ke'. Wana ihunni yunkan Kanġi-wicaśa kin ake wana iwakcipi ca okokpeya śkanpi canke iś-eya ekta ewawanyaka ke'.

16. El inażin yunkan hingnaku kin iyekiye c'eyaś tokeł h'an okihiśni ke'.

17. Canke wicoti kin iheyata wakpala wan ekta ki ke'.

18. Tokel h'ankta slolkiyeśni k'eyaś hel can-punpun wan hokśicala-kaġa ke'.

19. Heceś hokśi-kilowan ca żiżilowan hocoka kin okawinh hiyaya ke'.

20. Sam okik'ayela au kin ecel wacipi un hena ayuśtanpi na wana akiyunka ke'. Hecena hocoka kin itimahel hiyu na hingnaku awacipi un hecetkiya amani ke'.

21. Watohanl wacipi un hel ewanyaka yunkan wicahcala top yankapi eyaś oyas'in iśtinmap ke'.

22. Canke wana hokśicala-kaġapi un he tiyopa el owanżi eunkin na "Lena owanżi hpaya ye, niyate iwacukte," eya ke'.

23. Hecun na hingnaku kin wikan un yuakaġal otke un hena iyuha wapsakin na kul egnaka ke'.

24. Hecun na, "Oyakihi hecinhan wicaśa kin le wanżihcin waśpa ye," eya ke'.

25. Heyin na mila wan k'u k'eyaś waś'akeśni un okihiśni canke hecetuka keś iye wicahcala kin hena le glogle skala kin lel wawicaksa ahiyaya ke'.

26. "Lena cinkś hpaya ye, niyate tehanl ewegnakin na hehanl cigliyo-waukte," eya ke'; hokśicala kin he kin na.

27. Tehanl akiunpin na hektakiya hokśicala kin gliyoi ke'.

28. Wicahcala k'eya wicakte k'un hena unweya yuha yankapi kin hena ko icu ke'.

29. Ho he gnin na wicoti-ikiyela śunkakan nunp kaśka nażinpi ca hena wawicapsa kin na awicaki canke hena akan-yankapi na napapi ke'.

30. Ho he glapi ca wana tehanl kipi hanl le Lakota-oyate kin winyan kin le iś-eya olepi ca zuya au hcehanl el glapi ke'.

31. Ho, hetan taopi k'un he gluha glapi na Lakota-oyateta glokipi na iś-eya ehakela iwakcipi-tanka ke'.

32. Ho, hetanhan ca le winyan kin Lakota-oyate kin caś-tunpi na "Can-punpun Hunku" eciyapi ke'.

33. Na hingnaku kin he iś "Mnihuha-śina In" eciyapi ke'. Ho he, lolkunkeśni, he tawicu kin gluhpe unhan śina wan opemni na heyata aglignaka ca heun heyapi ke'.

34. (He taku-mnihuha-śina nacece';) ho, na hetanhan taopi k'un he ohakap ake lila okicize el wohitika keyapi'.

Stake Carriers

The English Translation

1. Some Indians, this kind that white men call Sioux, were on the warpath.

2. By the time of this story, they had been out perhaps about ten days.

3. And of all those who were on this trip, there were two young men of the kind known as ones-who-stand-tied (or "stake carriers"). They were young men who were held in great esteem.

4. Those known as ones-who-stand-tied are those who, when a battle is going on, have tied to them a rope about the length of four stretches of both arms, four times. [That is, four times the distance from fingertips to fingertips, with both arms stretched out to the side.] At the end of the rope is a stick, painted red, and sharpened; it is not the regular digging stick or propping post; it is only a slender stick, perhaps this long—about a foot.

5. Now when the enemy attack in earnest, then these ones-who-stand-tied may give out some bear cries, and turning sharply about, stop and peg themselves to the spot by means of the stake or stick they carry.

6. And there circling about the stick [around a circumference of which the length of the rope is the radius,] they remain, and when the enemy get to them, they delay there and fight with them. Meantime the weaker ones are able to get a head start in their flight; that is the purpose which the stake carriers serve.

7. Now back to the story. The Lakotas were at this time fighting the Crows, and the Crows were chasing them.

8. All day they had been fighting, and then one of the two stake carriers in the party suddenly turned about with a bear cry, and

right then and there he drove his stake into the ground, thus tethering himself, so the Crows concentrated on him alone, keeping him fighting them.

9. And, as he stopped there and sent the rest on, he said, "Now, if at least one of you should get home alive, see to it that you report events accurately."

10. Thus it happened that this one who stood tied was wounded, so when the battle was ended, the Crows took him and went home with him.

11. There at their home they erected a great tipi, and indoors they hung him with his arms and legs stretched apart, and they danced their Victory dances around him.

12. And now, about that same time the Lakotas also reached their home, and they reported the happenings: "That one who stood tied, was surrounded, and the enemy took him captive," they said.

13. And behold, the wounded one had a wife who set out to look for him. She went on horseback.

14. She first made for that particular place where the fighting had occurred; and from there she took up the tracks of the Crows and followed them.

15. In due time now she came to the Crow encampment. Having arrived there, it being just when the Crows were having another orgy of victory dancing, she went to the scene, and looked on.

16. As she came and stopped there, he recognized her (or she him?) but of course there was nothing she could do.

17. So she went back again to a stream back of the circle of tents.

18. She did not yet know how to proceed, but there she stopped to fashion a piece of light dry wood, that was rotting, into a doll.

19. And thus, by way of singing a lullaby to a babe, she went around and around the circle of tents, singing a humming tune between her teeth.

20. More and more she narrowed the circle, and as she did so, the dancers had stopped, and by now they had all gone to bed at their own homes. Going right on, she entered the circle and worked her way towards the place where they had been dancing over her husband.

21. After a time she got to the place where they had been dancing, and there were four old men sitting inside, but they were all asleep.

22. So she carefully laid the doll at the doorway and said, "Lie still here, while I take your father away."

23. So then she cut asunder all the ropes that bound her husband and held him stretched apart; and she laid him down on the ground.

24. Having done so, "If you can possibly do so, scalp at least one of these," she said.

25. So saying she handed him a knife, but he was too weak to try, so then she took the matter in her own hands without delay and cut the esophagus of all the old men, as she went along.

26. "Lie right here where you are, son, while I take and leave your father far from here; and then I shall come after you," she said, addressing the doll again.

27. Going far off, she laid her husband down and went back after her doll.

28. She even helped herself to all the food the old men (whom she had just killed) had standing by against the time they might wish to eat.

29. As she was going back to her husband's hideout, there near the camp stood two horses tethered, so she cut away their ropes and took them along; and those they rode to make their escape.

30. Now on their going-home trip, after they had gone far, the very Lakota tribe they belonged to was searching for the woman, and they met the war party bound on this errand.

31. Now it was from that point that the rescue party took over the wounded hero, and carried him homeward and arrived back in Lakotaland with him; and then it was their turn at last to hold a victory dance, which they did on a big scale.

32. It was from this incident that that Lakota tribe gave this woman a name; they called her "Rotting wood's mother."

33. As for her husband, him they called, "Wearer of a cloth blanket". By the way, it was because when his wife rescued him and took him down from his hanging, she wrapped him up in a shawl and laid him by.

34. (I don't know, nobody knows, just what sort of shawl that was.) It is said that after that, this one who was wounded later took part again in many fights, and he was always fearful and brave.

Notes

unit 4. *kaśka nażin* To stand tied down within a certain area, means "to carry the stake".

I do not know how general this custom was; I heard the term several years ago, and did not then know what it meant. I think it must be a Teton custom. It was explained to me thus, recently, by two different informants, neither of them old enough to have been to war, but drawing on their memory of other men's accounts.

The stake carriers, as I find it simplest to call them, were brave men, young men, who were selected by the older war chiefs, to serve in that capacity. They supplied the interference, by staking themselves down in the thick of battle, giving their comrades a chance to get away, when things looked very black for their side. Then the enemy came to such a hero, and was busy with him, shooting at him and dodging his arrows, till the retreating ones had gained a good start.

I am told that in each *tiyośpaye*, or clan within the band, there might be two at the most, but usually one stake carrier. They were picked for their valor; and a man so selected might not refuse, although he knew that it meant certain death to him sooner or later. Because if he refused, he would lose caste, and nobody in the tribe would respect him anyway, so that he might as well be dead.

When a stake carrier was killed, there was a special ceremony, a kind of memorial service, at which his war trappings, like his headdress, his standard, his beaded armlets and wristbands, his beaded or otherwise ornamented caparison, etc. were distributed to candidates who were chosen to become warriors, and presented by uncles or grandfathers or fathers who vouched for them and sponsored them. Those who received any such belonging of a stake carrier were expected to show some of his valor for owning it. But the one to whom the stake itself was presented had to be the next stake carrier in that particular *tiyośpaye*.

In the average war party there was always one, sometimes two, rarely three such. And nobody told them when to stop and drive their stake and set themselves up as interference; they must be guided by their own judgment in the matter, and do this when otherwise it would be entirely hopeless for their side. One who staked himself down in this way expected to remain there until he fell, or succeeded in turning back the enemy. Usually he fell, but that was part of the glory.

The stake was only a symbol, not strong enough to hold a man down if he wished to get away. Only a slender stick painted red, attached to a red painted thong rope four times the length of both arms outspread.

Note that 4 through 6 are not part of the narrative, but the speaker's own explanation from his general knowledge.

unit 11. *yuakagal*, from *yu*, held so; *a*, arm(?), *ka*, prefix, *gata*, reached, expended out. *a* by itself means armpit; but it occurs in such compounds as *akatinpi*, arm forced into a stiffened position; *aĥco*, sleeve; so I take it to mean arm in this case.

unit 13. "a wife of his" does not necessarily imply plural wives of which this one went looking for him; it means a wife hitherto unknown, because unmentioned.

unit 28. *unweya* I translated as lunch; it means provisions for eating, as on a trip. Here it was what the men had standing by so that they might eat during the night if they got hungry while guarding the prisoner. I can not analyze it. The Santee word is quite different; I can not recall it now.

unit 29. *wawicapsaka*, she snapped them asunder, as rope. This is of course a figure, she snapped the ropes by which they were tethered, because *psaka* can only be used with reference to things of the thread-wire-rope family.

unit 32. *punpun* is anything like bones, wood, fabric, which is so old that it is ready to disintegrate; dry rot; a falling apart. Rot in the sense of putrifaction, fetid matter, odors etc. is another verb. *ĥunwin*. Wood that is undergoing dry rot is light for its size; it was such a kind that she carried about, wrapped like a babe.

unit 33. *lolkunkeśni* is an idiom, serving as "O, by the by," only it does not mean that. I can not analyze definitely, though *śni*, not; *ke* from *ka*, as it were, and possibly *lol*, food, are recognizable.

unit 34. Another parenthetical bit; the narrator's own, so a glottal stop appears without *ke*, or other quotative.

A Woman Captive and Her Baby

The Lakota Text

1. Lakota-winyan wan wiyohpeyata wayaka akipi na heciyana yuzapi śke'. Yunkan tehan un k'eyaś iyotiyekiya un kin un hankeya iwatuka na kukte kin etkiya ece-wiyukcan śke'.

2. Hokśilala wan heceya yuha, na nakun wanźi ehantan-yuha eyaś tokeniś he mani okihilakteśni-iteke kin un ceyaya i ikputaktakin na unyan glicu śke'.

3. Eśeś le unma tokapala kin he lila kunśitku tehilapi canke tokśaś wicakiźeśniyan icaginkta wan ognayan kecin kin un ikope-śniyan ena ayuśtan'.

4. Woawacin kin he wi tona ataya nahmala awacin un kin un lila tanyan igluwiyeya kecin na hehanl glicu'.

5. Hanpa na woyute ko tanyan aigluha'; na wakanheźa kin eś ito nahahcin azinla canke heciyapya tokaśni'.

6. Ablezapikteśni iyacinyan wana oiyokpas aya hanl mni hiyoi-yayin na ektana cega kin can-aletka wan ekta kaot'ins egnakin na hecena glicu ke', wiyohinyanpatakiya ece ku'.

7. Otohanyan makiyekiya ke'; hecel oyate kin iglak-omanipi s'a kin un. K'eyaś wana tohanl tehiya iyeic'iyin na hehanyan tokiyotan taninśni'.

8. Eya hecena wi hinape cin etkiya ece itoheye eyaś maka kin iyekiyeśni hci'.

9. Hankeya ituya makoskanl nunni-omani ca akibleze'; tukte anpetu wan el otiweta wan iye tawa ca el ake glihunni'. Canke ena yankin na ceyahin na ake ya ke'.

10. Wanaś nakun ohaśunkecakta wan ogna ye'; wakapapi tawani kin glusota canke wakaheźala kin azin kin ekta imnaśni can ceyahe'.

11. Wana tehan ecel lila winyan kin hunkeśni aya eyaś hecena k̇acek̇cek̇ hanhepi koya mani'.

12. Iġuġa tankinkinyan wan egna ku śke; enana waṗamna saṗya han ke', canke wohankokipeya ececa'.

13. Iġuġa wan ohomni mani yunkan ungnahanla peta wan okśan wicaśa tona yank̇api ca k̇aiyaṗ iwicahan ke'.

14. Hena ozuye ca yank̇api na waceunṗahanpi'. Ṗte wan k̇tepi na tucuhu kin kceyapi na oiyokipiya yank̇api hanl el glihunni'.

15. Ṫokel ḣ'ankte cin slolk̇iyeśni'; wanyak̇api kinhan tokaś hena tok̇api hecinhan ena k̇tepi naiś ake wayak̇a yuzapikte kin hecela kiciyank̇e'.

16. Inaḣni nakipinkte eyaś ḣaṗḣaṗ hingle kinhan toka ca ana-wicaslata s'e wacinpi kinhan el iyeyapi na k̇tepikte'.

17. Ena cantiyapa ca wacinksaṗkic'un owanżilaḣcin nażin k'un lehanl ungna cincala kin asanpi icakiża un ohinni locinla canke t'ehowaya iyaye'.

18. Hecena wicaśa śakṗe seca ohitiya yank̇api k'un "Hantapo!" eyahingla buwicahingnin na hecena ake glipiśni'.

19. Tehan awicaṗe eyaś kupśni kin un hankeya peta k'un el i yunkan woyute henala cinpica kin oyas'in hel iḣṗeya napapi canke ena wiḣ'an śke'. Wicaśa kin hena Lakotiyapi ca naḣ'un'. Hecapi slolya yunkanś el wicaikta tka'.

20. K'eyaś tukte oyate etanhanpi hecinhan slolyeśni'; na nakun itahena tuweni he oyaka naḣ'unśni'. Iśtecapi sece.

21. Owekiś he tunweya ca hokśicala kuns ceye seca k̇ecinpi nacece'. Naiś wanaġi k̇ecinpi sece. K'eyaś tohunweni ek'eś he awicakeya wakanheża ca hel makoskanl ceya k̇ecinpiśni'.

22. Pilayapika, wiyohinyanṗatak̇iya oye otawicapin na ecel Ḣe-Saṗa kin el glihunni śke'.

23. Akotanhan ehanni hanṗa kin tatoṗ napota canke siiyoti-yek̇iya gli keyapi'.

24. Le ehanni wooyak̇e'; winyan kin he tuwe kin tunweni oyak̇api nawaḣ'un śni. Ikceya lecel ece-oyak̇api'.

A Woman Captive and Her Baby

The English Translation

1. There was once a Dakota woman who was taken captive to a tribe to the west, and there she remained, having married. She lived in that tribe a long while, but she grew tired of her hard lot, and at last when she got the idea of running away and coming home, it was all she thought on.

2. She had just had a little boy; and also one a bit older; but it was out of the question that he could walk all the way, so weeping she kissed him many times, and left him behind.

3. One thing she was sure of was that because the child was beloved of its grandmother and grandfather, he would grow up with few wants unmet, and she was not worried to leave him.

4. She had entertained this plan to run away for several months in silence, and so she got ready very carefully, and then when she considered it was right, she left.

5. She had provided herself amply with moccasins and food; and as for the infant, that was a simple matter for he was still at the breast.

6. Finding a time when she would go unnoticed, she slipped out to get water at the river, as night fell, and there she placed the water carrier in the crotch of a tree and its limb; and immediately she started, travelling eastward always.

7. For a time she knew the land. She had travelled with the tribe all over that region on camping trips; but when she placed herself in danger by going past that area, then she knew not where she was.

8. Of course she still followed the sunrise; yet she found the country unfamiliar.

9. At last she realized that she was wandering aimlessly through

the deserted land; one day she returned to the very site where she had herself stopped some days before; now she knew for sure she was lost; and she sat down to weep before going on.

10. Also by now she was facing disaster in that the pemmican she had provided was all gone, and the infant wept from the lack of nourishment in his milk.

11. As time went on the woman grew more enfeebled, but she staggered on, travelling nights as well.

12. She came to a region where great rocks of brimstone abounded. And here and there between them were large dark clumps of bushes that looked most foreboding.

13. She was walking around one huge rock when she suddenly came upon a fire around which several men were sitting.

14. They were a war party, roasting meat. They had killed a cow and were cooking the ribs in one piece over the fire, and were sitting contented and comfortable.

15. She did not know what to do; if they saw her, and if they were enemies, they might kill her there or else again take her prisoner; and that was all the prospect she saw.

16. Hurriedly she would fly to safety, yet she feared to make the least rustling sounds lest they might think an enemy spy was creeping up on them, and might shoot into the dark and kill her.

17. Right in her tracks she stood to calm her heartbeats, and try to get back her senses when suddenly the infant in her arms let out a great cry, because the poor thing was hungry.

18. Immediately the six men or so who had looked so formidable as they sat, now yelled, "Run!" and vanished in a second, and never returned to the fire.

19. She waited for them a good while but when they did not return, she went to the fire, and found nearby all the food anyone could wish for. They had left it behind in their fear, so now she found herself having her fill of good things. The men talked Lakota, that she heard. Had she known they were her tribesmen she would have gone directly to them.

20. But she did not know what band they were of, and even later she never heard anyone say, or tell this tale. Perhaps they were ashamed of running away!

21. Perhaps it was a spy, crying like a baby, they might have thought. Or else a ghost; but never probably did they think it was a real baby in that deserted place.

22. They did her this kindness: by leaving tracks she could follow eastward always till she reached the Black Hills.

23. Long before this she had worn out the four pairs of moccasins she had with her, and so she got home with her feet in very serious condition.

24. This is an old tale; I never heard anyone say just who this woman was. Simply they tell this about her as I have told it.

Notes

unit 1. *kukte cin* would be right. But this narrator is utterly neglectful of any shifts in all his speech.

unit 2. *i*, mouth; *i*, against; *putaka*, to press down. This is one of the class of verbs with the *pu* prefix meaning pressure on.

unit 3. his grandmother—they love him. This is an example of the custom of using a singular subject for a plural verb, wherein one person, the most important in a group, is mentioned though a party or retinue or family are meant.

unit 12. Rocks, big ones. This means a region of big rocks.

unit 16. *el*, in, at, to; *iyeyapi*, they send it. This came out in a previous paper. It means to shoot at, though the instrument, gun or arrow, is left unnamed.

unit 19. *ape*, to await.

unit 19. *hena*, those; *henala*, all such things; i.e., all that one could wish.

unit 23. *ta*, prefix, besides other things, means set, pair, etc.

The Prairie Dogs

Prefatory Remarks

This story of the prairie dog village where the Dakota societies were said to have been instituted, is a rationalized account, told by various old men, notably by one named Makula.

In trying to recall it I find that certain set forms have stayed in my mind, like the recurring question by each speaker, "Why is there no dancing, though the villagers wait anxiously to see some?" or words to that effect.

And the various words in which each animal "counts coup," before he dares to make himself heard instituting a society, are clearly remembered. These set forms bring in certain words that belong to them, which I can not wholly analyze, and which are not in my vocabulary.

But the narrative portions as I have them are only as I can recall them imperfectly, though essentially they are correct; and it is quite possible that some small details may be omitted.

I did not hear this often enough or systematically enough, as for instance the Buffalo story or the Iron Hawk tale in their elaborated versions. This uncertainty is apparent in the story here, which is therefore less unified. But it is the best I can do under those circumstances.

The Lakota Text

1. Heceś tohunwetuka wan oyate-tanka blok-yankapi śke'. Ho, iś le ehanni keyape lo—Iktomi maka akanl ounye c'un hehanni.

2. Oyate kin leś wacipi waśtelakapi seca yunkan anpetu wan el ungna hunk-eyapka, tuwenihcin waciśni, ecun-kapinpelaka owanżikżi yanka ke'.

3. Yunkan wicaśa wan cokap inażin na waci-wicaśa kin iyowica-kteka ke'.

4. Heya ke: "Toka yunkan le oyate blok-yankala wawanyak-cantokpani ahinażin k'un, wayacipśni he?

5. "Ito iwayinkta ce, hecel iyemayakiyapikte. . . . Oyate-ikce wicaśa el, tuktel cunkpaza can hel homatanin kin he eka yeś wokokipe canke oyate tanh mikiya ahiyaya ece ca le waun we lo!" eya ke'.

6. Yunkan he hinhan ca waktoglaka ke'.

7. Ho, yunkan iś hehanl wicaśa-cik'ala wan cokap inażin na heya ke:

8."Toka yunkan le oyate blok-yankala wawanyak-cantokpani ahinażin k'un, wayacipiśni he?

9. "Kola leca waktoglaka ca miś-eya wowaglakinkte lo!

10. "Anpiyopteya wimic'ignin yunkan wicaśa-wamanika nunp icaśtan mahiyankapi na can micunpikta tka wakuwawa ebluśtan na tima wagliyaku na le ni waun we lo," eya ke'.

11. Yunkan he iś hoka ca woglaka ke'.

12. Ho, heniyos itu-hotaninpi na hecena waci-wicaśa k'un itokapśni s'e nażinpi canke hehanl ake wicaśa wan wicaśa waśte ca iśta cikcik'ala k'eyaś sapsapawiyakpakpa ca cokap hiyu-ic'iya ke'.

13. Tansil ataya sap-ic'iyin na wacakiyela ska un iglazo ke'.

14. Liklila canzeka-waayuta na heya ke':

15. "Toka yunkan oyate blok-yankala wawanyak-cantokpani ahinażin k'un wayacipiśni he?

16. "Kola nunp waktoglakapi ca miś hehanl epinkte lo: Anpi-yopteya wimic'ignin yunkan wicaśa-wamanika nunp icaśtan mahiyankapi na can micupikta tka patak-wakinażin na hecegla iwakitapi ca cokan iyewicawayin na celożu-egna wagliyaku na le ni waun we lo."

17. Yunkan he maka ca ia śke'. Hecetu k'eyaś waci-wicaśa k'un wicayainceśni ke'.

18. Yunkan hehanl wicaśa wan tansinl sanic'iyin na wanbli-wiyaka nunp akiinskokecahcin na akiyehanyan waśteśte ca celogleya aopazan ke'. Wiyaka kin skaska ca inkpa kin el kitan ecinyela sapsapa ke'. Le tuwe kin kolatun ke'.

19. Heya ke: "Toka yunkan oyate blok-yankala wawanyak-cantokpani ahinażin k'un, wayacipiśni he?

20. "Kola yamni wana waktoglakapi ca miś hehanl epinkte lo:

21. "Oyate śunk-ok'in waziyatakiya oiglake yunkan peźiħotawapamna oħlate munka hanl akiglemayanpi canke wicikpitanhan inawaźin ye lo.

22. "Winunħcala koko sakye icicakakakya makuwapi na tona wan yuhapi k'un hena itazipa kannakśanyanpi tkaś takuni iyamapaśni wakpaptin na le ni waun we lo." eya ke'.

23. Yunkan he maśtinska ca ia śke'. Ho, keyaś hecena wacipiśni śke'.

24. Yunkan hehanl wicaśa wan ħol-ic'iya ca cokap hiyu ke, takolaku yamni op. Yunkan hena iyuha op akiyececa eyap-ca ke'. Tokel śkinciyapi cansna k'eħk'eħ hingla ke'.

25. "Toka yunkan oyate blok-yankala wawanyank-cantokpani ahinaźin k'un, wayacipiśni he?

26. "Kola top wana waktoglakapi ca miś hehanl homataninkte lo:

27. "Oyate kin iglak ayin na epage eyuħpapi canke wicitelake el inaźin wahiyaya canke tona wiyaħpeya okihipi k'un hena wanhinkpe kin itazipa kannakśanyanpi tka omakihipiśni; na hecela hi tanka ca nite kaħuħ iyemaya ca wapamna-oħlate teħiya munkin na niśtuśte kin omasota hanl hinħpaya ca le huiyamatala kin hemaceca ye lo," eya ke'.

28. Yunkan he iś śiyo ca woglake c'eyaś hecenaś tuweni waciwacinśni ke'.

29. Ho yunkan ohanketa, wicaśa wan sapa ca tokel-okihi tanka ca canħaka k'in na hinaźin ke'.

30. "Hehehe, miyeś le tokaheya wahi k'un, tokeśke, waktoglakahanpi ca wanaħ un-nawaźinhin na emahakelakte lo.

31. "Oyate blok-yankala wawanyak-cantokpani ahinaźin k'un, toka yunkan wayacipiśni huwo?

32. "Wana kola zaptan woglakapi ca miś ehakela epinkte lo:

33. "Waziyatakiya oyate kin oiglake kagapi yunkan etanhan hokśila kin mnaic'iyapi na caħunaptanyan wan el munka ca anpetu ataya okagamayanhanpi na wanhinkpe glusotapi yunkan nakeś hehanl amayuśtanpe lo;

34. "Ca hena apśunśunweheya waħpayin na omakizi ca iyuha kic'in le wahinawaźin ye lo." eye'.

35. Yunkan he tatanka ca ia śke'.

36. Ho, heceś śakṗe ataya waktoglakaṗe śan ataya waci kin ihunniwicayapiśni canke hehanl hena witaya mniciyapi ke'.

37. Ito lena epi: Tatanka, Śiyo, Maśtinska takolaku Śungila kici, Maka, Hoka na Hinhan—henakeca ca mniciyapi ke'.

38. Yunkan tatanka kin e ca tokeya lecel eya śke':

39. "Hunhi, cewinś waci-kapinpi ke! . . . . Wacipi kin he wicaśa ikibleze c'un. . . . hopo, cante silya wicicaginkteśni kin un ito okolakiciye wan oyate wicegna unkte lo.

40. "Tatanka kin he awanyakinkta ce. Wicaśa itancan ece hel opapi na oyate el oiye kic'unpikta ce," eya canke hetanhan ca he Itancan-okolakiciye kin u śke lo.

41. (Itahena Nige tanka ewicakiyapi kin hena epi'. Ecin ahcalaka ece opapi kin heun heyapi. Ca Nige tanka kin he Tatanka kin e ca okolakiciye wicakicaga śke lo.)

42. Hehanl heya śke: "Lena Itancan kin witaya ośpayepi na oyate kaśka wicayuzapi na akicita tośkinciye kin hena iye wicakicun-zapikte; hecel taku śica wanżini icaginkteśni.

43. "Kicicopi na lowanpi kin un oyate wiyuśkin na kibles-wicayapikte; hecel tunweni ake canśil, wihahaśniyan unpikteśni.

44. "Na tuktel oyate egna Itancan-okolakiciye kin he unni canśna el unhinagicala kin he eyaṗaha-unkte lo, iyokipiwica-yinkta un.

45. "Lena lecetukta tka nahanhcike lo. Tohanl kola nagi woslolye icupi na un oiyokipiya unpikte ca hehantukte lo." eya śke'.

46. Ho, tatanka kin lecel eyin na heyaṗ kinażin yunkan hehanl śiyo kin iś hehanl ia śke':

47. "Wicaśa maka akanl can śilya icaginkte cin he waśteśni kin un ito okolakiciye wan wicegna icaginkte lo.

48. "Ho, yunkan śiyo kin he hel waawanyaka unkte lo.

49. "Wowaci kin el śiyo kin ho uncapi un iyuha hlahla yuha wacipikte lo. (Kinyan iyaya canśna situpi kin hlahlaya iyaye c'un he.)

50. "Yunkan okolakiciye kin le oyate egna akicita-unpikta ca itancan-okolakiciye kin he tokel eye cin ecekce śkinciyapikte lo.

51. "Tuktel kiwitayapi ca hel ungnagicala kin he awicaglata unkte lo. Ohitika ece hel opapikta canke hena Cante-t'inza eic'iyapikte lo," eya ke'.

52. Ho, yunkan hehanl śunġila wan hinaźin ke'. He tuwe kin maśtinska kin kici ece-opiic'iya yunkan iś hehanl woglakin na maśtinska kin inila heyal ounyan ke'.

53. "Wicaśa maka akanl canśilya icaġinkte cin he waśteśni kin un ito okolakiciye wan wicegna unkte lo," eya ke'.

54. "Tohanl kola naġi woslolye icupi na oiyokipiya unpikta ca hehantukte lo. Maśtinska kin he tawaśicukte lo. Opapi kin iyuhahcin akicita-unpi na tunweya-wicoh'an yuhapikta canke un śunkmanitu tawoslolye na wowayupike kin hena tawapikte.

55. "Lena lecetukta tka nahanhcike . . ." eya śke'. Yunkan heciyatanhan ca le śunġila-okolakiciye kin un śke lo.

56. Yunkan hehanl kośkalaka wan hopyakel iśta cikcik'ala-wiyakpakpa ca cokap hiyu na heya ke':

57. "Wicaśa maka akanl canśilya icaġinkte cin hecetuśni kin un ito wicegna okolakiciye wan unkte lo.

58. "Un oyate imaġaġapikte; na un takuni icanhcinśniyan wicicaġinkte.

59. "Maka kin he tawaśicukte; na okolakiciye kin he Kanġi-yuhapikte.

60. "Maka kin woslolye wowayupika tawa kin hena iś-eya tawa-pikte; na wokokipeya wipe-kitunpi kin un oyate wanah'unkapikte.

61. "Lena lecetukta tka nahanhcike. . . Tohanl kola naġi woslolye icupikta ca hehantukte lo" eya canke heciyatanhan ca le Kanġi-Yuha kin upi śke'.

62. Na iś-eya hecel eya canke un ungnaġicala kin he tuktel mniciyapi can el hotanin ye lo.

63. Wanaś henalakte sece c'un, ake icizaptan wan cokap hiyu na heya ke': "Wicaśa maka akanl canśilya icaġinkte cin hecetuśni kin un ito wicegna okolakiciye wan unkte lo.

64. "Yunkan hel miye wamaśicukte lo. Na opapi kin hena ihokapikte lo. Akicita na tunweya-wowaśi yuhapikta tka miyehca ca owicawakiyinkte lo.

65. "Wobliheca mitawa kin unpikte lo. Lena lecetukta tka nahanhcin ke . . . Tohanl kola naġi woslolye icupi kin hehantukte lo," eya ke'.

66. "Na tuktel kiwitayapi can hel ungnaġicala kin unkte lo," eya ke'.

67. Hecel un Ihoka kin toka ekta kaǧapi śke lo.

68. Unhanketa wicaśa wan he wana iciśakpe hinaźin na heya ke': "Ho po, wicaśa maka akanl canśilya icaǧinkte cin he waśteśni kin un wicegna okolakiciye wan unkte lo."

69. (Yunkan he Hinhan-śun-Wapaha ewicakiyapi kin hena wicaka śke'. Ca okolakiciye kin he nakun ehantanhan u we lo.)

70. "Wicaśa sutunhca ece opapikte lo, na hena kicicopi na wacipi na witaya wakiyapi na wicoksape un kośkalaka wiwica-kiciyukcanpikte lo.

71. "Tokel eunpapi can he owotanlakte lo. Na he ogna akicita kin śkinciyapi kte lo.

72. "Na tuktel kiwitayapi canśna hel ohinni unhnaǧicala kin he ho kic'unkte lo." eya ke'.

73. "Tka, lehantuśni. . . tohanl kola woslolye naǧi eciyatanhan icupi kinhan hehantukte lo" eya ke'.

74. Ho, heceś toka ekta okolakiciye kin hena wamakaśkan ca kaǧapi śke'. Hecunpi na hena wiyeya egnakapi, na eyapi k'un ognayan tohanl wana wicaśa akantula wookahniǧe okic'ilepi un hanblepi yunkan wanźikźi naǧi eciyatanhan woslolye icupi na un ecekce oyate egna kaǧapi śke lo.

75. Ito tokeya kin he Itancan-okolakiciye śke; na he tatanka kin kaǧe'; na iye el waawanyak un'. He ośpaye kin epi ca itahena Niǧe Tanka ewicakiyapi śke'. Wawiyaksapa unpi na eś to tunweni iye iyunkala akicita-wowaśi yuhapiśni śke, oyate el wiyukcan ecela ecunpi'.

76. Na inunpa kin he iś Cante-T'inza kin epi'. He śiyo kin kaǧa śke lo, na he el iye ca waawanyak un keyapi'. Ośpaye kin hel akicita-wowaśi unśpa yuhapi'.

77. Iyamni kin iś Tokala kin epi'. Hel waawanyaka kin nunpapi, tokala kin e na maśtinska ki kicica, ho k'eyaś maśtinska kin he iyotan waawanyake'. Tokala kin ee ca okolakiciye kin kunze un he hecel eya ca ecetu'.

78. Itopa kin he iś Kanǧi-yuha kin epi ca he maka ki waawan-yaka yuhapi'. Tohanl śaic'iyapi canśna maka-ha kin he lila woilakyapi kin he un we lo.

79. Izaptan kin iś ihoka kin e śke lo. He hoka wan toka ekta wicakicunza ca ecel okolakiciye icicagapi na ecel unpi kin he epi'.

80. Na iciśakṗe kin he iś Hinhan wan wicakicaġa ca hena iś Hinhan-śun-wapaha eic'iyapi kin epi tka iśe lecala s'e miwatani ewicakiyapi'. Hena iś-eya aḣcalaka ece opapi kin un tunweni lila iye śkinciyapiśni, eya toketuke c'eyaś Itancan okolaḱiciye unpi kin he iś-eya iyecel unpi'.

81. K'eyaś tatanka kin he itancan canḱe okolaḱiciye wan ḱaġe c'un he el itancan ece opapi k'un he ataya-wanḱatuya unpi śke lo.

82. Toḱa ekta akenunpapi keyapi . . . itahena ol'ota opapi'.

83. Ho, yunkan le okolaḱiciye ḱunzapi oyaḱapi kin le ehanni wicaśa nahanḣcin maka aḱanl upiḣcisni k'un hehanni śke'.

84. Na le oyate wawanyaḱapikteḣcin keś tuweni waciśni k'un hena ṗisṗizaoyatepi śke'. Hena ecin ohinni blok-yankapi kin epi'.

85. Na winyan lehanl tuktel okolaḱiciye śkinciyapi can el wicaaglatapi kin hena iś unḣnaġicala keyapi k'un epi śke'.

86. Ecin lehantuke c'eyaś tuktel ṗisṗiza-oti can hel ṗisṗiza-taeyaṗaha wanzi un, yunkan he unḣnaġicala eciyapi'.

87. Ṗisṗizala kin tohanl wanżi ohitikinkteḣcin canśna, hinapela na "tokiyatanhan maopikte sece" ecinlakeśni, oḣloka tokeca wanżi ekta titokan yela keyin na icazoṗ s'e inyanḱe'.

88. Na wana ihunni canśna wicaaglatala kin "lilililililililii!" eya żahelas'e yaonihan un pan'.

89. Hecel un ṗisṗiza-otila kin el wayawiyuśkin, wayables unḣnaġicala unpi k'un, iyececa-kiya winyan kin iś-eya tuktel okolaḱiciye kin hena mniciyapi na el waktoglakapi canśna wicaya-tanpi un hotunpi kin hecetu'.

The Prairie Dogs

The English Translation

1. Once on a time it so happened that a great nation was living in a permanent village. O, long ago it was, they say—when Iktomi was still living on this earth.

2. Whereas the people had hitherto been so fond of dancing, there came a certain day when they said "Hunk," as it were; nobody at all danced; as if too indolent they sat quietly.

3. Then a man stepped into the ring and scolded them, telling them to dance.

4. He said, "Why is it that you do not dance, though the villagers have come and stand around, longing to be spectators?

5. "Now then, I am about to speak, in order that you may know me. Among the people, the common kind, the Indians, wherever there are dark woods, if my voice comes forth, just the sound of it is enough to inspire fear, so that men move sideways to avoid me always; and such I am!" he said.

6. And it was an Owl who had thus "counted coup."

7. And then a small man stepped into the ring, and he said:

8. "Why is it that you do not dance, though the villagers have come and are standing around longing to be spectators?

9. "My friend has just related his prowess; I shall do so next:

10. "Throughout the day I foraged for myself, when two men, walkers-on-earth, met me face to face without warning and would have used sticks to me, but I made repeated sallies after them, chasing them away, and reentered my cave; and so now I am alive." he said.

11. And it was a badger who had thus related his prowess.

12. Thus two spoke in vain, for still the dancers were as if un-

affected as they stood, so then a handsome man with small but very sparkling black eyes sent himself into the ring.

13. All over his body he was blackened, and he had only a single white line drawn on himself.

14. With very angry looks he surveyed the crowd, and then he said:

15. "Why is it that you do not dance, though the men who stay in permanent villages have come and are standing around eager to see some dancing?

16. "Two friends have counted coup, so I shall speak next: Throughout the day while I was foraging for myself, two men who walked the earth came at me suddenly face to face and would have taken their sticks to me, but I suddenly stopped short and sent 'it' into the very center of all they have to rely on for seeing, and then I disappeared into the rushes; and thus I remained alive."

17. And they say it was the skunk who had thus spoken. Even so, the dancers were not moved.

18. And then a man had painted his entire body white, and wore two eagle feathers of exactly the same size and of equal beauty, set upright in his head. The feathers were white and only slightly tipped with black. And this one was accompanied by his friend.

19. He said, "Why is it that you do not dance, though the men who are permanent village dwellers have come and are standing eager to look on?

20. "My three friends have already now related their prowess, and I shall do so next.

21. The people, using dog-travois, were migrating northward when they came upon me unawares where I lay under a sage brush, so from out of their very bellies, so to speak, I sprang up.

22. "Everybody, even old women with their sticks clanging against each other, gave me chase and those who possessed bows and arrows caused their bow sinews to bend, but I came through untouched and thus now I live on," he said.

23. And it was a rabbit that spoke. (jackrabbit.) But still they did not dance.

24. Then a man who had painted himself all over with grey stepped into the center with three of his comrades. And, they

say, they were all remarkably alike in appearance. Each slightest movement they made brought out a kind of buzzing sound.

25. "Why is it that you do not dance, though the men who are permanent villagers have come and are standing eager to see some dancing?

26. "Four of my friends have counted coup now, so it is my turn to speak out.

27. "The people were migrating and had stopped for a ceremonial pause, and right in front of them I rose up, so all who could throw on an arrow caused their arrows to bend the bowstring, but they missed me; and only one had a big enough arrowhead to impale my back, breaking through the bone, so I lay suffering under a clump until the meat of my back had all wasted away when the arrow fell out, which is why I am bony there," he said.

28. It was a prairie chicken who was thus talking, but still nobody had any intention of dancing.

29. Then finally a great giant of a black man carrying a pack of brush-wood on his back stepped up and stood.

30. "Alas, I was the first to arrive here, but somehow, through listening to others relate their deeds of valor, I am left till the last.

31. "Why is it that you do not dance, though the village people come and stand eager to see dancing?

32. "Already five friends have told their own stories, so I shall do so last.

33. "The people were making a migration northward, and from their group all the boys assembled (collected themselves) and because I lay amidst the wood of a hillside, all day they pinned me with arrows, and only when they had exhausted their supply did they leave me alone;

34. "So there I lay with arrows toppling about me, and when I was healed, I put them all on my back and carrying my load so, I come to stand here," he said.

35. And it was the buffalo bull who spoke.

36. Now all six of them had counted their coup, yet they failed all to reach the minds (wills) of the dancers; so then they came together to hold a meeting.

37. They were as follows: the buffalo bull, the prairie chicken,

the skunk, the rabbit with his companion the red fox, the badger and the owl, that many now held a council.

38. And the buffalo bull was the first to speak, and he said:

39. "Well, well, how disinclined to dance they must be! . . . and dancing is such a rouser of good cheer for man too . . . come now all, in order that men may live and grow without being gloomy, there shall be a society existing among them.

40. "The buffalo bull shall be the guardian spirit of it. Only chiefs shall have membership in it, and they shall use their word among the people," (their word shall be followed,) he said. It is said that since then the Chiefs' society has been in existence.

41. (Later this group was called the Big Bellies. This was because men somewhat past their prime, and going on towards old manhood were the members. So it was really the present Big Bellies for whom the Buffalo bull instituted a society, so it is said.)

42. Then he went on: "These chiefs shall be together in a group, and they shall lead the people and direct the movements of the camp police. In that way no evil may develop.

43. "By their feasts and their songs the people shall be caused to rejoice and to be aroused to good cheer. Nobody shall again live sad and cheerless.

44. "And where among the people that society of chiefs exists, then there shall be found the screech owl to act as crier for them, in order to add cheer. (To cause them to be pleased.)

45. "These things shall be; but not yet. What time my friends (human beings) receive knowledge through the spirit, and thereby can live more happily, then it shall be," he said.

46. Having thus spoken, the buffalo bull stepped aside, and then the prairie chicken spoke up:

47. "It is not good for man-on-earth to grow up without pleasure, so a society shall thrive among them.

48. "And there shall the prairie chicken be the guardian spirit.

49. "Men shall imitate the sound of the prairie chicken, in their dance, so they shall dance with buzzing rattles. (Like the buzzing sound of the tail as the bird takes off, as is well known.)

50. "And that society shall exist to be soldiers among the people, acting under the direction of the Chiefs' society.

51. "Wherever they assemble together there, the screech owl shall cheer and laud them. Only courageous men shall take part in the membership; consequently the society shall be called "The Stouthearted" (The Braves), he said.

52. And then the red fox stepped up. He always kept close to his companion the jackrabbit before this, and now it was his turn to speak, and the rabbit stayed quiet in the background.

53. "It is not good that man-on-earth should grow up without pleasure, so now a society shall exist among them.

54. "What time my friends shall take in knowledge through the spirit, and shall live agreeably, then it shall be. The rabbit shall be their guardian-helper; all the members shall be soldiers, and theirs shall be a scouting duty; so for it the knowledge and cunning of the dog of the wilds shall also be theirs.

55. "These things shall be . . . but not just yet," he said. And it was from that decree that the Fox society came to be, so they say.

56. Then a handsome man, one with small but sparkling eyes, stepped into their midst and he said:

57. "It is wrong that man-on-earth should grow up in sorrow, so now among them a society shall flourish.

58. "By means of it, the tribe shall be entertained; and through it, without anything troublesome, they shall grow up.

59. "The skunk shall be its guardian spirit; and the members shall keep a crow.

60. "They shall have the knowledge and cunning of the skunk; and because they shall be fearfully armed, people shall submit to obedience.

61. "These things shall be, but not yet . . . What time my friends derive knowledge from the spirit—when they do—that shall be the time," he said; therefore, from that fact it is that these "Keepers of the Crow" are in existence, so it is said.

62. And because the Skunk also decreed so, the voice of the screech owl is heard wherever these members congregate.

63. Now it would have seemed that was to be all; but a fifth man now came out and he said: "It is wrong that man should grow up on the earth in gloom, so now among them a society shall exist.

64. "There I shall be their spirit-helper. And those who belong

shall be *Iĥoka*. Theirs shall be soldier and scout duty, but I, my very own self, I shall personally assist them.

65. "They shall employ my energy. These things shall be, but not yet. When my friends through the spirit derive knowledge, then it shall be," he said.

66. "And wherever they congregate, there shall be the screech owl in their midst."

67. Thus was the Badger society first instituted, so they say.

68. Finally, a man who was the sixth in order, stood up and said: "Hear ye, it is not good that man should grow up on the earth in sorrow, so a society shall thrive among them.

69. (And it is said he referred to what are called the "Owl-Feather Headdress" society. So that society is also of very ancient origin, they say.)

70. "Only men who are thoroughly ripened shall be members, and these shall feast and dance and confer together in council, and with human wisdom they shall make decisions for the young men.

71. "Whatever they lay down, as their judgment, that shall be right. And soldiers shall act in accord with it.

72. "And wherever they assemble, there the screech owl shall always use its voice.

73. "But not now; when my friends attain to knowledge through the spirit, then shall be the time for it," he said.

74. So it is said that it was animals that first instituted these societies, in the beginning. Having devised them, they lay them by in readiness; and, as they had all said, when men on earth, seeking for wisdom, went questing for it through visions, certain ones acquired the idea and instituted the societies among the people.

75. Now, first was the Chiefs' society; instituted by the buffalo, who was himself the guardian-spirit of it. This was the group later called the Big Bellies. They existed as an advisory group, and never themselves acted personally as scouts; they were solely tribal thinkers.

76. The second were the Stouthearts. (The Braves.) This was instituted by the prairie chicken, which was its guardian-spirit. This group took some of the scouting-policing duty.

77. The third were the Foxes. They had two guardians—the rabbit and the fox, but the rabbit was the active guardian. It was as the Fox said in foreordaining the society.

78. The fourth were the Keepers of the Crow. They had the skunk for their guardian. Whenever they were ceremonially dressed, they employed a skunk skin conspicuously in their attire, in honor of their guardian.

79. The fifth were the *Ihoka*, or Badgers. A Badger first devised their order, and accordingly men made themselves a society, and so they lived as the badger had said; those were the members.

80. The sixth was instituted by the owl, and the members were the "Owl-Feather Headdress" society, but of recent times they came to be called the Mandan society, *Miwatani*. They also were oldish men, and so they never took very active duty, but instead, at all events, they existed in the same manner as the Chiefs' Society's members.

81. But the Chiefs' Society, started by the buffalo bull, because it was composed of men already leaders, held the very highest position of all.

82. Originally it is said the membership consisted of twelve chiefs. Later on, the membership increased to many more.

83. Now then, this account of the institution of the societies is said to refer to the very long ago, before human beings were thoroughly established on the earth.

84. And those villagers who wanted so to see some dancing but were denied it by the indolence of the dancers, so that these various men took action about it, were the prairie dog nation, it is said. For, of course, they are the people who always dwell in permanent homes.

85. And those women who are always on hand to give the screech owl cry in praise of the various members wherever a society is feasting and dancing, are the screech owls decreed to the societies long ago.

86. Even today it is true: wherever there is a prairie dog town, there is present its own village crier called the screech owl.

87. Whenever one of the prairie dogs chooses to display his

valor, he comes out, the little one, and without such a thought
as, "I might be shot at from somewhere!" off he goes like a streak,
towards another hole, saying he is going to pay a call.

88. And when he gets there safely, then his little crier screams,
"lililililililililili!" at the top of his shrill voice, to honor the brave one.

89. In such a way the screech owls live in the various prairie dog
villages for the purpose of making people happy and energetic; so,
in a similar way, wherever there is a society meeting, and coups are
counted, there women give their cry to laud and praise them.

Notes

unit 2. *hunk-eyapka*, an expression. "Saying '*hunk*' as it were." This
is used, in commenting on the sudden loss of interest on the part of
a person who is ordinarily overenthusiastic and eager.

As a child teases to be allowed to go swimming, because he is forbidden. Then, when he has permission, his enthusiasm is no longer
high, "*Hunk-eyeca.*"

unit 4. *blok-yanka*, to sit '*blok*' i.e., to stay put instead of migrating. cf. *bloka*, male; *bloketu*, summertime, *blo*, protuberance, ridge;
potato. (I do not see much connection, except in *bloketu*, summertime. Some reference is elsewhere made also to staying put for tilling
the soil.)

Blok-yankala is now nominalized; if *yanka* were verbal, it would
be *yankela*.

unit 5. The reason for counting coup is for the sake of establishing
prestige, in order to gain a hearing. Any man who endures such
hardship has a right to be heard.

unit 5. *tan*—body; *himi*—crooked; *kiya,* causing one's own. (To
move) body-caused-to-be-crooked, i.e., to sidle out of the way; to
get away by moving sideways. This is a common adverb.

unit 10. *wicaśa-wamanika* is part of the set speech of the badger,
but I do not know what is meant exactly. My free translation is
something of a guess. (*wamanica*, small animal, like a squirrel)

unit 16. *iwakita*, instrument for looking—the eye. Not usual

Teton to make such a verb. Ordinarily, *un wakita,* by means of/ to look about.

iwakita, verb, is good Santee.

unit 16. *iyeya,* to send it. The fluid emitted by the skunk is thought of as excrement, and the usual term for a skunk's reaction to danger is "*Išta ocešli*" to defecate into the eye. Because the eyes feel it most, the belief is that the skunk deliberately aims at his opponent's eyes.

(This fluid was sometimes regarded as a medicine for poor eyesight. So that it was a kind of mixed curse and blessing to have this experience with a skunk.)

unit 16. *celi,* reed; *ožu,* place of growth. I do not think this is a usual contraction. I have never heard the *i* dropped, except in this set speech of the skunk.

unit 18. *celogleya* an adverb, heard only in this connection. Probably refers to wearing feathers upright, perpendicular, like a reed set upright? Doubtful, except if it is that.

unit 22. *icicakakakya,* from *kaka,* the sound made of like things hitting against each other, wood on wood, paper on paper, etc.

unit 41. The narrator explained this, which I put in parenthesis. *ahcalaka* is colloquial for "on the decline" as elderly men, well past prime, and leaning towards old age but not yet there. *a,* somewhat; a bit, etc., *hcala,* a colloquialism for *wicahcala.*

unit 44. *unhnaǧicala* and *ungnaǧicala* used indifferently by Teton; *unhnaǧicana,* Yankton.

unit 49. This reference to the "rattle" of a prairie chicken's feathers upon suddenly taking off is difficult to translate. It isn't "rattle" in the ordinary sense; it is more like a sliding scale of *kdikdikdikdi,* as described in Yankton. Said rapidly, with the *k* very faint.

unit 70. *sutun,* to bear fruit; to be ripe; used here, and in special cases, in a figurative way, mature.

unit 80. *toketuke c'eyaš* is idiomatic, and may be variously translated as, "At all events," "taken by and large" and similar English idioms.

(It was always my impression, gained from this story of origins, that the standard societies were the two dignified ones, the Chiefs' the Mandan or *Miwatani* society, which were composed of elderly men who were the tribal advisors; and the four intermediate ones made up of younger men who were actively charged with keeping order; those six were all there were. And that later societies were spurious, largely, and didn't have the prestige of years. The White Horse society was especially modern, and I can recall as a child people making fun of it because it was not a "real society.")

The Buffalo People

The Lakota Text

1. Heceś maka akanl nahanḣcin tuweniḣcin unśni k'un he ehan nakeś heceya wicaśa-tokahe tawicu kici kal eti keyape lo.

2. Yunkan he waziya eciyapi na tawicu kin iś Wakanka eciyapi kin epi k'eyaś wana wicaśa akantula ahipipi śke lo.

3. K'eyaś Waziya atayaś tokatakiya ecaca wiyukcanśni, anpetu opta imaġaġa-ic'iyin na hanhepi can iśtinme cin hehanyela wiyukcan'.

4. Tawicu kin iyeśtuka tokeca . . . he iś ohinni tokatakiya wiyukcan na cinca yukinkteḣcin keyapi'.

5. "Wicaḣca, eśa wana cinca unyuke ceś," eya canke heceś wanżi kaġapi—canke wana iyehantu yunkan tunpi'.

6. Wicincala wan . . . hunhi, winyan waśtepi cinla, pehin kin sapsapa na hanskaska, iśta kin sapyela, iḣa ece-unla ca yunkapi śke lo.

7. Ho, yunkan nakeś hehanl Waziya wihaha . . . "Hunhe, micun-kśi, micunkśi, winyan miciwaśtela ye lo!" eyaśna kignala ke'.

8. Canlwaśteya cinca yukanpi canke awanglak icaḣ-kiyapikta un śkanpi ke'. Yunkan wana waniyetu yamni sap-iyayela na iyecinka oiyankela yunkan hehanl ake wana winyan k'un taku-cin taninśni na hankeya heya ke':

9. "Wicaḣca, eceś ake cinca-unyukinkte," eya canke "Ho wo, niś niyeke cin," eya ke'. Heceś ake wanżi yuhapi yunkan ake wanaś wicincala ca cuweku kin e eyap ca ke'.

10. Winyan nunp akeyecelya ḣopḣopapi caś wana canlwaśteya unkte sece c'un, hehe, wana akeś Wakanka k'un canl-waḣteśni taku ce taninśni, na unhanketa wana ake cinca-yukinkteḣcin ke'.

11. Heceś wana iciyamni-cincatun yunkan hehanl nakeś hokśi-lala wan t'insyela icaska-kaġap s'e yuhala śke'.

67

12. Ho, hetanhan yin na ake wana wicincala wan yuha k'eyaś he ośteka śke'. Pehin na iśta ko zizi na ite yeś ko ziya-ska ca wicaśa iyececaśni ke'.

13. Itankaku wan hehanl yuhapi ke'. Ake iś-eya zi-winla ca cuweku iyekceca . . . . wana yunkan tokaheya wincincala nunpa iśta kin na pehin kin sapyela na yunkan hokśila wan wana hanskela ca waś'akya opeiciya yuhapi; na hakakta kin heniyos wicincala zizipila ke'.

14. Ho, henakecapi yunkan hehanl inayanpi kin imna hunśe inunpa cante śiceśni, wana eyaś wicaśa icahyinkte cin k'un igluśtan ke'.

15. Kahmi wan oblaye-owaśtecaka ca el iśnala tipi . . . ecin tuweni unśni, nahanhci oyate wanica . . . .

16. Wamakaśkan waśkuyeca ko ota canke takuni icakiżeśni hecel unpi na wakanheża kin iś hece śkaltukel icah ayapila . . .

17. Hecel tohanhunniyan kin unpikte s'e wacinpi k'un, anpetu wan el cincapi kin kośkalaka ca atkuku yanke cin el hi na heya ke':

18. "Ate, leceya lila omani-wakinica ye lo . . . Ito ka wi mahel iyaye cin hecetkiya mninkte," eya yunkan atkuku kin wacin-nunpa-hingnin na iyokiśni'.

19. "Hehehe, cinkś, nakun tuwa ihanhan mninkte ecin k'eyaś takunl ikuśekta yunke lo," eyaya k'eyaś hecenaś wanahunśni kakena icimani-iyaya ke'.

20. Tohinni tokiyani yapśni canke iyaye c'un hetanhan hakataku kin iwatokiyapihca ekta etunwan unpi ke'.

21. Yunkan anpetu wan el iyuha enanakiya wowaśi ecunpi na atkukupi kin tankal tiyopikiyela cankażip yankahan ke'.

22. Yunkan ungna, "Cunkśi, nisunkala le-anpetu kin glikte lo," eya ke'. "Ito tokaś," nahmahma eyapi na heceś wowaśi ecunhanpi yunkan ungna iś hehanl anatanpi ke'.

23. "Ate, ate, wicayake, misun lehanl glikta kehe c'un, ma ka wiyohpeyatanhan ku tka iśnala kuśni ye. Winyan wan aku we!" eya okaśkap s'e unpi ke'.

24. Wi kuciyela canke iyuha iśta nape un aohanzi-kiya nażinpi yunkan kiyela sam kupi kin ecel winyan wan iśta na pehin ko sapsapi na iś-eya lila owanyakwaśte ca aku-he'. Iśta kin tankinkinyan-mimama na pehin kin wiyakpakpa ke'.

25. Heceś ścepanku-tokapa k'un nupin itkop inyankapi . . . hena iyewicaceca canke wancagna iśna-ścepanyeic'ilapi.

26. Isto anunkatanhan koyakyapi na akupi ke', yuonihanyan. "Ścepan, ścepan," eyaya wiyuśkinyehcin akupi na timahel akiyagla ke'.

27. Waśtelakapi na ehaś iwitkotkoke s'e ahan-nażin kuwapi ke'. Taku waśte yuhapi kin iyuha k'un ahiyayapi na wana kal owank-pikiya śkanpi canke kohanape wicayanka yunkan tankakupi zi-winla k'un tiyopa el hinażinpi na ahiyokas'inpi . . . iś-eya ścepanku wanglak-wacin.

28. Ho, k'eyaś cuweku kin wicakiśica ke'. "Ako glapi na," eyapi na akeś "Ektan ścepan wanunkinciyakaktehcin!" eya okiciżiżipi canke śika zi-winla k'un śiglapi na hehanyela el yeśni maniltukel ece-unpi ke'.

29. Hetan tonacanka yunkan ake kośkalaka k'un atkuku yanke cin el hi na ke': "Ate, leceya omani-wakinica ye lo. Hehanl wi hinape cin hecetkiya mninktehcin . . ." eya ke'.

30. "Hehehe, cinkś, tawicu-yatun na wana owanżila yaun na mitakoża icagakte sece c'un . . . tehiya waehe lo . . . nakun tuwa ihanhan-mninkte ecin k'eyaś takunl ikuśekta yunke lo," eyaya k'eyaś hecenaś ake kakena iyaya ke'.

31. Tankeku k'un ecanl ścepan-tunpi kin iwinktapi un atayas le misun toki iyaya ce ecinpiśni; k'eyaś tankakupila k'un hena ekta etunwan unpila ke'.

32. Tonacan yunkan wana hinhanna wi u kin eciyatanhan ku ke'; ho, k'eyaś ake wanaś iśnalaśni, winyan wan ake kicica ke'.

33. Kiyela kupi kin hehanni winyan wan pehin zizi waśteśte, na iyeke c'eyaś nakun wi iheye cin lecel zi-ska ca owanyak wowinihan s'e lececa ke'. Ścepanku nunp iyewicakceca canke hena epi ca iś hehanl itkop yapi na istokoyakyak itokakinkin iyuśkinyehcin akupi na aglipi ke'.

34. Wana wikośkalaka kin śakpepi, yamni iśta pehin ko sapsapapi na yamni iś pehin zizipi, na eya toktuke c'eyaś iyuha winyan-waśte-iyakapapi ke'.

35. Nake kośkalaka k'un hehanyela omani-wacinśni, winyan nunp awicagli na op iyuśkinyan un ke'.

36. Heceś unpi k'un wana tawicu-tokapa k'un igluś'aka ke'.

Canke ścepanku nunp iyewicakceca k'un hena epi ca itomni
s'e iyuśkinpi un ehaś taku tokeya ipatakta taninśni śkanpi ke'.
Taku cikcik'ala wakanyeźa-tawa kin hena iyuha kitanyan swuyela
ipatahanpi ke'.

37. Iyecala s'e wana iś hehanl inunpa-agli k'un he igluś'aka ca
tanka aya ke'. Canke ścepanku zi-winla kin nupin iś-eya iyecehcin
wakah iyankapi ke'.

38. Wana wi tona hecel śkanpi yunkan ungna anpetu wan el
wicahcala kin tiyopa-itankal yankin na can-kaźipahin na cinca kin
kipan ke'.

39. "Cinkś, kaki ka wiyohpeyata bloya wankin na itokaga ihanke
kin el mni kin ekta ipuś'inyan ihunni kin hetulahcin mitakoś iyayin
na toki iyaya taninśni ye lo," eya, canke hecenahcin kośkalaka k'un
ektakiya inyankin na hel iguga tankinkinyan canke oko wan etan
aokas'in ke'.

40. Yunkan wicayuś'inyaye s'e, pte-winyela wan wayaślaśla
hiyayin na cincala wan heceya-tunpila ca hu ogloglokaheya ihakap
yela ke'.

41. "Hehehe, tokeśke wah'an huwo? Pte-winyan wan bluze lo!"
ecin na hecena lila glicu ke'.

42. Tiyata wana hecel-okahnigape laka tankeku k'un nupin el
upi ke': "Misun, misun, toka he?" eyap canke, "Tanke, niścepan
hokśila wan miciyuha ye lo," eya ke'.

43. Hecenahcin napatakiciyus inyankapi na wana ke c'un el
ihunnipikte hcehanl iguga-oko wan ogna ścepankupi k'un hokśicala wan waśte tancan t'inzehca ca aloksohan glinapa ke'.

44. "Ścepan, miye," eya okiciscis icupi na ho, hetanhan ihanhan
s'e yuha ece-unpi ke'.

45. Ake inunpa-can seca hanl wicahcala k'un tiyopitankal
cankaźi-yankahan yunkan ungna heya ke':

46. "Cinkś, kaki ka canpa-hu k'eya pamna he cin hel mitakoś
mahel iyaye c'eyaś etan kuśni ye lo," eya canke wana ake he taku
toka kin nupin slolyapi un kośkalaka k'un ekta inyank ihunni
ke'.

47. Canpahu kin paokoko na sam etunwan yunkan wagmeza
santuhu wan suta na waśte ca hanskeya icaga ke'; na isakip wanźi
iś-eya ula k'eyaś nakeś hinapela ca nunuźela ke'.

48. Kakel tate-hiyu canśna icikoyake seśna kawins-iyaya hanpi ke'.

49. Hecena hehanl tankśitku hakakta k'un hena agli-owicaki-yaka canke ekta niyaśniśni ihunnipi ke'.

50. Kaglayapi hanl wanaś ścepankupi k'un hokśi-waśte wan aloksohan wapamna aohomni glicu ke'.

51. Śehanl eś wicincapila canke psipsil ehaś tukte-unma tokeya icukta taninśni kuwapi na yuha inyank kiglapi ke'. "Mitośka, mitośka," eyaya kigna aglapila. . . .

52. Ho, hetanhan ihanhan-s'e tośkakupila kin lila tehilapi na ohinni awanyak yuha unpila canke ehaś ścepankupi kin takuni iksapeśni un ke'.

53. Wakanheża tuktel yukanpi can oiyokipi canke tiwahe kin ataya canl-waśteya unpi yunkan tohanl ungna wicahcala k'un tankal yankahin na heya ke':

54. "Mitakoża tokapa kin micicaupi ye!" eya canke tunwincu nunp ohinni gluha unpi k'un hena ahipi na tunkaśitku śiyute akanl egnakapi ke'.

55. Kakel aisiya kiglapilaka ca hecena wicahcala k'un heya ke':

56. "Ho, takoża, anpetu kin le tanyan wanyanka yo. . . . towan-żica na waśte ye lo, iwicakibleze cin heca ye lo . . . Le nitaanpetu ce . . . anpetu-lececa ca el maka ayalikta ce. . . .

57. "Maka kin le awali tka wakan ye lo . . . canke heun ohinni wakan-laya amawani ye lo . . .

58. "Niś-eya hecel ayalikta ce . . . ho, takoża, si-leciyatanhan un ihan yo . . . hecel. . . . ho, hehanl unma kin. . . . hecel!"

59. Tohanyan hecel wakaneża kin mani-unspekiyahe c'eyaś unmapi kin iyuha otakiya śkinciyapi canke tuweniś ableześni ke'.

60. "Ho, cunkś, nitośkala icupi ye!" eya-pan canke tunwincu k'un nupin hiyupi na glakiyagla ke'.

61. Ihinhanna yunkan ake ecehcin ecun. . "Mitakoża-hakakta kin micicaupi ye!" eya canke wana iś-eya tunwincu k'un ahipi na tunkaśitku śiyute akanl egnakapi ke'.

62. Kiciśnala yunkan hehanl heya ke':

63. "Ho, takoża, anpetu kin le tanyan wanyaka yo. . . . ahanziya, iśtiyowicaśniżeśni . . . asasyela wanke lo . . . le nitaanpetu ce. . . . anpetu lececa ca el maka ayalikta ce . . .

64. "Takoża, wanmayaka yo. Maka kin le awali ye lo . . . Ho, tka wakan, kin he un ohinni oholaya amawani ye lo . . .

65. "Niś-eya hecel ayalikta ce . . . ho, takoża, si-leciyatanhan un ihan yo . . . hecel . . . ho, hehanl unma kin. . . . ho!"

66. Hecel otohanyan takożakpaku mani-unspekiyahe c'eyaś unmapi kin abeya śkanpi na tuweni leś taku tokun ce ecankinpiśni ke'.

67. "Ho, cunkś, nitośkala wana icupi ye," eya-pan canke inyank hiyupi na ikikcupila na wana ake yuha śkatakta ca taniś tokiyotan lena eyayap.

68. Ihinhanna yunkan hehanl heya ke: "Ho, takoża awicaupi na niye ko iyuha upi ye . . . taku wanlakakte lo . . ." eya canke tiyopa kin ikanye hel ahinażin ke'.

69. Hokśilala kin wana lila śkehanhanpi canke tunwicu wicayuha hinażinpi k'eyaś glicu-wacin waś'akya iglaśpa-huns'e śkanpi ke'.

70. "Ho, lel ewicagle po," eya canke ecunpi ke'. Yunkan napatakiciyuzapila na akiciyulyuta, tunkaśitku kin hehanl ayulyuta ikopeyehcin ihanpila ke'.

71. "Hecetu we lo, takoża!" eya canke ake ihanpi na hankeya ohitika ayapila kin ecel kaoh'ankoya s'e ca eglepi, na hankeya, tankapi kin. "Hinun!" eyeye wanwicayakapi canke hecena ihatata inyank iyayapi ke'.

72. Hecenahcin manipila . . .

73. Akeś wicahcala k'un heya ke: "Winunhca, tehmiso etan yagnaka hecinhan glou ye!" eya canke heca ota kahi.

74. Hecena wahinpaspe-ohloka kin aohomnimni soso na wikan hanskaska kaġa ke'.

75. Canyatanhan psehti-hato k'eya kcankcanla na laplapela k'un heca wan agli na tanyehcin yuktan na cangleśka wan kaġin na hehanl imahel ataya wikan kin glakikinnyan icipasisasa yut'insya iyeyin na cokayelahcin cante-kahiya hlokya ayuśtan ke'.

76. Ho, he maka akanl toka-painyankapi kaġa śke lo.

77. Waśe un cangleśka kin yuhophopin na tuktektel un iyawapikte cin ecekce wapetokya iyun na heya ke:

78. "Ho, wawanyaka kin gli-witaya po . . . tima kiyotakapi na tiyopa kin iyublasya okatan po . . ."

79. Eya canke ecunpi, yunkan hehanl hokśila kin kinunkan

can wicak'u na painyankapi kin pacangle iyeyin na tokel el can
yekiyakte cin unspe-wicakiya ke'.

80. Waśtelaǩapi na ohinni ecunktehcin canǩe awanyak-śna
wicayankin na unspewicakiya ke . . . ecel hankeya sam glawa
ko-wayupikapi na imaġaġa-iciyapi ke'.

81. Hinhanna na wi u can hokśila kin nupin tunkaśitku kici
tankal inaźinpi na anpetu-ikignipi ke'. Towanźica can he hokśila-
tokapa kin tawa; na ahanzi na ablakela can he is hokśila-hakakta
kin tawa-iglawa ke'.

82. Yunkan tohunwel wana ake anpetu-ahanzi hanl painyankapi
unpi na śkatahanpila yunkan can kin tokel ecunpi na iciha-
hinglekiyapi na ecel unma sipa-wakaśe na hihpaya ke'.

83. Tuweni unśni, tunkaśitkupi kin ecela el yanka canke wana le
hicahin na ġahe s'e ceya yunkan-tunwincu kin iyuha, topapi kin,
inyank hihunnipi na, "Ate, tokeśke h'anpila he, mitośkala?" eyapi
ke'.

84. "Iśe tokaśni ye lo, cunkś. Nitośkala wanun-hicahela k'eyaś
lilahcin ksuyeyeśni ye lo. . . . inaźin yo, takoś, heca wica can
makicapśa icaġe lo!" eyaya ke'.

85. Tokapa k'un he e ca ceya canke tunwincu nunp ohinni gluha
unpi k'un hena ena kignapi ke . . . zi-winla k'un ehanni tokel
kiglapi, tośkakupila kin e ca ksuyeyeśni canke . . .

86. Wana yuasnipi na ake hokśilala kin nupin itap, wakanheźa
eyap śeca, śkatahanpi canke tunwicu kin kiglapi ke'.

87. Maninl taku ecunpi ca ektakiya glapi yunkan hel ścepankupi
tokapa k'un he wahatkahan ca slohan-kel śkan ke'.

88. Cinca hoiyekiya hunśe, el upi yunkan awicayuta canke
heyapi ke: "Iśe mitośkala unma wanu-hicahela ye ścepan, k'eyaś
ksuyeyeśni . . . wanaś ake he ihat'a śkatapi kin!" eyapi na iyayapi
ke'.

89. Yunkan ścepankupi kin hecetula s'e iha, k'eyaś ite-tokeca-
hingla ke'. Taku iyokipiśni . . .

90. Iyecala s'e, wana ake tuwe kin iyuha abeya śkanpi hanl
ungna tantaninśniyan wiwoha-tokapa k'un e ca hokśi-napatayus
gla ke'.

91. Tunkaku kin eca-tankal yanke ca, tokeya wanyakin na
cunwintku-tokapa kin owicakiyake'.

92. "Cunkś, niścepan takomni taku iyokipiśni-iteya kaki ka gle

hu wo. Anpetu-cokaya na kata ca hoksi-temnite-yinkte lo . . . ekta yapi na kigna po, cunks'," eya iwatokiyahca ke'.

93. Hecena wikoskalaka k'un inyank-ic'iciyapi k'eyas owas-yapsni, wanas wiyohpeyata he wanglakinya yanke c'un tuktel okiksahe wan el taninsni ke'.

94. Hecena inyankapi na is-eya etulahcin taninsni ca atkukupi kin tiyatahan ekta etunwan nazin yunkan iyecala ake glinapapi na lila kupi ke'.

95. Itkop wicayin na "Toka huwo, cunks, niscepan tayankel yegnapi na lucanl-asnipisni," eyaya k'eyas ecanl ceyapi na heyapi ke':

96. "Ate, taku yake, ma k'eya he winyan sni, he pte ye. Ca paha-akotanhan blaye-opta cincala iyowas'inyan icato-naunk gla ca tuweni wicasa-akantu wanzi kiglega okihikktesni ye," eyapi ke'.

97. Hecena iyuha ceyapi, na hoksila wan kakiyaglapi canke, koskalaka k'un iyotan tehi slolya ke'.

98. Yunkan hehantu ca tawicu-hakakta kin el hi na kigna ke. "Cante sicesni ye; tecihila kisto; u wa, kaki unyinkte," eyin na canpa-hu pamna he c'un heciya ai ke'.

99. Hecena can kin etan top wasteste owotantalahca ca waksin na cancan s'e wanhinkpe kicaga ke'.

100. Na heya ke: "Gnin na tunkasi icalu wan kangi-hupahu ca yuha k'un he makau," eya, canke hiyoi na kaki yunkan etanhan wiyaka wan icu na un wanhinkpe kin iyuha akiyecehcin inyak-tun na hehanl wase iyun na k'u ke'.

101. (Kangi kin isnala owotanlahcin kinyin nasna tehanlhanl ihunni kin he un hecun ske'.)

102. Hecena wanhinkpe kin hena yuha-kiyin na heya ke: "Ho, lena yuha ya. Le wanzi iyaye-yeya cansna owotanla yin na tuktel glihan can hetu ca owicayakile kin hena yankapi kte kisto.

103. "Wan le nakun yuha ya . . . tohanl taku tehika wanzi el nayazin can le itazipa el ikoyak-yin na kahomnimni na ho-umakiya," eyin na tohantan hi kin hehantan wacinhe wan zi, osteka ca yuhahaya peslete kin el eca-unka yunkan he e ca gluzun na k'u ke'.

104. Yunkan he le wagmeza hu kin sutun cansna santuhu inkpa kin ekta pahtapi s'e he c'un heca ske'. He un lehantu kin Lakota

wapaha-mima ḱaġapi canśna peslete kin el wacinhe wanżila
hanśkeya eglepi ḱ'un hecunṗe lo.

105. "Ho, wanżi yeya ye," eya canḱe ecun yunkan waś'aḱyeḣcin
ḣmuyela iyaya canḱe tawicu kici awanyaḱ nażinpi ḱe'.

106. Hecena wocetunglaya wiyoḣṗeyata bloya wanḱe c'un
atayela el ye śan wana tahepiya hinḣṗayinkta iyecetu yunkan ungnahanla ḱawanḱal ḱas'a-iyayin na ṗaha kin iwankaṗ aisinyan
iyaya ḱe'.

107. Wakan ca hece. . . . Heceś wana wicaśa ḱ'un tawicu unma
iḣṗeya iyayin na unma iś okile-ya ḱe'.

108. Anṗetu okise ataya mani na wana ṗaha kin iyuha toḱa can
ḱitan ecinyela ahanzi ḱ'un hececa ḣcehanl wakṗala wan el ihunni
na iyuweġinkta yunkan hena ohuta kin el lece wanhinkpe wan wi
coḱa hiyaye c'un e ca owotanla gliheya maka-paḣli
han ḱe'.

109. Yuslul iḱikcu gluha iyuweḣ iyaya yunkan akotanhan oblaye-
owaśtecaka wan el tipi wan ćisćila han ḱe'.

110. Itanḱal wakanheża wan śkal un ca wanyakin na wanaś
cinca ḱ'un he e ca iyekiya ḱe'. Yunkan iś-eya, oiśta-blesya, iyekiyin
na śkatela ḱ'un ayuśtan tiyoṗa kin ektakiya inyankin na itanḱal
nażin ḱe'.

111. Ohitiyela wiyutata tuwa timahel ḱici woglaḱin na eciyatanhan inyank u ḱe'.

112. "Micinḱśi, micinḱśi," eyaya iḱikcu ḱ'eyaś ecanl nihinciya
iela ḱe'.

113. "Ate, lecala, 'ate wana u we lo,' epa yunkan ina lila canzeḱe
lo . . . 'Taḱu, cewinś wicaśa aḱantu wan ca-hanśḱaska naiś tehanl
hi ye! . . . Iś iyeḱa ca hece, tehanl et'inkta wanś!' eye lo, ate.

114. "Nakun leye lo: 'Hinhanna ḱinhan wakṗa wan ibluweġinkta
tka hecamun ḱinhan mni kin naskeṗ-iwahinkte śan; iyeke hel
ohokta ca! . . . tokel ḣ'an ḱ'eyaś ipuza-t'inkte śan!' eye lo, ate.

115. "Tka tanyan anaġoptan yo: Oye unkiyayapin ki mitoye-
catḱayatanhan ki hel etunwan yo!" eyela ḱe'.

116. Wana waḱeya kin el ḱipi yunkan winyan wan lecaś canzeḱe
c'un, waśtecaka ḱe'.

117. "Unśika, maka kin okise anṗetu-wanżila yahihunni ḱiśto
. . . Tokeḣcin wanituḱa ye le! . . . Tima hiyu; ecala asniyakiyinkte,"

eyin na owinś pikiyin na wok'u ko śkan canke canl-waśtehca
iyunka ke'.

118. Iś unmake cin, watuka-iyakapa canke kakel iyunke c'un
hecena iśtinma ke'.

119. Anpa-o canke oguga yunkan tuweni-hci unśni, iśnala-
hci blaye-cokaya hunska kin pehan ikpahin hpaya ke. Wakeya na
owinża akanl iyunke un hena ko takuniśni . . .

120. Iyotak hiyayin na hunska kin ecekce okitun na hecena ake
wanhinkpe wakan kin wanżi iyaye-yin na ecel ya ke'.

121. Cu-nakankan iyayapi canke un islolya ke'.

122. Oye kin eciyatanhan naunk kiglapi-iteka canke iś-eya
anpetu-okise ataya inyankapi ece ecun na ipuzat'inkta hanl wico-
kanhiyaya ca mni-akilkil ya yunkan kaki tokata tehanl cunkpaza
canke wana hel mniyatkinkta ic'ila piyabliheic'iya ke'.

123. Ho yunkan wana el ihunni na wanyake c'eyaś atayaś mni
wanice . . . ee tuktel mni tka k'in ecel maka kin wana naksaksa na
opapun kin hena wi-kata u nakaś'inś'inya ececa'.

124. Ho, k'eyaś haakapyela ecela puzin na ohlate nahanhcin
upsiża-lolope.

125. Hececa kin un le oye iyayapi k'un mahelhetuya nalop
ihanpi ca wanyakin na cinca oye kin ole yunkan niśkośkola
mimeya hin na wanżi el mni sni waśte ya blesya he.

126. Hecena blaska-ihpayin na mni kel i un yage-yatke' . . .
lila ipuza k'eyaś mni-ognakela kin lila ciścila canke imnaśnihan
yahepinkta-ikope c'eyaś wakan caś tokel-yatke cin ecel nawankal
mni kin u.

127. Heceś mni-sni ipiic'iyin na nakun etan un ca peslete na
maku ko akpawintin na iglubleze'.

128. Yunkan hehanl mni kin tokah'an ke . . . ho, k'eyaś eyaś
hecetu wanaś hetan ake ya okihi ke'.

129. Ake wana htayetu-eciyatanhan paha kin tokecela opapun-
yan ahanzizi hanl wanhinkpe wan he-hinhanna kin iyaye-ye c'un
iyekiya ke'. Na wakpa-akotanhan hel ti-ska wan han ke'.

130. Hokśilala k'un atkuku aktunwan śkata hunśe kakel taninyan hiyu kin hecena wiśkate kah'ol yeyin na tipi kin ektakiya
inyanka ke'.

131. Wana ake hunku kici woglakin na hecena akiś'aś'a atkuku
anakitan ke'.

132. Ake ikikcu k'eyaś niyaśniśni ecanl wokiyak inyanke.
"Ate, ate, wana ake ina ikcapte lo, 'ate wana u we lo,' epa yunkan
hecena . . . 'Wi, cewinś wicaśa-akantu wan hu-waś'aka nacece
ke! . . . Etanś toka, iś iyeke cin, ... hinhanna kin hlihlila wan
opta wakiyuweginkta tka miyeka yeś tawat'el-wayeśni yeśan!
133. " 'Eś hel ake ohitikta kecinhca! Toki tahu-ecela tanin ni;
toki eś eś ataya mahel iyaya ni! . . . Tokel kpapte-pica ka!' eye lo,
ate; ce tokel h'an-wacin yo!" eya ke'.
134. Wanaś ake ti-skala k'un ekta kihunnipi yunkan winyan kin
waśte eyap ca ke'.
135. Kihaha na heya ke: "Śika, śika, til glicu! Nanicit'e kiśto;
ca htayetu-amna inunkinkte . . . hinhanna ciyuhica-iyawecunni na
unyan cihiyu k'un. Nakeś ecala asniyakiyinkte," eya yustosto ke'.
136. Wicake s'e lececa canke wana akeś gnayan ihpeya ca heya
ke: "Ho, eca wakanheźa kin ako hpayekiyin na niye misakip hpayi
ye," eya canke ecun ke'.
137. Wana lila iśtinme seca canke wahwakiyehcin iye taipiyaka
ihanke kin zezeya otka canke he tawicu taipiyaka kin ekta aiya-
kaska ke'.
138. Hecun na hehanl pehin ki waśteśte hanskaska canke
napogna etan icu na isto el tonakel aiyakpehin na ihanke kin hena
sutaya yus hecel iśtinma ke'.
139. "Tokśa nakeś iyayinkta-igluwinyeya kinhan omagunginkte
cin," ecin na hecun ke'.
140. Ho, yunkan ake wana anpa-o ca kikta yunkan iśnalahcin
blaye-cokaya maka kin iyatala hpaya ke'.
141. "Wahteśni!" wana ecin na iyayapi ca ecel cu-nakankan
oyepi kin etkiya ake wanhinkpe wan iyaye-ya ke'.
142. Ecel yin na wana kal ake glihan ca yuślul ikikcu na gluha
ya yunkan hel maya ke'. Na hukuta wakpa-tanka iyehanyan s'e
maka kin eca-unpśiźa ca sloślola, alipicaśniyan yunka ke'.
143. Yunkan cokaya s'e wana tawicu k'un hokśi-kic'in na ahco-
kaśeya taninyan naźin ke'.
144. He gla keyehca nacece c'eyaś otehiya gla canke ehaś ena
naźinhe s'e lececa ke'.
145. Heceś wicaśa k'un tawicu-unma kin wacinhe wan wakanyan k'u k'un he ikikcu na itazipa-ihanke el ikoyak-yin na wankal
yuzin na kahomnimni ke'.

146. "Ho wo, winyan, wanmayaka yo . . . omakiya yo . . . niye womayakiyakin na le mayak'u k'un ognayan!" eya.

147. Yunkan kahomnimni kin ecel wamniyomni wan ciscila k'eyaś waś'aka ca kaicaga ke'.

148. Canke iyukap icu na le wokokipeya hlihlila wan glakinyan yunke c'un akotanhan maka-suta akanl glihe ke'.

149. Can kin woihanbleta s'e tankinkinyan canke kal ituhu-can wan iyotan tunweni icageśni s'e han ca hute el kaicanyan iyotakin na asnikiya ke'.

150. Yunkan itehan hanl wana wicaho tanin . . . sam kiyela u kin ecel taku kapi kin ko nah'un . . . Yunkan tawicu k'un e ca leya u ke':

151. "Śicaya k'eyaś cinkś, takomni tokel h'an-picaśni ye . . . niyate iye ic'icage . . . wicaśa akantu unpi kin ektana keś unśni, he tokel mihakap u-wacin . . . śika, okihiśnihce śan! . . . hecel un wana lehanl unpśiźa kin cete ekta niyate hpaye!" eya ke'.

152. Yunkan "Hiya, ina, hecetuśni ye lo . . . kaki ka can-tanka wan hute kin el ate yanke lo!" eya ke'.

153. Ho, nakeś hehanl pte-winyan k'un awicakeya-canzeka ke . . . "Wahiteśni śice cin, ektan mayucanze-ktehcin ye! . . . tokel wana naic'iśpe-pica ka!

154. "Lecegla wana mitamakoce kin el ya ca tokśa ekta i kinhan nakeś winunhcala kin wicaśaśni kapinkte! . . . Tokel tiyopa-wakan kin el zaniyan iyayinkte kecin. . . . Winunhca ke, 'Wipe kin hena nitawin tawak'in kin akanl egnaka' eye, cinhan tokeśke tona mitawa kin slolyinkta ca!

155. "Na tohanl, 'Nitawin kin isakip yanka' eye, cinhan tuktel hiyayinkta ca! Untopapi k'eyaś iyuha akiyeuncecapihce c'un, iyeśtuka tokeśke iyemakiyinkta keyehcin na witkohcin na ipaweh iyotake-cinhan tokśa wana t'inkte . . ." eyaya itomni s'e iya gla ke'.

156. Ho, k'eyaś hokśila ku atkuku yanke ci ekta ihunni na "Ate, nayahun we lo . . . wakta yo. Unci cunwintku topapi kin iyuha nico-u-wicakiyinkte lo.

157. "Wacin-ksapa yo, ate; ina iyuha akilececape lo . . . wanźi nignayinkta keś tiyatakiya etunwan yo. Taninmic'iyeśni kin hehan ena yanka yo.

158. "Tokśa tohanl ina e ca u kinhan wahinapinkte lo," eyin na

inyank kignin na hunku kici wana kuya pte-tamakoce kin ekta hocokatunyan wicoti-tanka ca ektakiya glapi ke'.

159. Kaiyuzeya k'eyaś tanyan tanin canke ekta awanwicayak yanka ke'. Yunkan kal tipi wan tanka ca el tima kigla ke'.

160. Yunkan hecena winunhcala wan inayanpi kin cunwintku topapi kin iyuha can wicakicun nuns'e howaya ke'.

161. "Hinun, hinun, le wicaśa akantula wowicunk'ukta ca unkunpi kin, wicincala k'eya uncikpani it'a wicabluha ye le, miyelahcin!

162. "Inażinpi na cancan s'e lol-ih'anpi . . . na mitakoś kico-yapi na!" eya u canke wana wanżikżila kicohipi'.

163. Ho, k'eyaś wanżi ake u can he tawicu kin ee kecin ke' . . . akiyececapi kin un eceś ośtekapi kin un.

164. Lila tantanya kicopi can gnayanpi nuns'e lececa . . . "Eceś u na, ungninkte . . . nikun wan unniyuonihanpiśni keyin na kte nuns'e unkuwa pe . . . Coka-ki-wakapin ye, unśimala na!" eyapi ke'.

165. Winyan wanżi unśisi-ia can wicaśa gnayan canke iś-eya le gnayanpikta keś icukiya ke'.

166. Wana kitanhcin icitopa kin u k'eyaś wanaś hehanyan tukte yuze c'un e taninśni canke hecel ayutaśni yanka yunkan hinażin na iś-eya ecekce eya ke'.

167. Ecanl, toke-wacinka, tipi kin ektakiya etunwe hcehanl hokśilala k'un hinapin na wankatakiya wiśkate-wanhinkpela k'eya yuha canke hena utahan ke'.

168. Wanyak iheye cin hecena nażin hiyayin na wana ka winyan kin gla canke ihakap yin na el i ke'.

169. Kunku k'un wana itkop hinapin na winunhcala-hpecakeśni canke "Ito miye iyatayela mitakoś wakiyugan-kte," eyin na tiyopa kin kiyugan ke'.

170. Canke til iyaya yunkan oh'ankoyehcin tiyopa kin ayuhpa ke'. He inyan canke agliheyin na kte kecin'.

171. K'eyaś ake tawicu-hakakta kin wacinhe wan k'u k'un he gluha canke iyowas'inyan wiyaka s'e kahwok-tima iyaye'.

172. Winunhcala k'un inahma s'e nihinciye c'eyaś waśte-kic'un ke'. "Ho, takoś, lecel le untipila ye . . . wipe kin nitawin tawak'in kin akanl ekignaka, wayatinkte," eya canke opehantakiya etunwan

yunkan wak'in hiyeye cin iyuha akiyecelya waśteśte na okaġe ko
owanżila ke'.

173. Toṗ hel tanka-kiciyapi ca iyuha tawoyuha akiyececapi . . .
canke unc'unnica s'e iyuha wanyak nażin yunkan kal ihankeya
wank'in kin akanl wana ehanni ake cinca-tażila k'un wanhinkpela
kin ekignaka canke iś-eya akanpatahan ekignaka ke'.

174. "Ho, takoś, micunkśi kici iyotaka, takomni he luze," eya ke'.
Yunkan ake hokśila kin peżi wan hunku pe kin el ayuśtan canke
un iyekiyin na ṗat'a nuns'e iyotaka yunkan winunhcala k'un ihata
ke'. "He-he-yo! Miyeś hena wicawatun weś icignuni-wicawaye s'a
k'un. . . . Ho, k'eyaś cin heca wicaśa can tawicu iyekiya ca hece!"
eya ke'.

175. Wana iyunkapi na anṗa-o canke kośkalaka kin inapin na
okśankśan etunwan nażin ke'.

176. Taku kin iyuha tokeca s'e wicoti'—takomni lena iś-eya
oyatepi k'eyaś ptepi kin he un.

177. Yunkan lena wana ake winunhcala k'un ikcapta kikta ca
tioġeya tanin'.

178. "Kiktapi! Kiktapi! . . . He le wicaśa-akantu wowicunk'ukta
ca unk'upi, caś slolyayapi kin, tokel le nunkapi he? . . . wicaśa
akantula cehupa gluśkanśkankta un ece anṗa can inażin ye . . .
kiktapi, kiktapi!

179. "Miyekeś le pte-winunhca mniciyapikta ca ekta mninkta ce
wok'upi!" eyin na wana hocoka-opta cancan s'e kicico-ya ke'.

180. Hankaku kin waśtecapika canke hunkupi kin iyaya yunkan
oihateya canl-waśteya wok'upi canke oṗ wotin na hehanl iyuha
akiyecel pehin olotapi canke tawicu kin kicisun na hehanl unmapi
kin wicakicisun na oṗ woglak yankahan ke'.

181. Tanyanś yankapi k'un wana ake winunhcala k'un cinktakta
ku na el gli na canpa-hu wan nunhnunhyela wicitokaṗ ihpeyin na
heya ke,

182. "Cunkś, tokel nankapi so! Mak'eya lecala nihunpi kin
ihahaṗe! Pte-winunhca wotapi kin el wanżi wiceśkipasise waśteśte
tekteca ota yuha canke 'Cepanśi, etan mak'u ye, henakehcin
tokanunkteśni hecinhan,' epa yunkan heye: 'He takole! Owehcaś
hanhanke! Mitakoś he lena micaġe cinś, wicawak'u ka! . . . . Niś-

eyaś takoś-yatun kin, toke etan nicaġe śni?' eyin na le aiḣpemayan
canke imaḣa ṗe!" eyin na itogmus glus ceya ke'.

183. Hecena takośku k'un naic'ipsicin na "Tuktel canpahu
yukan huwo?" eya, yunkan hankaku kin wanżi okiyaka ke':

184. "Ma, kaki tehanl ka can wan iyotan-hanske cin hel okśan
canpahu waśteśte ye," eyin na hehanl, heya ke': "K'eyaś tunweni
tuweni heciyatanhan ni gliśni k'un!" eya ke'.

185. Hececa k'eyaś kośkalaka k'un iyaya ke . . . Na wana kiyela
ya yunkan can kin okśan enana wicahu aociptelya-śekśeca hiyeya
ca wanyaka ke'.

186. Na cankin iyohila hute el zuzeca kaśkan yunkapi ke'.

187. Heceś napinkta-iyecelya ye c'eyaś katinyeya yin na wana
kiyela inażin na hehanl tawicu-wagmeza-winyan k'un wacinhe
tawa kin ake kahomni yunkan wamniyomni wan kaicaġa canke
can kin iyuha yuweḣweġin na zuzeca kin wicakte ke'.

188. Canke iye tokel cin ecel can-kaḣniḣ omanihin na wihin-
ṗaspe na wiceśkiṗasise-waśte ece waksa agli ke'.

189. Kunku iyokipi-kiyinkte sece c'un ecanl eha winunḣcala kin
bleześni s'e howaya ke'.

190. "Ako ayapi! ako ayapi! Hena zuzeca-wakan kin tipi
etanhan ca gliyoupikte! Tase zuzeca wati el upikta ca caś! Mayata
eiḣṗeyapi!" eya, si yuzaṗ s'e howayin na heyatakiya napa ke'.

191. Canke cunwintku hakakta kin canpahu kin iyuha ṗahi na
mayata ai tkaś kośkalaka k'un tawicu kin kiṗan na heya ke: "Iyayin
na canpahu kin etan waśteśteḣca wanhinkpe-waśte ece aku wo,"
eya canke agli ke'.

192. Hecena wagmeza winyan kin wanhinkpe-wakan kaġe c'un
kiksuya canke eceḣcin iś-eya wanhinkpe-wakan toṗ cinca-hokśila
kin kicaġin na kal pusya otkeya ke'.

193. Yunkan inunpa-hinhanni ake eceḣcin kunku kin kikta na
ikcapta cunwitku wicayuḣicin na pte-winunḣca kicicopi wan ekta
iyaya ke'.

194. Na tanyan yankahanpi hanl el ceya gli na heya ke: "Cunkś,
lecala owemaḣaḣapi na le aiḣpemayaṗe! . . . pte-winunḣca wan
unżicala k'eya waśteśte yuta canke 'Cepanśi, wanżi mak'u ye,
miś-eya watinkte,' epa yunkan, 'Ece, tase takowe! . . . Nitakośku

yukeśni ye laka?' eyin na lecela tamaheca na iyut'int'inya ececa caś
ena eħpeya yunkan he e ca akaħ'ol hiyumaye!" eyin na wana ake
zahela s'e ceya ke'.

195. "Ho, tuktel le unźicala yukanpi huwo?" wana ake wicaśa
kin eya, yunkan hankaku kin heyapi ke: "Ma kakiya maya-sapa kin
he e śni, akotanhan wanźi yanka ca hetu we". . . . . eyin na, unmapi
kin okicizizipi yunkan, "Niś hehanl okiyakapi na," eyin na tima
kigla canke heyapi ke:

196. "Śice, akśaka tunweni heciyatanhan gliśni k'un," eyapi ke'.
Tkaś hecena wicawoha canke iyaya ke'.

197. Kiyela ya yunkan enana wicahu aociptelya sekseca hiyeya
canke wanyakin na can kin iś lila hanskaska ca ableza ke'.

198. Tokeni ali-picaśniyan aletka kin wankalkatuya canke
hecetuka keś ake wacinhe k'un he itazipa el ikoyak-kiyin na
kahomnimni yunkan tate wan iyumniyan tan-ataya yuwankal icu
na can kin wanźi iyotan-hanskin na inkpa ekta topakiya okiźata
yunkan hel cokayelahcin wahohpi-tanka wan ekta egnaka ke'.

199. Yunkan wahohpi kin ekta unźincala top waśteśtepi na
tanktankapi ca iyohi tate ouye kin wanźi etkiya etunwan yankapi
ke'.

200. Canke wanźi toktok nata akanl awicapin na kat'a awicahi-
yayin na wana wanźila okapte hcehanl can kin iwankaptulahcin
hel mahpiya wan mimeya kuciyela yanka yunkan etanhan wakan-
gli hiyu na can k'un kte na topakiya hute kin ihunni ohangleya
wosleca canke cokaya osloheic'iyin na makata glicu ke'.

201. Hecena mahpiya-cik'ala k'un ekta lena wakinyan kin
iśikcin hotunpi yunkan tokiyap wicaho wan tanka ca heya ke:

202. "Ayuśtanpo! Tunweni he yaktepikteśni ye lo! He iś-eya
wakanyan un we lo. Ituya le can wan el hokśi-icah-yakiyapi k'un
niye iyunkala ihankyakiyape lo!" eya ke'.

203. Yunkan Wakantanka-wayasu kin he e śke'.

204. Hecena wakinyan kin nake ñah'unpi hunśe, mahpiyala wan
eca-yanke c'un iyopteya iyayin na hankeya ataninśni ke'.

205. Canke eciyatanhan wicaśa-akantu k'un unźincala top
awicaku na kunku kin iyokipikiyinkta-ic'ila gli ke'.

206. K'eyaś ecanl winunhcala k'un ake bleześni, "Ako awicayapi
na! Hena he wakinyan cincapi ca wokokipekapi kin, tase wati el

hena yanka kte ca caś! Wakinyan-aute-mayanpikta tka!" eya ceyaya
iyayin na napa ke'.

207. Cunwintku wanźi wanah'unka canke manil eihpe-wicaya
tkaś wicaśa kin tawicu hupahu wanźi kin hiyoyeśi ke'. Agli ca etan
wiyaka icu na cinca tawanhinkpe k'un iyaktun ke'.

208. Ihinhanna, wana he hinhanna-iyamni yunkan wacipi ke'.
Hokśilala k'un ake atkuku el i na nahma-wokiyakela ke'.

209. "Ate, wacipikte lo. Pte-hokśila kin iyuhahcin mnaiic'iya
anpetu ataya wacipi na pte-owaci kagapikta śke lo," eya ke'.

210. (Lehantuka yeś makośkanl tuktektel pte-owaci mimeya
ośkokpaya yanke c'un hehan hena toka-kagapi śke lo.)

211. "Ca ate enakiyapi kinhan imayakikcuśni hantanhanś unci
niktekta keye lo. Ca tanyan wanmayaka yo. Hokśila henawicakca
keyaś ihankeya s'e opimiciyi na amayaluta canśna nakpa-catkaya-
tanhan wagluśkanśkankte lo," eya ke'.

212. Na wana wacipi k'eyaś okokipeka ke'. Tohinni ake hecel
wowayanke tukteni yukeśni iyecel pte-oyate el hokśila wicayuhapi
k'un hena iyuhapi canke hocoka wan wakanyan kah-enaźin na
kakel-spapi kin hecena witayelahcin ehanni iglutapi s'e wacipi ke'.

213. Koktopawinge tona witaya wacipi na maka sota s'e anpetu
ataya śkanpi canke maka kin wankatakiya mahpiya iyagleya sutaya
tate-kawinźeśni han ke'.

214. Wana hitayetu canke enakiyapi yunkan winunhcala k'un
ake takośku kin na, "Ma takoś, nicinca kin ikikcu, iyeśtuka
wicaatkuku kin iyuha hokśi-ikigna owicatantunke," eya canke
waci-gliśtanpila na watuka-asnikiya glinaźinpi canke egna iyaya
ke'.

215. Wancagna taźila wan kal nakpa ogloglokahe s'e ohitiya
wanyakap-cin-yankel pipiya-inaźin k'eyaś wanyakeśni kuns omani
na wana eyaś kunku kin imnayin na hehanl ungna cinca ikikcu na
heyata glogliyaku ke'.

216. Eśeś iyekiyinkteśni kecin na tamahel iyuśkin tkaś atayela
ikikcu canke tokel etunweca nuntka ke'.

217. Hecetu keś, "He-he-yo! Toś, toś, heca wicaśa can cinca
iyekiya waś" eyaya ihaha naźin k'eyaś ho-aecetukeśni ke'.

218. "Ate, ehanni wanmayalake śni, kal eś nakpa-oglohoho
nawaźin k'eyaś iśta-nigunga s'e lececa yelo," eya canke, "To, cinkś,

wicotapi ca hece," eya ke'. Icunhan tokyehcin-wiyukcan canke
takeye cin el ewacinśni.

219. Wana hinhanna-icitopa k'unhan oiyokipiyela painyankapi
unpi ke'. Canke pte-owaci wan heceya-kaġapi k'un hel oyate kin
ataya s'e wawanyakapi ca wicaśa akantula k'un cinca kici egna
naźinpi . . .

220. K'eyaś icunhan tuweni oslolyeśni, winunhca-wicaśaśni
k'un he e ca manitakiya inyanka ke'.

221. Heci osmaka-mahel tipi wan iśnala, tośu-inkpa ece taninyan han yunkan ekta ihunni na tankatanha hoyeya ke':

222. "Tatanka-gnaśkinyan, el nanka he?" eya yunkan tuwa
timahetanhan ayuptin na "Ho!" eya ke'.

223. "Ma, taku slolyeśni nanka he! Leceya le wicaśa akantula
kin htayel cunk'inta nitawin-hakakta kin okiya keyapi na oyate kin
ikik'op kin, tokel nanke!" eya ke'.

224. Hecena hnahna tankatakiya hinapinkta ca lena śkan k'eyaś
apeśni hetan icazop s'e glicu na wawanyaka kin pazanzan takośku
okile ya ke'.

225. Tuweniś hecunkeśni, isto el yunini na, "Takoś, iyaya!
. . . Heceya, oyate waaiyap s'a ke cin wana ake tuwa tatanka-
gnaśkinyan ki tawicu-hakakta wan oyakiya keye-okiyaka ca hinske
uye-kiyin na takpe-niu we! . . . Iyaya! . . . iyaya! . . . takoźa icu na
kici napa!" eya ke'.

226. Tkaś ecanl wanhinkpe-wakan ikikcu na wiyeya naźin, na
wana tatanka-gnaśkinyan k'un gloglo maka k'ak'a u tkaś owanźila
apaha nazin ke'.

227. Oyate kin ataya icak'oyela napapi canke tuweni unśni ca
atayela u na capinkta tkaś pahte-cokaya iyeya ke'.

228. Hecena tatanka kin pomnamna yukśanyan inyankin na ake
piya-u tkaś ake iśta-cokaya iyeyin na wobleześni canke kawinh-
kigla ke'.

229. K'eyaś ihakap inyankin na wana ka kaiśutata ya ca ake
wanźi tuktel iyeya yunkan kaslohan glihpayin na hehanyela
inaźinśni ke'.

230. "Ate! . . . . Leciyatan!" hokśila k'un eya ca iglamna hcehanl
kunyapi waśteka, winunhca k'un he iś-eya wana pte-winyela ca

wokokpeya anatan tkaś he nakun el iyeyin na wahinkpe wanżila
un kte ihpeya ke'.

231. Okśakśan wicaśa kin etunwe c'eyaś ehanniś oyate kin ataya
paha-akotanhan aisinyan tokah'anpi ke'.

232. Yunkan ehankec'un le tatanka-gnaśkinyan kin e na pte-
winunhca waniye kunye cun heniyoś ehantanhan oyate kin le ataya
tehiya wicakuwapi ca lila wokokipe-wacayapi hunśeca . . .

233. "Ho, cinkś, ekta yin na kuwicaśi yo . . . henala han-
kokpapikte . . . Wana toka kin nupin wicawecikte ye lo, hena
makipażinpi kin un hecamun, na pte-oyate unmapi kin iyuha
tawacin waśtepi kin un miś-eya waśtewicawalake lo." eya ke'.

234. Canke hokśila k'un paha-akotanhan i na oyaka ke'. Yunkan
mahpiya kin iyapat'oya akiś'api na eciyatanhan agli ke'.

235. Tohanyan inilakel agliyotakin na hehanl ungna wicaśa-
okinihan akenum, hena oyate-wakicunzapi kin epi ca tanyehcin
igluzapi na yuowecinhan hocokatakiya yapi ke'.

236. Hel pte-owaci k'un etu ca yapi na inila yukśanyan wiyohinyanpatakiya etunwan iyotakapi ke'.

237. Ehantanś taku tokakte s'e oyate kin icinapeya unpi caś
ableza ke'. Yunkan wana lena upi kin hehanni oyate kin ataya
yuocik'aya upi na mimeya ahinażin ca wakicunza kin cokata
yankapi ke'.

238. Tuwe kin oyas'in el yapi canke iś-eya opeya yin na inażin
yunkan cokap kicopi na kal tuktel iśnala egnaka ke'.

239. Na heya ke: "Ho, wicaśa-akantula, anpe-lehanl oyate wan
yucik'a s'e pilayaye cin un iś-eya wopila eniciyape lo.

240. "Pte-winunhca gnaśkinyan wan cinca ca luze cin he
ihpeyin na wikośkalaka waśteśte le ahinażin kin hetan winyan
iglahniga yo.

241. "Ena yaunkta ce; wicaśa maka akanl un kin e, na unkiye
iyotahena yaun na iyeniskakta ce." eya ke'.

242. Heceś tehiya wakicunzapi kin un ehaś waayuptinkta cin
oiyanica canke inila tehan-nazin ke'. Ungna pa yuwankal icu na
okśankśan etunwe c'eyaś pte-oyate kin iyuha inila pamagle, taku
wakta s'e nażinpi ke'.

243. Yunkan heci: "Ohan, ehank'un le wowilake-waunkta

hunśe . . . Ho, eya cin takel iglaśpe-pica ka!" ecin na ohanketa "Ha o!" eya ke'.

244. Hecena pte-oyate kin henawicakeca k'eyaś wanźini okapteśni himu s'e "Ha-ye! Ha-ye! Ha-ye!" eya ke'.

245. Yunkan hehanl ake kin nupin inaźinpi na inapapi ke', hocokaya ahinaźin k'un etanhan. . . . Tuwenihcin takeyeśni ca, iś-eya, "Toka huwo?" ecin k'eyaś inila naźin ke'.

246. Iyecala s'eś ake kupi . . . Pte-wicahca wan tokel-okihi kan ca yus aglipi na kal, yukśanyan wakicunza yanka k'un wicitokap iś-eya wiyohinyanpatakiya etunwan iyotak-kiya ke'.

247. Wicahcala na kan k'eyaś woimnaka ca, nap-coka na ite ko tanyan wase kic'un, na kanpeska k'eya owin ke'—hena wakan-tawoyuha ye lo—na wokoyake ko tanyehcin un; na sakye wan śayapi ca iikpatan yanka ke'.

248. Na pehin kin nata-sani iśle yatanhan ataya glakcaśni ca winawizi tokeni heyap icupicaśniyan iyuwi ke'. Wakanyan yanka ke'.

249. Hecena ake iyayapi na inunpa wanaglipi ke'. Iś-eya iyecahcin na oigluze koya yugnayeśni; tka le iś nata-sani ataya peźi-hota iyuwi ke'.

250. Ake iciyamni wan aglipi, yunkan he iś nata-sani isle-yatanhan ataya pte-iciyuha iyuwi', na icitopa wan aglipi yunkan he iś wahca-zi hu kin heca ca pehin iyuwi ke'.

251. Lena-top wosla yankapi k'eyaś sakye k'eya luta ca iikpatan iśtogmus wanah'un yankapi ke', paoglayeya, wakicunza yankapi kin wicitokap.

252. Heceś wana henala hunśe wayutanpi kin iyotakapi yunkan hehanl wanźi iyeskakta ca inaźin na heya ke':

253. a. "Ho, lena wohinape kin ektakiya manipikta ce.

    b. "Tasiśake nagwes, canku śaglogan manipikta ce,

    c. "Owanka wan waśte ca kagapikta ce,

    d. "Owanka wa wakan ca kagapikta ce;

    e. "Hena hokśicanlkiyapi kin wanyak manipikta ce;

    f. "Wakpa guheya wanke cin kicapta manipikta ce;

    g. "Anpetu-kata opta manipikta ce;

    h. "Niya taninyan manipikta ce.

254. i. "Heci ognake wan imanipikta ce.

    j. Ikce-wicaśa kin imanipikta ce;

    k. Mniwan luta imanipikta ce;

    l. Waluta wan imanipikta ce;

    m. Kanpeśka wan imanipikta ce;

    n. Wanbli śun wan imanipikta ce.

255. o. Wicincala wan wotiyemnaśni (wakaśte śni) ca icupikta ce.

    p. Na kiciic'iya mni-yatkanpikta ce;

    q. Sakye śayapi kin napiyusyapi kta, na

    r. Tatiye wan iye tawapi ca iyopteya maka nakiptanyeśni yuhomnipikta ce;

    s. Na hinaśte-ska ohtayetu ekta wakicunzapikta ce.

256. "Hunhi," wicaśa kin ecin; "iś-eyaś lena ecun-kapinpikta naceca yeś lecel mitaoyate un yapikte cin; ito miś-eya canl-waśteya iyowinmic'iya ke. Miye kin tokaśni' . . . mitaoyate nipikte cin he e iyotan ye lo . . . ." ecin'.

257. Heciyatanhan ca le Tatank-awicalowanpi kin u śke lo. Na tohanyan tatanka kin el unpi kin hehanyan Lakota kin nipikta keyapi k'un he iyecetu'. Canke Lakota oyate kin tatanka-hokśila k'un he etanhan wicicaga keyape lo.

258. He un ca le Lakota kin pte-talo ecela woyute-tokapa-yawape lo.

259. Maka kin ihukuya pte-tamakoce kin ekta lecel owolitatun k'eyaś icunhan maka akanl wicaceya ke'.

260. Tiyata yankapi kin hena anpetu canśna wana hehanl glipikte seca ca ape wicayankapi k'eyaś tokiyayapi taninśni ke'.

261. Yunkan ungna Wagmeza-winyan k'un e ca tokeya taku slolya śke'. Inapin na kaki maninl iyotakin na canke śica-yankahan canke tokeya ścepanku ziwinla k'un hena ekta hipi na gleapehanpi k'eyaś iyakcunnipi ke'.

262. "Ścepan, glapi ye; tokśa tohanl owakihi kinhan wakukte, towaś cante akiśni-mic'iyinkte," eya canke unyaglipi'.

263. K'eyaś atkukupi k'un takośka gluonihan canke hehanl cunwintku tokapa kin ekta yewicaśi ca ipi k'eyaś iś-eyaś yahlo-kapśni canke coka-glip ke'.

264. Wana tehan-yanka ca hecetuka keś Wakanka iye iyunkala ekta i na heya ke': "Takoś, nitunka umaśi ca wau we . . . wana ku ye!" eye c'eyaś itkop heya-ayupta ke':

265. "Eś miś-eya wacinko-iblamninkta kecannipi nacece . . . Tokiyani mninkteśni kiśto," eya canke iś-eya winunhca k'un iśnala gli ke'.

266. Ho, unhanketa, wicahcala k'un ekta ya ke'. . . . inażinżin tawat'elyeśnihce c'eyaś nakun akukte cin lila cantokpani canke el itohanyan inazin na lila wiśtelkiye cin un ayutaśni ia ke':

267. "Hehehe, takoś, le tohanyan-miglawa na un namayah'unkta kecin-wauśni ye lo. . . . Unmapi kin epika yeś nawicayah'unśni k'un, . . . hehehe, takoś," eya ceyaya iyaye, wana kan na oceye-wankala canke.

268. Ho, k'eyaś winyan kin iś-eya tunkanku gluonihan canke tanyan ayupta ke'. "Tunkaśi, gla ye, tokśa tima yakiyagle cinhan miś-eya wakukte, niye yahi kin he unhca ca wakukte." eya ke'.

269. (Hetanhan ca tunkanku na takośku ohowicakilapi kin le wicoh'an kin u we lo.)

270. Wana wicahcala k'un tima kiyotaka yunkan hehanl wagmeza-winyan kin inażin na ku canke kohan ścepanku kin sicawacin woyute kiyuwiyeyapi, anpetu ataya woteśni kin un.

271. Tima gli canke wok'upi ca wotahin na igluśtan na hehanl heya ke': "Tunkaśi, unciśi, ścepan, tanyan nah'unpi, taku wan eciciyapikte . . . Tuwe wan waśte-unkilapi k'un he le-anpetu kin ihpeunyanpi na pte-oyate kin op ohinni unkta-ic'ic'u we.

272. "Hecun kin un wana unkiyepi etanhan heyap iic'ikcu canke he un ca le waceye. . . ihaunktapśni, cinca kin le eka yeś ko kiksuyeśni . . ." eye, cin hecena unmapi kin iś hehanl ceya iyayapi na otohanyan hmu s'e wicaceya ke'.

273. Kit'api s'e kicanpi na hehanl wana eyaś ceya-imnapi can caokit'api k'un hecunhanpi yunkan wagmeza-winyan k'un heya ke':

274. "Wana eyaś hecetu we . . . inila yankapi ye, towas take-pinkte," eya canke tehilapi kin un nah'unpi na inila yaśtanpi yunkan heya ke':

275. "Tecihila ce: ca tunweni tokanl mninkteśni kiśto. . . .

Wicaśa wan iyecinka tokanl icicu ca tunweni ake he lel canl-
waśteya kici unkunpikteśni ye.

276. "Ho, hecetu kin u, ito letanhan unkiglakapi na wiyohin-
yanpata mitamakoce kin etkiya unglapikte.

277. "Hecun tuktel owaśtecaka wanżi el piya-unkitipi na
tohanyan ni unk'unpikta hecinhan hehan hel cante-waśte unkiyu-
tapikte . . . tokaś unkokihipikte sece . . . Eceś lel oiyokiśice," eya
ke'.

278. Iś-eyaś tuktel etunwanpi kin iyuha el wakiksuyapi kin un
iyayapikte cin hecetulapi canke wana iglakapi na wiyohinyanpatakiya yapi ke'.

279. Tonacan hecel eti yahanpi na unhanketa kal wakpa-
cunśoke wan enana mni kin kawiyakpakpak s'e taninin ca ikiyela
etipi ke'.

280. Can kin yukśanyan kahmi ca oblula wan el ticagapi na
tokel waśtekta iyecekce iyotakapi'.

281. Tipi kin iheyata hel blaye-owaśtecaka yunkan heci anpetu
wan el wagmeza-winyan k'un tiwahe-ataya ye-awicape canke kici
ipi ke'.

282. Yunkan iyuha paogla-yeya wiyohinyanpatakiya etunwan
inażin-wicaśi canke oko-tuntunyan inażinpi ke'.

283. Heceś wana iyohilahcin taku k'eya zizi, suksuta ca cikci-
k'ala wicak'u, top ece-wicak'u na heya ke':

284. "Nayażinpi kin itokap maka kin k'api na el lena oyuśnapi
na hehanl ake ecel akantapi, tanyan inaskapi na hehanl tokatakiya
caglepi wanżi inażinpi," eya canke ecunpi ke'.

285. Oblaye kin ohanskeya k'eyaś ohangleya ataya hecel ecun
yapi na ehake kin ekta ihunnipi yunkan hehanl iyuha ake atokan-
yan hektakiya ecel ku-wicaśi canke ecel kupi'.

286. Ito tunkanku na kunku kin epi na ścepanku kin topapi,
na iś cinca kicica canke ohiye śaglogan ece ehunnipi na wana
oblaye kin ataya yuśtanpi canke pahala sekse cankuyetuntunyan
otkunseyehcin kagapi ke'.

287. Hehanl ake hel ikanye cik'ayela mni-ikiyela oblaye canke
hel iś taku k'eya blaskaska zizi tanhanskeya ececa ca maka kin el
hapi ke'.

288. Hecel yuśtanpi k'unhan glipi na hetan anpetu ota taku toktokeca un śkinciyapi na hehanl itehanka yunkan ekta ye-awicape canke kici ipi ke'.

289. Oblaye-tanka wan el taku k'eya cikcik'ala ca top ece-hapi k'un hel apepeya maka kin eglepi k'un cokayelahcin etan hu wan toyela nunużela ca hinapa ke'.

290. Na unma-oblaye cik'ala k'un hel iś wanyakapi yunkan hucan ptelyela hinape c'eyaś ape k'eya tanktanka lila mimama ca icah aya ke'.

291. Glipi, na etan itohantu hanl ake awanyakapi yunkan tokeya k'un heci wana santuhu nunsekse tohanyankel u ke'; na unma kin el iś hucan k'un he slohan ya ke'.

292. Iciyamni-ipi yunkan wana oblaye-tanka kin el santuhu eca-hanskaska can inkpa kin ekta wagmeza-winyan ki wacinhe wan eca-un k'eyaś hingnaku kin kaeyaye c'un heca icaga ke'.

293. Oblaye kin ataya cankuyetuntunyan hena hin na tate-hiyu can akiyecel kawinś iyayin na akeśna iyuha-kaśka ecel kigla can oiyokipi ke'.

294. Na unma-oblayela k'un hel iś taku toto k'eya pśunkaya wiaślayela ikoyaka ke'.

295. Icitopa-ipi yunkan wana wagmeza wahuwapa-hanskaska waśteśte suntun ca tonana hu kin iyohi tkeya ikoyak hin na unma kin ekta iś wagmu k'eya niskosko yanka ke'.

296. Hunhi, heceya maka etan woyute slolyapi canke lila waśtehce s'elececa ke'.

297. Iyuha, tuweni teic'ihilaśni, ekta ipi na śina ognagna k'in aglipi nawiyuśkinyan kicanyanpi'.

298. Wagmeza kin unge śpanyanpi, na yutapi; na unge iś pusyapi; unge iś takapi na unge yukpanpi na wagmeza-wasna toka-kagapi; na sutunhce cin hena iś yuganpi na ha kin sunpi canke wagmeza kin woicaśyela wikan tanktanka sekse pusya otka ke'.

299. Kunku na tunkaku kin kici wana h'anhiyakel opiic'iyapi canke anpetu al-ataya wagmu sosopi ece ecunpi ke', tuktel owanżi yankapi na.

300. Yuśtanpi yunkan wagmeza-winyan k'un heya ke': "Tunkaśi, canpata yin na psehtin hato etan aku," eya ca ecun yunkan un cunkśu wan kah-kiya canke he tokaheca unpi śke'.

301. Akanl owinśtunpi na ataya wagmeza na wagmu-ośpula ko mnipi canke wi-kate cin un puza ke'.

302. Hehanl akeś tunkanku kin maka k'e-kiya canke mahetakiya mimeya k'ahin na yuśtan yunkan wicaśa ekta wosla nażin k'eyaś peslete yeś taninkteśni hehanyan mahetuya kaġa ke'.

303. Cete kin ekta coħi-wanżica hu, ape iyowas'iya owinżapi na heci woyute wagmeza na wagmu tona waniyetu kinhan yuta kte cin hena heciya kiħapi na heceś woħa toka-kaġapi śke'.

304. Wana waniyetu na icamna, iwoblu ko k'eyaś hecel tan-yan can ko gnakapi canke takuni icakiżeśni waniyetu ataya tima ocosya yankapi na tohanl woyute kin glusataktaca akeśna woħa k'u etanhan tokel cinpika icuhanpi canke canl-waśtepi ke'.

305. Ecel wana wetu aya ke'. Wana taku oyas'in, zintkala na can-waħe yeś ko kinipi yunkan tokiyatanhan oyate wan etan kośkalaka wan pehin zizi ca lila owanyak-waśte hi na wagmeza-winyan kin tankeya ke'. Kici akiyececa kin un.

306. Yunkan ścepanku kin tima awicaki na, "Ścepan, misun wanżi yecicapikta ca hi kiśto," eyelaka can hakaktaħce cin eha tokeya, (wicincala eyaṗ-seca) psipsil, "Miyekte, miyekte!" eya un na wana hingnayan ke'.

307. Yunkan hanhepi-iyunkapi kin ekta wokiyakin na, "Kola iś-eya ukta keye c'un," eya ke'.

308. Itonacan yunkan kośkalaka wan ake iś-eya owanyak-waśte ca, pehin iśta ko saṗsapin na wiyakṗakṗa ca, hi ke'. Hecena wicincala-tokaṗa k'eya iśta na pehin ko saṗsaṗapi k'un he unma hakakta kin iś-eya wancagna akśiża ke'.

309. Heceś wana kici iyunka yunkan "Kola iś-eya ukta keye c'un," eya, yunkan wana ihinhannaka yunkan ake kośkalaka wan pehin zizi na iśta ko ġiġi wiyakṗakṗa ca, ake wagmeza-winyan k'u iyekceca ca hi ke'.

310. Canke he iś-eya aiyopteyaka canke zi-winla unma k'un he iś hingnayan ke'.

311. Yunkan wana kici iyunka ke', hanhepi hanl. Na woglak ħpayapi yunkan, "Lolkunkeśni, kola iś-eya ukta keye c'un," eya ke'.

312. Heceś itohantuka yunkan ake kośkalaka wan tokiyatan taninśni hi ke'. He iś-eya pehin saṗsapin na akiśokin na iśta kin petaġa kin hececa na iyeś ihankeya owanyak-waśte s'elececa ke'.

313. Canke, eya cin wana iśnala okaptapi ca, witokapahce c'un he iś he hingnayan ke'.

314. Icunhan, wagmeza-winyan kin cinca k'un wana iś-eya wiawacinka hunśe tokiyotan iyaya yunkan itokaġatanhan winyan wan lila owanyak-waśte ca iglogli ke'. Wagmeza-winyan k'un ececlahcin wana witanśnaun ke'.

315. Kośkalak k'eya hipi k'un hena iyuha ścepan-wicaya ece wicayuzapi canke hena iś hakata-wicaya ke'. Unśiwicakila na iś itkop lila tehilapi na ohinni yuonihanpi ke'.

316. Taku ka kaśna kicipatitan ecakicunpi canke wana ake, "Misun, tipi wanżi miye wacin kin ogna kaġapini ecanmi ye," eya yunkan hecena iyuha okiciya śkanpi na tipi wan cankaġa tanktanka un kaġapi ke', ti-mima-tokaheya kin he e ke'.

317. Tanyan oko wanilya, osni hiyukteśni iyacinyan kahwicakiyin na yuśtanpi yunkan hel kunku, tunkanku kici, wana kanpila ca tiwicakiya ke'.

318. "Hel iyotiyekiyeśni yankapikte," eya śke'. Ake wanżi ecehcin kah-wicaśi k'eyaś he kitanla-tanka ka canke ecel kaġapi yunkan hel iś ścepanku k'eye pehin sapsapapi k'un heniyos hingnaka opop eti-wicakiyin na hehanl ake wanżi la ca yuśtanpi yunkan hel iś zi-winla kin nupin hingnaku opop ewicagnaka ke'.

319. "Ho, misun, hehanl micinkśi tipi wanżi cin-wakiye," eya yunkan, "To, cin he nakun eheśni k'eyaś unkaġa kta ca le ehanni unkigluśtanpi kin," eyapi na tunśkakupi kin waśtekilapi canke tipi wan acik'ala ke c'eyaś lila ayucoya kiyuśtanpi ke'.

320. Ho, wana ti-gmigma ece top tantanya na yunkan hehanl tankekupi kin takuni eyeśni k'eyaś iyecinka ti-kicaġapi ke'. Ihankeya waśte wan kiyuśtanpi.

321. "Tanke ksapin na un tanyakel le unk'unpi ca tipi wan ihankeya waśte otikta ce," eyapi ke'.

322. Canke iyuśkinhca, "Misun, pilamayayape, hecel wawaktaśni k'un!" eyaya ekta wak'in ekignakahan ke'.

323. Na hehanl tohantuka wan ohtayetu hanl can-aglagla iśnala tawa-ziya ca śkanhan yunkan tokiyatanhan wicaśa wan hopiyakapa ca el i na kici nażin han ca wanyakapi ke'.

324. K'eyaś lila oholapi canke wanżini un takeyapiśni'. "Tokśa

iye tohanl cin kihan oyakinkte," eyapi na gli k'eyaś takuni slolyeśni
s'e unpi ke'.

325. Yunkan, wana hececakta c'un, ścepanku kin iyuha tima
wicakico na heya ke': "Ścepan, nihakatapi wan ihpeya imayaye
c'eyaś hecena ihacinktapi na nitośkala he niś-eya iyoniważapi kin
un tokanl amninkta ca ececa wacinśni . . . . lena lel titakuye op
unkta cin wakiye ca wana tanyan winyan yuha canke miśnala lecel
waunkte seca yunkan nitiblopi wan hi na wecicakta keya ce," eye'.

326. Canke ścepanku k'un iyuha lila cante-waśteya hecetu-
kicilapi'. Ecin ohinni iyepi un htani na canl-waśte-kic'un k'eyaś
mahetanhan iyokiśice s'a ca ablezapi'.

327. Heceś wana winyan kin iyuha wicaśa yuhapi, na wicaśa kin
iyuha winyan yuhapi śke lo, owotanla kin ognayan, hecel waśte
kin un.

328. Na hetanhan ca wicoicage wan iś-eya sutaya, waśteya,
tanzaniya upi yunkan hena Palani kin epi śke lo.

329. Ca lehantuka yeś le Palani-tawagmeza na Palani-tawagmu
kin ihakeya woyute waśte kin hena e ye lo.

330. Pte-oyate kin Lakota wawicakicunzapi na un okiwanżila
iglaka woyute igni omanipi k'un he iyecel iś-eya wagmeza-winyan
kin he Palani kin wawicakicunza canke ohinni blok-yankapi ca
lehantuka yeś totiwota kin enana mimeya hiye yelo.

The Buffalo People

The English Translation

1. It so happened, they say, that when as yet nobody lived upon this earth, there were recently camped at a certain place first man and his wife.

2. And his name was Waziya; and his wife was named Wakanka; it was those two, but they had now taken up their abode as men-on-earth.

3. But Waziya did not think about the future, only contented with enjoying himself throughout the day, and then thinking only of sleep when night came.

4. With his wife it was otherwise. . . . she always thought ahead and was longing for children.

5. "Husband, what if we should have a child!" she said, so they made a child, and in due time it was born.

6. A girl . . . my, how beautiful indeed! Hair and eyes black, hair long, always she smiled.

7. And now at last, Waziya was pleased . . . "Well, well, my daughter, my daughter, how pretty she is for me!" So saying, he would pet her.

8. They were happy in their parenthood, so watching carefully over it, they worked to bring it up. And now when the little thing was past three years, and ran about of her own accord, then again the woman was yearning for she knew not what, and at last she said,

9. "Husband, I wish we might again be parents of a child," so he said, "Very well; it is you who say it!" he said. So they had another child, and again it was a girl, so exactly like her sister.

10. Two girls equally beautiful, by now they should have been

content, it would seem; but alas, now again Wakanka was restless and irritable, not knowing what she yearned after; and at last she again wanted to bear a child.

11. So she bore her third child, and then at last she bore a man-child, solid, as if formed by compressing firmly, such he was.

12. From then, time went on and next she had another girl, but this one was peculiar. Her hair and eyes were light, and even her face was light yellow, so she looked almost inhuman.

13. A younger sister to her was next born. She also was a little *ziwin,* exactly like her sister . . . now then, first two girls with black eyes and hair, and then a boy, now tall and well able to go about with strength; and the two youngest were little light-tawny ones.

14. That was their number then; and now at last their mother was probably satisfied, for she sorrowed no more, now at last she had completed her work of creation.

15. They lived in the bend on a pleasant level ground . . . of course nobody else was about, people were yet lacking . . .

16. Animals, and fruits abounded, so thus they stayed, lacking nothing, and the children, unmolested, grew up, playing . . .

17. But whereas they supposed that was the way they would go on living always, a day came when their son, now a young man came to his father and said,

18. "Father, over this way, I have an uncontrollable wish to go on a journey. . . . I want to go where the sun goes down," he said; and his father suddenly encountered doubt in his mind, (his mind went double), and he forbade him.

19. "Alas, alas, my son, for even though one might say, 'I go but for a little while,' there might be something to prevent his return." But the son, disregarding him, went off yonder on a journey.

20. Since nobody had ever gone anywhere (before), after his departure his sisters were much concerned, and kept gazing into that direction for him.

21. And then on a day, while all were at various tasks here and there, their father was sitting outside the doorway whittling on wood.

22. And suddenly, "Daughters, your younger brother shall return

this day!" he said. "We shall see!" they whispered together, and went on with their work; and suddenly it was their turn to run to their father, saying,

23. "Father, father, you were right! You said our brother would return today; why, over in the west there he comes, but he comes not alone. A woman he brings home!" So saying, they ran hither and yon, (as though corralled).

24. The sun was low, so they all gazed shading their eyes with their hands, and as the ones coming drew nearer, it was a woman with black eyes and hair, and very beautiful, which he was bringing. The eyes were large and round, and the hair shone on her.

25. So her two elder sisters-in-law ran to meet her. . . . Because she resembled them, they immediately claimed her as their special sister-in-law.

26. They hooked arms with her on each side, and brought her courteously, "O, my! Sister-in-law, Sister-in-law!" they kept saying happily, as they escorted her and brought her into the home.

27. They thought her lovely, and so much so that they were a little foolish as they fluttered about her. They could not keep from giving her all the nice things they had, and now they were busy making up her couch yonder while she sat waiting; when the younger sisters, the *ziwinla* came to the door and peeked in . . . they too would have liked to glimpse their sister-in-law . . .

28. But their elder sisters ordered them off. "O go away, will you?" and then they said to each other in whispers, "Why must they insist on casting their eyes on our sister-in-law!" So poor things, the *ziwinla* resented this, and came no more near, but stayed out from the tipi as much as they could.

29. From that day, several days passed and then the young man came again to where his father sat and said, "Father, right now I have the urge to go on a journey . . . Next I want very much to go where the sun comes up!"

30. "Alas, alas, my son, you have married, and now it had seemed likely that you would remain at home, and my grandsons would grow up . . . dreadfully have you spoken . . . For even though one might say, 'I go but for a little while,' there might be

something to prevent his return," he said, but disregarding it, again
he went off in yonder direction.

31. His elder sisters were at the time (instead of caring about
his absence) so proud of their having a sister-in-law that they did
not have time to think so much as "my younger brother has gone
somewhere," but his younger sisters continued looking always for
his return.

32. Several days went by, and then now the morning sun was
coming when from that direction he was returning; well, but again
now he was not alone; there was again a woman with him.

33. As they neared, it was a woman with hair that was yellow
and fine, and she herself too was yellow-white as the sunshine,
supernaturally wonderful to behold, so she seemed. The two
sisters-in-law which she resembled had their turn now to run and
meet them coming, and linking arms with her, gazing into her face
with great rapture, they escorted her and brought her home.

34. Now there were six young women at home; three with black
eyes and hair, and three with golden yellow hair; and no matter
how taken, they were all handsome to see, surpassingly.

35. And now at last the son had no further thought of traveling,
and lived happy with his two women he had brought home.

36. Thus they lived; and now his first wife was pregnant. So
the two sisters-in-law whom she resembled were drunk with happiness, and were so eager they could not decide which garment
first to beautify with quills. With infinite care, they did minutely
beautiful quillwork on the tiniest of baby things.

37. Soon after, rather soon, the second wife to be brought home
was also with child, and grew large. So her *ziwinla* sisters-in-law
both had their turn to fall avidly to porcupine quill work.

38. This went on several moons, and then one day the old
man was sitting outside the doorway whittling when he called to
his son:

39. "Son, over there to the west where the ridge runs along, and
at the south end it juts towards the river, right there my daughter-
in-law disappeared and it is not plain where she is, (she had not
appeared again,)" he said. So at once the young man ran thither,

and there were great crags with spaces between, so he peeped beyond.

40. And, frightening sight!—there was a buffalo cow moving about grazing, and a newborn calf with his limbs still loose, following her.

41. "Alas, what has happened to me! . . . have I married a buffalo cow?" he thought, and at once he hurried home.

42. Those back home must already have sensed what was the matter for his two elder sisters were coming, so they met and said to him, "Brother, Brother, what is it?" So, "Sisters, your sister-in-law has borne me a son," he said.

43. Immediately, hand-in-hand they ran there, and as they were reaching the spot he had indicated to them, just then, through a space between crags, their sister-in-law came out, carrying a beautiful and perfectly formed man-child in her arms.

44. "Sister-in-law . . . me!" saying so, fighting over it, they took the child, and then, from that instant, as if temporarily at first, they always made him their special charge.

45. Again perhaps two days or so, the old man was sitting outside the doorway whittling, when suddenly he said,

46. "Son, yonder where the chokecherry bushes cluster together, my daughter-in-law disappeared and has not come forth again." So again both were aware of the reason, and the young man ran hurrying there.

47. Pushing the chokecherry bushes asunder for an opening, he looked through and past, and there stood a corn stalk, ripe and perfect, and grown tall; and close by it a little one was also coming, but it had only just sprung up, and it was tender. (unfirm.)

48. As a breeze suddenly swept past, the two bent and swayed like one, in unison, as they stood.

49. So then he came home and reported it to his two younger sisters, and so they arrived there breathless.

50. As they neared, already there was their sister-in-law carrying a perfect babe, and coming around the chokecherry clump.

51. There was excuse for them, being still girls, that they jumped about struggling over the babe until it was uncertain which should hold him first; and they came running home with it. "O, my

nephew, my nephew!" they repeated, cooing to it as they took the little one along.

52. From that hour, though it seemed temporary at first, they held their little nephew very dear, and always guarding they carried him, and so much so that their sister-in-law had nothing to occupy her with as far as child-care went.

53. It is ever true—where there are little ones, there is happiness; so the entire household lived on happily, and then one day suddenly the old man who was sitting outdoors called,

54. Bring here my elder grandson to me!" So his two aunts, who always took care of him, brought and placed him on his grandfather's lap.

55. The minute they went out of sight, the old man said this:

56. "Now, Grandson, observe this day well. . . . See it is continuously blue, and beautiful . . . intense, rousing men to action, such a day is this . . . this is your day . . . on such a day shall you step upon this earth.

57. "I walk upon this earth; but it is a holy earth . . . therefore always walk upon it, reverently . . .

58. "You are to do the same . . . now, Grandson, this foot, step with it . . . that's it . . . now next with the other. . . . that's it!"

59. For a time he was instructing the child to walk, but the others were all busy in various ways, and nobody took notice of him.

60. "Now then, Daughters, take your little nephew," he said, calling. So the child's aunts both came and took their own away.

61. The following morning he did the same thing. "Bring my younger grandson to me!" he said, so *his* aunts next brought him, and placed him on his grandfather's lap.

62. When he was alone with him, the old man said,

63. "Now, Grandson, mark well this day . . . overcast, easy on the eyes; a gentle calm prevails; this is your day . . . on such a day you are to step on the earth . . .

64. "Consider me, my grandson. I tread this earth . . . but it is a holy earth, and so always I tread it with awe.

65. "You are to do the same . . . now, Grandson, with this foot, step; that's it. . . . now with the other, next. . . . so!"

66. Thus for a time he instructed his grandson in walking, but the others were scattered at their tasks, and nobody thought, "here he is doing something." (Idiom for: Nobody paid him the least attention.)

67. "Now, Daughters, take your grandson, please," he called, so they came running and took up their little one, and again, to play with him as usual, they whisked him off somewhere.

68. Next morning he said, "Now, bring my grandsons here and all of you come too . . . you shall witness a show . . ." so they all came and took their places near the doorway.

69. The little boys were now very active, and they tried to get down out of the arms of their aunts who held them, and struggled to get loose, almost succeeding.

70. "Now, set them down here," he said; they did so. And the two little boys took hands, and looking occasionally at each other, and then at their grandfather, they stepped very cautiously, the little ones.

71. "That is right, my grandsons!" he encouraged them, so they took another step; and gradually they grew braver, and advanced by stepping out more rapidly; and at last, because their elders admired them, saying, "*Hinun!*" as they watched, they immediately started off, running and laughing.

72. Immediately from that time, they walked.

73. Then once more the old man said this: "Wife, have you any *tehmiso?* if you have, bring it out!" so she brought a good deal of it.

74. Then, avoiding the holes made by the pins when it was staked down to be dressed, he cut strips into long thongs.

75. From the wood, he brought home some ash, the kind with a blue bark, smooth, and supple, and he carefully bent it into a circle, and then with the thongs running across each other, in and out, he filled the inside tautly, leaving only a heart, an opening in the center.

76. Now, they say that was the introduction of the hoop-and-stick game upon this upper earth.

77. He beautified the hoop with red paint, and here and there he applied paint to indicate marks for counting, and then he said:

78. "Now then, spectators, come back to assemble! . . . go inside and sit down, and stake the doorway opened out wide."

79. This they did; and then he gave each boy a playing stick, and sent the hoop rolling, and taught them how to throw their stick into it correctly.

80. They liked the game, and were always eager to play at it, so he always sat watching them, and teaching them . . . thus in time they grew more skilled, also in counting their points, and they derived pleasure from it . . .

81. When it was morning and the sun came up, the boys both went outside with their grandfather and stood and claimed their day. Whenever it was continuous blue, it was the older boy's; and when it was hazy and calm, the younger boy claimed it.

82. And it happened once when it was a hazy day, they were playing at hoop-and-stick, and playing nicely, when something happened and their sticks were caught together suddenly, and as a result one of the boys tripped and fell down.

83. Nobody was about, only their grandfather sat near by, so now as the boy fell and yelled, crying, all his aunts came running, all four of them; and "Father, what happened to the little ones? my nephews?" they asked.

84. "O, it was nothing, Daughters. Your little nephew tripped accidentally, but he was not really hurt . . . stand up, Grandson, it must be so that if one is man, he must grow up, crashing against the earth now and then," he said.

85. Now it was the elder boy crying, so his two special aunts stayed to soothe him . . . the *ziwinla* had already disappeared, satisfied it was not their special nephew wanting attention . . .

86. Now they had him restored in temper, and almost at once again the two boys, childlike they were playing, so his aunts went away.

87. They had work to do, off far from the tipi, so they were returning to it, and there they had to pass their elder sister-in-law who was on her knees, sort of crawling about, fleshing a robe.

88. She must have recognized her child's voice, for she looked up as they passed; so they said, "It was nothing; one of our little nephews tripped and fell, accidentally, Sister-in-law; but he wasn't hurt . . . already now there they are, laughing and playing again!" and so they passed on.

89. And their sister-in-law seemed to accept that, for she smiled;

but her countenance had suddenly changed. Something displeased her . . .

90. Rather soon after that, when everyone was again scattered and at their respective tasks, suddenly, quite unobserved, the elder daughter-in-law was going off homeward, leading her child by the hand.

91. Her father-in-law, who habitually sat outdoors, saw her first and told his elder daughters.

92. "Daughters, it is without doubt a fact that your sister-in-law is displeased over something, for yonder she is going. Look! . . . it is midday and hot; she will exhaust the child . . . go you to her, and soothe her, Daughters," he said, most upset over it.

93. At once the two young women forced themselves into a hard run, but they came nowhere near her; already the sister-in-law was disappearing in a ravine that cut through the high ridge that flanked the west.

94. Still they ran and they too disappeared into the exact spot; so their father stood looking there, from home; and soon again they emerged and hurried homeward.

95. He went out to meet them, and said, "What's the matter, Daughters, why didn't you take pains to beguile your sister-in-law and restore her humor?" he said, but instead they burst into tears and said,

96. "Father, you can't guess! Why, that was no woman, it was a buffalo cow! Such, across the plain beyond the ridge, with a calf at her side, she is loping westward, and no human being could ever catch up with her!" they said.

97. At once, they all wept; and because a son of his had been taken off, the young man was especially grieved.

98. And lo, it was then that his younger wife came to him and comforted him. "Please do not be sad-hearted; you know you are dear to me . . . come let us go over yonder!" and she took him to the clump of chokecherry bushes.

99. At once from their stalks, she cut four sticks, the best and straightest, and quickly she made him some arrows.

100. And she said, "Go home and bring me that fan my father-in-law carries, the one from a crow's wing." He brought it, and

from it she drew out a feather, and winged all the arrows with it, making them all alike; and then she applied red paint to them, and gave them to him.

101. (The crow, of all birds, flies straightest and goes farthest, and it is said that is why she did this.)

102. She made him hold the arrows, and said, "Now, you are to go with these. Whenever you send forth one of them, it will go straight, and where it lands, it will be there that they whom you seek will be.

103. "And take this along too . . . when you stand before a trial, fasten it to your bow, and spin it round and round, and call to me," she said; and she gave him a yellow feather-ornament of peculiar type, in a cluster which she habitually wore at the very crown of her head, from the time she came. This she extracted from her head. (as if planted there, yuȟun.)

104. (And they say it was of the kind which surmounts a ripened stalk of corn, and appears like a clustered plume. That is why to this day when Lakotas make their warbonnets of plumes, they always have one single central one, coming out from the crown, apart from the rest.)

105. "Now then, send one forth," she commanded, and when he did so, he sent it with such power that it sang through the sundered air, so he and his wife stood watching its flight.

106. So it went, and incredibly, although it went directly towards the ridge to the west where it should have struck the hillside and fallen, instead it suddenly rose and curved upwards, clearing the ridge and disappearing over it.

107. That was because it was magic; so now the man took leave of one wife to seek the other.

108. Half of a day he travelled, and now as all the hills first cast a very edge of shadow, he arrived at a creek, and was about to ford it, when there on the bank was his arrow which he had sent off at noon; it stood perpendicular, its head deep in the earth.

109. Pulling it out, he carried it, and crossed the stream, and there on the open prairies beyond where it was very pleasant, a small tent was pitched.

110. Outside it a child was at play; and now he recognized him

as his own boy. And he too, so keen to see him, recognized him and left his play to run to the doorway where he stopped outside it.

111. Energetically he was gesticulating, talking with somebody inside, and then he came running.

112. "My dear boy, my dear boy!" so exclaiming, he picked him up, but instead (of responding to the caress) the little thing talked frantically:

113. "Father, just now when I said, 'My father is arriving now,' my mother was very angry. 'Well, of all things, how long must be the steps this mortal can take, that he should have come this far! . . . it's his own fault, that he shall die far from home!' she said, Father.

114. "Also she said, 'Tomorrow I must cross a stream, but as I do, I shall step into it, causing it to dry up; does he think he will be safe there! . . . No matter what he does, he must die of thirst!' she said, father.

115. "But listen well: As we leave our tracks behind us, look to my left track!" he said.

116. Now they reached the tent, and the woman so recently raging was most agreeable.

117. "You poor thing, do you know you have traversed half the world in a single day! . . . How tired you must be then . . . Do come inside, you shall take your rest early." So she made his bed, and gave him food, and he lay down quite content.

118. He, for his part, was exceedingly weary, so the instant he lay down he was asleep.

119. When it was dawn, he wakened, and lo, there was nobody about; just he alone on that prairie, with his leggings folded into a pillow under his head. The tent and even the robe he had slept on were gone . . .

120. He sprang into a sitting position and put on his leggings, and again he immediately shot off an arrow and started after it.

121. They had gone off, knocking off the dew from the grass with their feet—thereby he knew which way.

122. Judging by their tracks, he decided they had gone off at a gallop so all he did was to run too, for a whole half-day, and when he was about dead for water, it being noon, he went along, try-

ing to sight some water and way off yonder, far away, there was a wooded-dark (a timbered stream), so thinking he would get his drink there, he braced himself again to go.

123. Now then when he got there, there was no water at all . . . instead where it had once been water, there the earth was now cracked into cakes whose edges were curled upward in the sun's heat.

124. But that was on the surface only where it was drying; underneath it was still soft loam.

125. That being so, they who had left their tracks behind.left deep imprints into it. So he looked for his son's foot-marks, and there one stood, tiny and round, and water, good and cold and clear, filled it.

126. Instantly he fell on his belly, and placing his lips to its surface, he drank the water by drawing it in . . . so thirsty he was; yet the little water vessel was so small, he despaired of drinking it dry before he should be satisfied . . . but it was magic, so as he drank, more water welled up to fill it.

127. So he filled up on cold water, and had some to rub on his head and chest to refresh himself.

128. Then the water disappeared . . . but it was enough; now he was able to go on again.

129. Again it was towards evening, the hills were just lining their borders with a rim of shadow, when he came upon the arrow he had shot off that morning. And beyond the river there stood a white tipi.

130. The little boy must have kept watch for his father even as he played, for the moment he came into sight, the child threw aside his toys and ran to the tipi.

131. Again he talked with his mother, and then with shouts and whoops, he came running to his father.

132. Again he took him up, but the child was talking breathlessly. "Father, Father, again my mother scolded when I said 'My father is coming now.' 'Well, how stout must be the legs of this man-of-earth, indeed . . . I don't care, it is his own fault. . . . tomorrow I must cross a miry stretch which even I dread to attempt, indeed!

133. "'Does he think he is going to be so brave there again! May he stand with only his head visible! Or, instead, may he go entirely under! How can he come through that!' So she talked, Father; so try to think what you may do," he said.

134. Now again they arrived at the white tipi, and the woman was sweetness itself.

135. Greeting him with smiles, she said, "Poor thing, poor thing! Do come back in (where you are welcome, you belong.) You have made yourself tired unto death by walking, so you shall retire at once; this morning I gave up trying to rouse you and had to leave you behind. This time you shall rest at once!" With such sweet words she stroked him affectionately.

136. It seemed she meant it, so now again she succeeded in persuading him, but he said, "All right; but in that case, place the child beyond you, and you lie by my side." And she did so.

137. When it appeared she was really asleep, he very gently took an end thong of his belt, which hung dangling, and tied it to his wife's belt.

138. Having done so, then he took a handful of her beautiful, abundant hair and wrapped it several times around his arm, and held the ends in a tight grasp—and so he went to sleep.

139. "By and by, this time when she prepares to leave, I shall be wakened by her preparations," he thought, as he did this.

140. And lo, once more when he wakened at dawn, there he was, all alone lying in the midst of the bare prairie.

141. "The rascal!" he now thought that of her; and seeing the dew knocked off by their departing feet, he again shot off an arrow that way and started off after it.

142. As he went along that way, he came upon it where it had landed, and drawing it out, he took it along, and there was a high bank. And below there lay like a big river, a perpetual mire, soft, impossible to step on.

143. And about the middle of it was his wife, with the child on her back and she stood, visible only from the line below her arms. (even with the armpits.)

144. She probably thought she was advancing on her way, but with such difficulty it looked as if she stood still.

145. So the man took the sacredly bestowed plume which was his second wife's, and tied it to the tip of his bow, and held it aloft and spun it.

146. "Now, woman, look at me! Help me . . . you yourself made me a promise when you gave this to me—accordingly do," he said.

147. And as he spun the plume, a whirlwind was generated which was small but powerful.

148. So it snatched him up and set him down on firm earth, over and past this miry stretch.

149. The trees were giant-like, as in a vision, so there where an ancient oak (which seemed never to have had a beginning) stood, he sank at its base and sat leaning his back against the trunk to rest himself.

150. And long afterwards, voices were sounding . . . as they came nearer he could tell what they were saying . . . and it was his wife who said:

151. "It is bad, but Son, there is nothing to be done about it . . . your father brought it upon himself . . . why didn't he remain where mortals belong? Why must he try to follow me? Poor thing; he couldn't do it. Therefore by now your father lies down there at the bottom of the mire!"

152. But the boy said, "No, Mother, that is not so . . . over yonder sits my father at the foot of that great oak!"

153. Now at last was the buffalo woman really raging . . . "The wretched one, the bad one, why does he insist upon maddening me! . . . But now, how could he escape what lies ahead?

154. "Right close now is my country, he is walking right into it, so pretty soon now when he gets there, this time he shall match wits with the tricky old woman! . . . how does he think he can get past the magic doorway safely? . . . When the old woman says, 'Lay your weapons on your wife's luggage,' how will he know which are mine?

155. "And when she says, 'Sit by your wife,' where will he go, just? We are four, but we are exactly alike; just how is he (where others fail,) going to know me, does he think, indeed! If he is fool enough and makes a blunder, certainly now he shall die." So saying, as one insane, she went on, talking.

156. But the boy ran to his father. "Father, you heard her . . . have a care, then. My grandmother had four daughters, and she will send them all to invite you.

157. "Keep your wits about you, father; all my mothers are exactly alike . . . when one of them has you just about persuaded, first look towards the home . . . I shall keep out of sight, and so long, you stay where you are.

158. When it is my own mother who comes, I shall come into sight." Then he ran to join his mother and they went on into the great tribal circle of buffalo-land, down below.

159. It was a trifle remote, but in plain sight, so he sat watching them go. And there where a very large tipi stood, there they entered in.

160. Instantly the old woman who was their mother shrieked at her four daughters, all but taking a stick to them.

161. "Dear me, dear me! Are we not in existence to furnish food for men-of-earth? Why should it be I, of all people, who must have daughters who are lazy unto death?

162. "Get up and hurriedly make some food . . . and go call my son-in-law, she commanded. So now one after the other came to invite him.

163. But each time a new one approached, he thought it was his wife. They were almost freakish in their resemblance to each other, that was why.

164. With fine words they invited him, and each time they all but had him. "Do come now, won't you, let's go home . . . your mother-in-law says we are not honoring you, and is dealing with us almost with blows! I dread to go back unsuccessful . . . do pity me!" they said.

165. When a woman uses humble language to gain her point, she deceives man; so in this case too, they would about have him tricked, but then he would retract.

166. Now at last the fourth one was coming, but by now he was so confused as to which he had had for a wife that he didn't even look at her, as he lay there on the ground; and she came to a stop and she too used similar pleadings.

167. Instead of listening to her, he happened casually to glance

towards the home; and just then his little son came out and was shooting off his play-arrows into the air, overhead;

168. Seeing him, instantly he sprang to his feet, and now followed the departing woman, and arrived at the home.

169. Now his mother-in-law came out to meet him, and being an aggressive old woman, she said, "Well now, it shall be I, personally, who shall open the door to my son-in-law." And she did so.

170. So he entered; and very suddenly she let the doorway fall again. It was made of rock, so her intention was to let it fall hard upon him.

171. But once more his younger wife's gift of the magic feather, which he carried, was blown into the room on the air and took him along.

172. Secretly the old woman was disturbed at her failure, but she feigned sweetness. "Now, Son-in-law, this is how we manage to live, such as it is. . . . place your weapons on your wife's luggage for you are to eat," she said. So he took a glance at the rear of the tent, towards the base, and saw that all the luggage belonging to them was exactly alike, fine and of one style only.

173. There were four sisters, and they had belongings exactly alike; so he stood looking as if frozen into inaction, when suddenly he saw there on the end, the things where his little buffalo calf son had already placed his tiny bow-and-arrows; so he too placed his there.

174. "Now then, Son-in-law, sit down by my daughter, for at all events, she is the one you married," she said. And again the boy had laid a blade of grass on his mother's head already, so he recognized her and crowded beside her, as though to crush her; and the old woman laughed. "*He-he-yo!* . . . even I who bore them confuse them sometimes . . . well, but of course a man recognizes his own wife!" she said.

175. Now they retired; and at dawn the man went outside; and stood surveying the scene.

176. Everything about the camp seemed a bit strange—of course they were people, too; but they were buffalo people, that was why.

177. And now, the old woman was up and scolding, which he heard through the tent.

178. "Get up, get up, we live to feed the men-on-earth, and you know it; why do you lie there? . . . and man rises with the day but to move his jaws . . . get up, get up!

179. "As for me, I am going to the feast of the elderly buffalo women, so give him food!" and she started off across the camp center, as if shaking and jarring with each step, (so vigorous the walk.)

180. His sisters-in-law were very agreeable persons, so when their mother was gone, they served him with laughter and good cheer, and he ate with them; and then they were without exception blessed with beautiful, abundant hair, so after he had combed and braided his wife's hair, he dressed that of the others too; and they sat visiting.

181. They were sitting pleasantly when once more she came upon the scene, returning, half-crying, and said, throwing a bit of gnarled chokecherry stick in their midst:

182. "Daughters, how can you sit there! Why, just now your mother has been mocked! At the feast of the older buffalo women, one had many fine new tipi-front pins, so I said, 'Cousin, give me some, if you have no need for all of those,' and she said, 'Why should I! . . . Of all the nerve. My son-in-law made me these, why should I give them away. You too have a son-in-law, why doesn't he get you some?' and with that she flung this warted stick at me, and all of them laughed at me!" And she cried, covering her face with her hands.

183. Her son-in-law sprang to his feet and said, "Where are there some chokecherry trees?" and one sister-in-law told him:

184. "Why, far off over there where that one especially tall tree stands; all around that are many fine chokecherry trees," and she added, "but nobody ever returns alive from there, alas!"

185. Nevertheless, the young man went off. And when he neared it, here and there around the trees were skeletons in varying degrees of decay.

186. And at the base of each tree lay a snake coiled around it.

187. So he went, though it was enough to make him run away; directly he advanced and when he stopped near, he took out his corn wife's plume and again he spun it, and generated a whirlwind that broke all the trees and killed all the snakes.

188. So, as he pleased, he selected suitable sticks, walking all around, and brought home cut-pieces for tipi-front and tipi-base pins.

189. He thought to please his mother-in-law, but instead the old woman was nearly insane, as she howled,

190. "Take them away! Take them away! Those came from the abode of the holy snakes, so they will surely come for their own! I certainly will not have them coming to my tipi! Throw them down the hill!" So screaming, as if somebody held her foot fast, she went running away to the hills.

191. So her youngest daughter collected all the sticks and took them down the hill, but the man told his wife to go and bring him four of the very best ones, and she did so.

192. So the corn woman's method of making magic arrows being fresh in his memory, he made some exactly like them, four magic arrows for his boy; and hung them up to dry.

193. Next morning it was the same thing: the old woman got up scolding her daughters to rouse them, and then went off to a feast of elderly buffalo women.

194. And then when they were sitting agreeably visiting, she returned in tears, and said, "Daughters, just now I have been insulted and this has been thrown at me . . . an elderly buffalo woman had some fine birdlings for her meal so I said, 'Cousin, give me one, so I can eat it too,' and she said, 'The idea, why should I? Don't you have a son-in-law?' And this one was so poor and wrinkled that she had discarded it, but now she flung it at me!" And again she screeched as she wailed.

195. "Well, where are there birdlings to be found?" again asked the man, and his sisters-in-law said, "Why, it is not that cliff appearing black, yonder; but one beyond it," said one, and the others whispered among themselves, and she said, "Well, you tell him next then!" and went into the tipi, so they said,

196. "Ah, but Brother-in-law, what is so bad about it is that nobody has ever returned from there alive!" But being son-in-law, he went anyway.

197. As he neared he saw that skeletons in varying stages of decay lay here and there, and that the trees were excessively tall.

198. Certainly not possible to climb, the lowest branches were far above his reach, so then without further ado, he again tied his magic plume to his bow and spun it, and a wind that whirled was started, and it lifted him bodily and raised him to the top of the tallest tree, where it branched into four equal parts; and in the very center of the fork they made, there was a huge nest, and he was placed in its midst.

199. And in it sat four fine birdlings, large ones, and each sat facing one of the four directions.

200. So, one after another, he struck them on the head and killed them, and was about to attack the fourth, when from a tiny cloud that stood low and round immediately above the tree, lightning came forth and struck the tree and split it into four parts, all its length, to the roots; so the man slid down the crack, and landed on the ground.

201. Instantly up there in the tiny cloud the thunders roared in anger, and then from somewhere a voice called out, saying,

202. "Let be! Never can you kill him: He too has magic power. In vain do you with your own hands destroy the very tree where your young are reared!"

203. And it was the Great Spirit Judge who called that out, it is said.

204. At once the thunders, evidently heeding at last, that permanent little cloud passed on and faded out.

205. So the man came home, bearing the four birdlings, and thought to gladden his mother-in-law with them on his arrival.

206. But instead she was again insane. "Away with them! They are the children of the thunder, and they are to be feared, never shall they lie in my tipi! Or they will bring the lightning to my abode!" so she ran away, howling.

207. One of the daughters being very obedient, took them away and left them, but the man sent his wife after one of the wings. When she brought it, he took out a feather and winged his son's arrows with them.

208. Now it was the next morning, the third morning in his visit, and there was a dance. Again the boy came to his father and communicated something secretly to him.

209. "Father, they are going to dance. All the buffalo boys are to assemble, and dance all day to make the *pte-owaci* (buffalo wallow).

210. (To this day, out in the wilds, now and then these *pte-owaci* are found—circular depressions, with weeds growing tall there; and it is said this was their first making.)

211. "So, father, when it is over, if you do not claim me out of the group, my grandmother will kill you, she says. So look carefully. Of all the boys, I shall keep to the end, and when you look my way, I shall move my left ear," he said.

212. Now they danced; but it was terrific. Never again was such a sight to be seen anywhere; in such a way, all the boys in the buffalo nation took part, so they took their places forming a giant circle, and with the first beating (of the drum), at once, all together, as if formerly rehearsed, they danced.

213. Several thousands danced together, and with the earth rising like smoke, they were at it all day long, and they raised the dust reaching to the sky in a mass, a column that stood solid, unbent by the wind.

214. Now it was evening, so they adjourned, and the old woman came to her son-in-law, saying, "Well, Son-in-law, take out my grandson, other fathers are all looking for their sons, at a great rate!" she said, so they, having finished dancing, now stood resting from fatigue, and he went in among them.

215. Immediately a little tawny one stood there, obvious, wriggling his ear as though it were very loosely fitted, trying so hard to be noticed, shifting ever his position all the time; but pretending not to notice the man moved about awhile, and when he had given his mother-in-law enough hope, he suddenly drew his son out and brought him from the masses.

216. The old woman thought he would miss, and rejoiced inwardly, but he went directly and took him out, so she didn't know which way to look.

217. And then, "*He-he-yo! He-he-yo!* Of course, but of course, a man should recognize his own child!" she said, smiling as she stood, but her voice failed her.

218. "Father, you should have seen me at first: Right there I stood, moving my ear, but you were like a blind man, I declare!"

he said, so, "Ah, yes, my boy, because the crowd was so great!" he said. Meantime his thoughts were so far away, he wasn't thinking what they said.

219. Now it was the fourth morning, and a gay hoop-and-stick game was on. So all the people were out on the newly made *pie-owaci*, and were looking on; the man of earth was standing amidst the crowds with his little son.

220. But meantime, without anybody aware of it, the tricky old woman was running away to the wilder parts.

221. There, in the ravine, a solitary tipi stood, its tipi poles showing only the tips; from the tribal camp there she went and called from outside,

222. "Crazy Bull, are you at home?" and from within came the reply, "Yes!"

223. "Why, say, sit you here, unaware of anything? . . . They are saying that this man-of-earth was seen courting your youngest wife at the woodgathering last evening; and all the people are in an uproar over it!"

224. At once, growling, preparing apparently to dash out, the crazy bull could be heard, but without waiting for him, she ran like a streak to the center, and worming her way in the crowds, she sought out her son-in-law.

225. Quite improperly, she nudged him on the arm, and said, "Son-in-law, go off! go off! Right now, true to the habit of gossiping, which people have, somebody has again told the crazy bull that you courted his youngest wife, so he has allowed his tusks to grow out, and he is coming to attack you! Off, go off, take my grandson, and run away!" she said.

226. But, contrarily, he took out his magic arrows and stood ready to meet him, and now the crazy bull, grunting, pawing the ground, came at him, but he stood aiming at him.

227. The people, like one, had fled and the space was clear, so he came directly at the man, but he sent an arrow at him between the eyes.

228. At once the bull, shaking his head, ran in a circle, and came at him anew, but he shot him in the eye, and set him crazy, so he turned away.

229. But he followed him, and when he went staggering along, he shot another arrow somewhere into him, and with that he fell, sliding to the ground, and rose no more.

230. "Father! . . . . This side!" cried the boy, so he turned in time to see that fine mother-in-law, now a buffalo cow in form, charging him fiercely, but that too he shot into and killed with only one arrow.

231. The man then looked all about, but long since the tribe had fled to a place out of sight, beyond the hill.

232. And then it was clear that these two were the pests of the whole tribe, this crazy bull, and the buffalo cow which was his mother-in-law; and it seemed that the people had always held them in great dread.

233. "Now, Son, go and tell them to return . . . they no longer will need to fear . . . now I have killed for them their two arch enemies; I did it because they bore me ill will, but the other people are kindly disposed, and I like them," he said.

234. So the boy went beyond the hill with the news. And a shout that rose and hit the sky went up, and then the people came home.

235. For a time, everyone was quiet, as they settled back in their home, and then without warning twelve men of eminence, the magistrates of the whole tribe, beautifully appareled, came out and walked single file towards the center.

236. There was the new *pte-owaci*, and there they went and sat down in a crescent shape, all facing the east.

237. Already with a something-is-going-to-happen air, the people seemed unsettled in their mood, and this the man had observed. And now these men came and then all the people narrowed down their circle to that focal point and stood round them, with the magistrates sitting in the midst.

238. Everybody went there, so the man also went and stood, and they drew him inside the ring and placed him to one side by himself.

239. And they said, "Now then, man-of-earth, on this day you have rendered a favor to a whole tribe as if to one man, and they in turn would reward you.

240. "Discard the wife you have, who is a child of the late crazy

buffalo cow, and choose you a wife from the many fine young daughters who stand about.

241. "For you are to remain . . . Between the men-on-earth and ourselves you are to be forever the interpreter," they said.

242. So it was a hard thing indeed that they were decreeing for him, and he could not find the voice to reply, so he stood quiet a long while. At last he raised his head and looked about, but he saw all the buffalo people standing with lowered heads, waiting on his answer.

243. And he thought this: "O yes, so that's it, that I am to be cast as one who is of use; well then, all right; to be sure, how could I free myself from this, anyway?" and after a long time he said, "*Ha o!*"

244. Immediately a full cry went up from that host of buffalo people, without a missing voice, the air hummed with a rumbling, "*Ha-ye! Ha-ye! Ha-ye!*"

245. And then the two (after ten, i.e. eleventh and twelfth) stood up and withdrew, out of the circle of onlookers; nobody said a single word, so he too, "What is all this?" he thought, but stood quiet.

246. Soon, rather soon after, they again returned . . . and they led in an ancient buffalo man, very very aged, and sat him down there, in front of the twelve men of eminence, with his face also towards the east.

247. He was old and full of years, but how majestic; with the palms of his hands and his face too well anointed with red paint, and abalone disks in his ears—those are supernatural properties—and he wore his apparel well; and he sat, braced against a staff painted red.

248. And half of his head was unkempt, and it, the right half, was inextricably tangled with sandburs. Unspeakably holy he sat.

249. Again they went out, and brought in a second ancient one; and he was exactly like the first, and his dress was the same; but this one's right half of head was tangled with sage.

250. A third one was then brought in, and the right half of his head was tangled with buffalo-plant; and the fourth with sun-flower stalk.

251. These four sat upright leaning on their scarlet canes, with eyes closed while they listened; in a row, somewhat ahead of the men-of-eminence.

252. Then, apparently that was all, for those who officiated now took their seats, and then one who was to be their spokesman stood and said of them:

253. [Deloria supplied only a word-by-word translation of the oration. The editor's free translation follows:]

   a. Ho, towards the east they shall walk.
   b. With ridged hoof nails on eight paths they shall walk,
   c. A good altar to make,
   d. A holy altar to make;
   e. Seeing those children beloved, they shall walk;
   f. Cutting through rivers lying at right angles, they shall walk;
   g. Through the day-heat they shall walk;
   h. With breath showing they shall walk.

254. i. For a container, a vessel, there they shall go.
   j. To the Indians they shall go;
   k. To a scarlet water they shall go;
   l. To a scarlet they shall go;
   m. To an abalone-disk they shall go;
   n. To eagle-down they shall go.

255. o. A pure girl they shall take.
   p. And bringing her with them they shall drink;
   q. A red cane they will have her accept;
   r. In the wind-direction that is their own on the earth, and without oversetting hers, they will turn her;
   s. And for her, locks of white at evening-tide they shall decree.

256. "Well," thought the man. "They too, these probably get tired of their relentless errand, yet they are going out thus, for the sake of my people. Now then, I too, willingly I must surrender. What am I? That my people should live, that is of supreme importance!" he was thinking.

257. It is from there that the Buffalo ceremony comes, they do say. And as long as the buffalo were present, the Lakotas should

thrive, they said, and it was true. So it is said that the Lakota people sprang from the buffalo boy.

258. That too is why the Lakotas place buffalo meat as the highest kind of food.

259. While all this excitement prevailed in the buffalo country below the earth, back home on earth there was wailing.

260. Those who remained at home spent the days thinking, perhaps on this day they will return—and they waited for them, but there was no sign of them.

261. And then one day the corn woman first knew something. She left the lodge and sat down far away and sat sorrowing, and first her two golden sisters-in-law came and kept inviting her to go home, but finally they gave up trying.

262. "Sisters, go on home; when I can I shall return too; first I want to cure my heart," she said, so they left her.

263. But their father, who honored his daughter-in-law, then sent his two elder daughters, but they had no more success than their sisters; so they came back alone.

264. After a good while, the old mother went out herself, and said, "Daughter-in-law, your father-in-law sends me, so I come . . . do come home now!" but she said in reply:

265. "Mother-in-law, do go home; later, for a time, as long as it helps me, I shall stay here; and later I will return. Doubtless you think I too might go off, pouting . . . I shall go off nowhere, be sure of that!" So the old woman also returned alone.

266. Now, at last, the old man went out. Pausing now and again, dreading his task but also so very anxious to bring her back, he went and stood a short distance apart, and because he held strict avoidance for her out of politeness, he talked, not looking her way:

267. "Alas, my daughter-in-law, I do not come here thinking I am so very important that you should obey me . . . the others even, you did not heed . . . alas, my daughter-in-law"; so saying he wept, now old he was and easily provoked to tears.

268. Now, but the woman too honored her father-in-law, so she gave him a kindly reply. "Father-in-law, go home now, do; later when you have gone inside, then I too will come, it is because *you* have come for me that I am coming in now," she said.

269. (From that day forth it is said, the precedent was made for

children in law and parents-in-law to love and defer to and avoid each other out of courtesy.)

270. When the old man reentered his home and sat down, the corn woman rose and came homeward; so meantime her sisters-in-law hurriedly got food ready, for all day she had eaten nothing.

271. As she entered, they gave her food which she ate slowly; and when she finished, she said this: "Father-in-law, mother-in-law, sisters-in-law, listen well, I have something to say to you . . . that somebody we all loved has this day abandoned us and given himself up forever to live with the buffalo people.

272. "By that act he has gone from us, and that is why I have been weeping . . . he feels no pull back to us, even this child of his he has not remembered . . ." she said, so at once the others wailed next, and for a time like a great roar, the weeping went on.

273. As if he had died, they mourned him, and then when at last they were all satiated in weeping, at that period when only deep long sighs are possible, the corn woman said,

274. "It is enough . . . hold back your grief now, I have something to say." So because they loved her they listened quietly, having stopped weeping, and she said,

275. I love you all; so never shall I leave you, that is certain; there is a man who has of his own free will given himself away, and so never again can we live here happily with him.

276. "That being so, let us remove from here, and migrate eastward toward my country.

277. "There, at some pleasant spot let us remake our home and as long as we live, however long that is to be, there let us try to be happy; it may be we might succeed, who knows! It is too unbearably desolate here now!"

278. It was the same with them all; no matter where they looked, they recalled something, and so they thought it advisable to move away; and now they had packed and were traveling eastward.

279. For several days they went, camping on the way; and at last they found a place to settle near a river, heavy with timber, through which here and there the beautiful water sparkled.

280. The timberline curved gently, forming a sheltering bend, and there they settled in the best sort of way.

281. Back of their location, towards the hills, there was a fine

level ground, and there one day the corn woman took the whole family, inviting them to accompany her.

282. She told them all to take places, side by side, facing eastward in a straight line. They did this, leaving spaces between each one.

283. So now to each she handed four small yellow hard objects, quite small ones, and said,

284. "In front of you as you stand, dig into the ground and there drop these; and then cover them up again with the earth; and then trample the earth down firmly over them, and all step ahead one pace." They did accordingly.

285. The ground was long, in its stretch ahead, but they went its entire length in this way; and at the end they all stepped to the next section, in the same positions, and returned as she instructed them.

286. There was the father and mother-in-law; then four sisters-in-law, then she and her son, so they made eight rows each time, and now the whole place was finished, a field with tiny hillocks, as it were, in even rows, forming straight pathways.

287. Then a little more towards the water from this was a smaller plot, and there she gave them some different kinds of objects, flat, long, and yellow; and those they buried in the earth.

288. So when they finished this, they came home, and from that time for many days they were engaged in various tasks, and then after a reasonable time she invited them to visit those places, and they went.

289. The larger plot, where they had buried tiny things in fours and left little hill-like bits of dirt, showed in the very middle of each such hill a small greenish stalk, still tender and yielding, which had sprung out of the ground.

290. And they looked to the smaller plot, and there they saw some short tender stalks that were holding up some very large round leaves.

291. They came home, and after a time again they went to see, and at the first ground, the stalks were taller and almost sending out a top; and in the other the stems were creeping along the ground.

292. The third visit showed the stalks well formed and tall, with

a plume surmounting the top like the ornament the corn woman used to wear, which her husband had taken with him.

293. These all stood evenly in rows over the whole level land, and with every breeze they all swayed and bent together and then all together righted themselves again, creating a beautiful motion.

294. In the other plot certain green things, spherical and bare to the sun, were attached.

295. The fourth visit showed corn, long beautiful ears, all ripened, several borne on each stalk making a heavy burden for it; and at the other field were great pumpkins.

296. Well, well, how wonderful! It was their first knowledge of food out of the earth, so it seemed extra marvelous and good to them.

297. All, nobody withholding himself, went to the field and brought home the first fruits of the soil, in great blanket loads, and they worked with it, rejoicing.

298. Some of the corn they cooked, and ate; and some they dried; some they parched or roasted, and some they ground up and made the first corn *wasna*; and they took the ripest ears and husked them, and braided them in long ropes by their husks, and the corn in prosperous abundance and beauty, like great ropes, hung drying.

299. The parents-in-law, now at the stage when they moved about more slowly, sat all day long each day cutting pumpkins into long strips.

300. When they finished, the corn woman said, "Father-in-law, go to the wood and bring some of that blue-bark ash"; when he did, she taught him to make the first drying rack in use.

301. On top they spread a robe, and there they spread out corn kernels and bits of pumpkin to dry in the heat of the sun.

302. Next she had her father-in-law dig the ground, downward, circularly, and when he finished, a man standing upright in it would not even show the top of the head; that deep it was.

303. The base they spread with willow boughs with their leaves on; and there they put food, corn and pumpkins, whatever they were saving to use during the winter to come; these they buried there, and thus they made the first cache.

304. Now winter came on, it snowed and there were blizzards, but comfortably with plenty of firewood also on hand, and with no lack, all winter they sat cozy within; and whenever food was needed they drew on their reserves in the cache as they pleased, so they were happy.

305. And so spring came on. Now everything, birds, and even the leaves, everything returned to life and was astir; and then from some unknown people, a young man with golden hair, very handsome, came and said he was the corn woman's brother [had the corn woman for an older sister]. She and he resembled each other, that was the reason.

306. And she called in her sisters-in-law and said, "My younger brother has come to be with one of you," and instantly the very youngest first, like a little girl, jumped up and down, "Let it be me!" she said; so now she was married to him.

307. And when they went to bed, he talked with her. "A friend of mine says he too is coming here," he said.

308. Several days later he came; a young man, just as handsome with black eyes and hair that shone. At once the younger of the two dark girls preempted him and took him for her husband.

309. Now she lay down with him, and, "A friend of mine says he too is coming here," he told her. And now, a morning or so later, again a youth appeared with golden hair and eyes that sparkled, and again he resembled the corn woman.

310. So he too seemed appropriate for the other *ziwinla,* and she took him for her husband.

311. And when she lay down with him, and they lay talking, he said, "By the way, I have a friend who says he too is coming."

312. So a while later again a young man arrived from somewhere, it was not known where. His hair was black and thick, and his eyes were like coals of fire; and he seemed more handsome than all.

313. So of course the eldest sister, who had been left so far, took him for her husband.

314. Meantime the corn woman's son, now also turning his thoughts toward women apparently, went off somewhere southward and returned with a very beautiful girl. Only the corn woman was unmated.

315. The young men who had come, because they married those she called sisters-in-law, became her respect-relations, brothers, etc. She felt kindly toward them, and they in turn thought highly of her, and always showed her great respect.

316. Whatever she indicated as her wish, they crowded each other to do for her; so now again, "Brothers, I wish a house might be made according to my plan," she said; and at once they all co-operated on it, and built it of great logs, and it was the first circular house of logs.

317. Carefully, without open spaces, planned to keep the cold out, she had them make it, and when it was done she placed her parents-in-law there, now so old.

318. "There, lacking nothing, they shall live," she said. Again she wanted one exactly like it but slightly larger; and they made it, and there she placed her two black-haired sisters-in-law and their husbands; and then a third was completed, and there she placed her two golden sisters-in-law and their husbands.

319. "Now, my brothers, next I want a house for my son," and they said, "Of course; had you not said so, yet we were already agreed to make it," and because they really liked their young nephew, they built him a little smaller but very nicely con-structed house.

320. Now there were four of those circular houses standing up, splendidly built; and then although she said nothing, of their own accord they built their elder sister a house, and it was the finest of them all.

321. "Our sister is wise, and thereby we live in a good way; so her home shall be the finest," they said.

322. So she was very happy. "O, my younger brothers, how grateful you make me! I did not expect this!" she exclaimed now and again, as she removed into it and settled her belongings there.

323. And then one day in the evening she was all alone over at the timber's edge tanning a skin, when a man from some unknown quarter, whose beauty surpassed them all, came and stood talking with her where those at home could see.

324. But they respected her so much that nobody mentioned it to her. "Later when she wishes she will tell," they said. She came home but they went about as though they knew nothing.

325. And then now, as it was bound to be in time, she invited all her sisters-in-law to her home and said, "Sisters-in-law, a brother of yours left me behind and went away, but even so I was bound to you with ties of attraction and could not leave you; moreover your nephew is yours as well as mine, and for me to take him away never entered my thoughts . . . right here with his relatives I have wished him to live always. Now he is nicely married, so I had thought to live on alone like this, but now an elder brother to you has come and says he and I are to be together," she said.

326. So her sisters-in-law were all very happy in accord with her news. For always she had labored for them and put on a happy exterior, but underneath she was often lonely, as they had observed.

327. So now all the women had husbands and all the men had wives, and that was as it should be, in the right way.

328. And from them came the sturdy, fine, healthy Palani, it is said.

329. So even today the Ree corn and the Ree squash are the sweetest foods there are.

330. The buffalo people decreed for the Lakotas that they should always migrate, following their food; and in that same way the corn woman decreed for the Rees, so that they always remained in permanent homes to till the soil, and even now their old home sites are to be found here and there.

Notes

unit 2. These are the nicest characters attributed to Waziya, the cold, cruel cold wizard and Wakanka, the witch. Ordinarily they are very inhuman and cruel people.

unit 9. a common expression, like, "It's up to you!"

unit 12. "Not like man," i.e., supernatural looking was this type, personifying corn, a golden rich brown and yellow body.

unit 27. *ahan nazin* means "always hovering about somebody," from a solicitous or otherwise cause, but always staying around, ready for the slightest wish of the one attended. I know no English for it, and I can't analyze it absolutely.

unit 50. *kagla,* "close at hand." Not usually used today, except to mean "alongside of," as a river or road; *kiyela* would be a better word for "near."

unit 52. This is very correct, for the father's sisters to make over their nephew or niece. The mother *loves* it, doesn't resent not having personal care, but takes it as a compliment instead. Neglectful aunts are disgraceful things for a child to have.

unit 73. *teḣmiso* is the strip of hard border cut away from the edge of a dressed hide. It is characterized by continuous small holes where the skin was staked down for treating. Not good for anything but to be trimmed for narrow strips of thong.

unit 76. Every so often these parenthetical rationalizations on the art of the narrator take place. Editorial comments too occur now and then, on customs, attitudes, the decline of old ways, etc. This is true of most good speakers.

unit 84. *takoża,* "grandchild," *takoś,* "daughter-in-law," etc., but in talking to children, grandparents often shorten their kinship term to *takoś.*

unit 86. *eyaṗ śeca,* idiom. *eyapi,* "they say"; *śeca* I can not translate. When anyone does anything true to type, good or bad, this is used. Here it is, "childlike, they forget promptly and are hard at play." Grown-ups would make slower recovery; refers to tempers, humor, etc.

unit 92. *hu wo,* man's word in calling attention, as here. Strictly idiomatic use.

unit 225. *Tuweniś hecunkeśni* "Nobody does this." The narrator, also a teacher of custom, wants to forstall any false impression the children might get as to the correct behavior of a mother-in-law. To poke your son-in-law is not done, ordinarily.

units 253–258. This is all in reference to the Buffalo ceremony, said to have been devised by the kindly buffalo people for the good of the Dakotas. The various articles mentioned, under (k)–(n) are all requisites.

Under (o) of this I am confused. I think it is *wakaśoteśni,* unsullied; instead of *wotiyemnaśni* pure, which I used in the record when I spoke it.

(s) *hinaśte-ska* is said to mean "white hair," a worthy crown at the close of life for a good life of a child-beloved. The term occurs only in this symbolical use.

units 259–340. This part, referring to the origins of the Arikaras with their agricultural background, as an afterthought to "The Buffalo People," is quite good in the matter of kinship attitudes. It is characteristic all the way. Exception cannot be taken to the corn woman's ordering her parents-in-law around. She does it kindly and is so easily of a different order, and acting for the good of the humans—they would accept and welcome her attitude under such circumstances, of course.

The inflections all through this tale are varied, and interesting, in the spirited conversational sections especially.

Editor's Note

unit 225. *hinske uye-kiyin* "he has allowed his tusks to grow." In presenting instances of insanity in pre-reservation days, Deloria describes a bear dreamer who became violent while recounting his vision: " 'He grew tusks,' the narrator said, meaning he lost all reason as 'a bear enraged.' With knives drawn he roamed growling about the common, all ready to stab anyone who dared to cross his path. Terrified women pulled up the anchoring pegs in the rear of their tipis and fled from the camp circle in all directions, many dragging small children by the hand and carrying babies on their backs. Luckily, before the man could harm someone, strong men knocked him down from behind and restored him to sanity by dousing, with quantities of coldest water" ("Camp Circle Society" 70).

"And So I Remained Alive"

Protective Theater in "The Prairie Dogs"

Though it is not nearly as long and elaborate as "Iron Hawk: Oglala Culture Hero" or "The Buffalo People," "The Prairie Dogs" is wide-ranging in its allusions to centrally important values. The story also displays narrative conventions and their masterful use by Makula and Deloria. In prefacing this tale, Deloria suggests that her technique resembles that of the traditional Lakota narrators and perhaps of oral traditions in general. Certain set speeches and formulaic word patterns remained fixed in her memory, while she improvised the rest of the telling in her own words. The set form she recites is "Toka yunkan le oyate blok-yankala wawanyak-cantokpani ahinazin k'un, wayacipiśni he?" 'Why is it that you do not dance, though the villagers have come and stand around longing to be spectators?' (unit 4). This question is repeated in almost exactly the same Lakota words, and similar though less identical English words, six times in the story.

It may be that the set forms Deloria remembers were also those remembered by the older narrators. Perhaps the most significant cultural meanings are perpetuated through exact repetition between and within individual tellings, while nuances of meaning and feeling can be freely varied to suit changing times, occasions, and listeners.

In this case the "bound motif" expresses the responsibility of each adult to contribute to the confidence, energy, and morale of Lakota society. The "free" specific message may have to do with the cessation of dancing and other traditional cultural expressions prior to the advent of John Collier and the Indian Reorganization Act of 1934 (see Collier 154–58, Rice, *Iron Hawk* 4–6, 10–13, and Standing Bear 237).

By telling how the strongest forces for social cohesion, the warriors' and chiefs' societies came to be, "The Prairie Dogs" forecasts the reinstitution of traditional customs encouraged by Collier's reforms. The immobility and depression of the dwellers in permanent houses, the prairie dogs, corresponds to the enforced cultural dormancy of the Lakota during the first fifty years of the reservation period. In addition to the banning of the Sun Dance and all religious ceremonies, warrior dances had been forbidden as potentially provocative to dangerous regressive impulses in the "warlike Sioux." "The Prairie Dogs" repeatedly refers to the warrior societies as practicing a form of community theater promoting cultural vitality and joy. Their members are as responsible for producing educative and inspirational dance theater as they are for the governmental, military, and police duties they routinely perform.

The other verbal formulas that Deloria remembers comprise the *waktoglaka,* the "kill" or "coup" talks spoken by the animal guardians of each society. In a coup-talk a warrior recounts his own deeds, partly as a form of boasting, but also to define his individual contribution to the nation's life. Each of the six animal guardians represents a particular type of courage and skill, and after describing its differing physical expressions, each affirms the result, "ca le waun we lo" 'and so I remain alive' (unit 5). If the nation is defended by warriors of several particular virtues, then all of their virtues together make the people more secure than they would be with only one form of defense. They are covered from all sides both militarily and spiritually. The kill-talk, as part of a warrior society performance, is a theatrical element that creates cheerful confidence, just as each whole society joined the other societies to make the Lakota nation physically secure.

The repetition of "waktoglaka" (six times) underscores this sense of spiritual self-defense. Although the term literally means kill-talk, it is used to direct the people's love toward their own relatives rather than to evoke hatred of an enemy. The responsibility of individual adults to cheer the people is further emphasized by the repetition of "Kola leca waktoglaka, ca miś-eya wowaglakinkte lo" 'My friend has related his prowess. I shall do so next' (unit 9). The repetition enhances the cumulative effect of individuals lending their strength to a common effort. The object of all this vigorous persuasion is capsulized in another set phrase, included in each animal's exhortation, "wicaśa maka akanl canśilya icaġinkte cin he waśteśni kin un, ito okolakiciye wan wicegna icaġinkte lo" 'It is not good for men on earth to grow up without pleasure, so a society shall thrive among them' (unit 47).

Repeatedly the founders allude to each society's purpose as artistic and inspirational. Deloria reinforces the performance concept with the additional repeated allusion to the *unhnaġicala,* the screech owl cry trilled by women specially privileged to accompany the "waktoglaka" and "wicayatanpi" 'kill-talks' and 'praise-talks' at each society meeting. The owl, founder of the *Miwatani* society, is the first animal to attempt to revive the soporific prairie dogs, and his presence highlights the story's emphasis on the non-military function of the societies. Although the owl could frighten its enemies in the manner it mentions, it was also noted for its gentle habits (Densmore 181). As the guiding spirit of the essentially peaceful group of elders, the *Miwatani,* the owl keynoted a story about cultural expression. The women whose trilling accompanies (*awicaglata*) the kill-talks epitomize the ideal role played by everyone, including the audience, in each society ritual and in Lakota society generally. They demonstrate the proper use of the body, mind, voice, and spirit by helping their relatives to creatively know and define themselves.

But the story also makes it clear that society dances were not calculated forms of social propaganda. Their message was expressed in symbols rather than explicit exhortations. These forms gave the message motivating energy and an immense potential for varied meanings. To achieve this they required the originating force of inspiration. The animal guardian of each society tells the prairie dogs that the societies they foretell will not come into being simply because they can be verbally proposed. Visionary instruction alone can supply the power to implement and differentiate the initial conception (unit 45).

Deloria's emphasis on the purpose and development of cultural forms does not necessarily replicate a similar emphasis in the various tellings she had heard. Other narrators may well have spoken more of the military than the social function of the societies. Some may attribute this to a personal bias. Her novel *Waterlily* has been said to take "an unequivocally negative stance toward warfare," because it "mirrors" her personality rather than Lakota society itself (see DeMallie, Afterword to *Waterlily* 242). In most of her work, however, Deloria included historical deeds of war-like bravery enacted by both men and women, and the male protagonist of "The Buffalo People," like the heroic wives of "Sioux Captive" and "Stake Carriers," does not spare his enemies (see also *Dakota Texts* 268–73). The warrior societies in "The Prairie Dogs" define the larger society's values through ritual drama, not because Deloria tried to conceal their military function, but because the members of the societies contributed to the preservation of Lakota consciousness as much as they protected its physical and territorial integrity.

To describe such *akicita* (soldier) societies as Badger, Crow Owners, Fox, and Brave Hearts as theater companies does not romanticize or demilitarize them but rather acknowledges the activities that would have most influenced Lakota society at large. When a warrior verbally reported his own coups, only a few fellow society members had actually witnessed them. The rest of the onlookers, by lending their presence, helped to create a collective portrayal of all courage and sacrifice. Men of Makula's age would have remembered the late nineteenth-century warrior society ceremonies described by Wissler in "Societies and Ceremonial Associations" (1912) (For Makula's own description, see Appendix). Mythically, "The Prairie Dogs" refers to pre-history "when Iktomi was still living on the earth" (unit 1). Thematically, it refers to any present telling or reading, since Iktomi is an eternal presence. Unlike tricksters of other tribes, Iktomi has virtually no creative or beneficial influence. For the most part the recorded Lakota oral tradition presents him as a threat to social cohesion and survival (see Deloria, *Dakota Texts* 8–

46, 109–12, 116–19, 124). If people imitate Iktomi, they will live only for themselves, egotism and pleasure-seeking will spread like disease, and everyone will die.

The warrior societies maintained civil discipline in such matters as punishing overeager hunters who risked stampeding buffalo herds by not awaiting the signal to charge (see Walker, *Lakota Society* 34). But their ceremonial acts also stressed the psychological discipline necessary for tribal as well as fraternal unity. When the animal spirits in "The Prairie Dogs" scold the dormant dancers "with very angry looks," they evoke the official "whippers," who drew delinquent society members into the center of the dance circle while lightly beating them on the calves to make them dance. This was the dramatized, instructive punishment for being truant from meetings, remiss in donning regalia, or insufficiently generous in feeding the poor. The scolding in the story and the whipping in the dance are single elements in the society rituals that reiterate the same message in a rich abundance of expressive forms in speech, dance, clothing, ceremonial objects, and settings. The participants are primarily members of the societies, but the other onlookers also knew their role. Before describing a nineteenth-century society performance in detail, it should be made clear that the message of unremitting sacrifice has been effectively adapted to contemporary forms of ritual drama.

Since 1987 hundreds of young Lakota have participated in the non-competitive 500-mile Sacred Hoop Run around the Black Hills between June 18 and 23, the time of the summer solstice. The run serves to demonstrate Lakota devotion to the sacred places the runners pass, and to inform the general public of the spiritual and historic significance of *Hinhan Kaġa* (Harney Peak), *Mato Tipila Paha* (The Bear's Lodge or Devil's Tower), *Mato Tipi* (Bear Butte), and Fort Robinson (where Crazy Horse was killed). Showing continued reverence for the Hills in this way reinforces the tribe's refusal to accept monetary compensation for them and their will to fight for the recovery of the land.

The rigors of the run demand the traditional spirit of sacrifice now channelled into a legal and spiritual form of war: "Remember your prayers when you're running for the loved ones back home. This is what the run is all about. Instead of thinking about competing against each other, remember those who are sick. That is why you are sacrificing yourself" (Ted Standing Soldier, qtd. in *The Lakota Times* 10 July 1990). Dave Brings Plenty, the original organizer of the run, emphasized that the runners risk its dangers to protect and express "the Lakota belief system" (videotape, 18 June 1989, Oglala Lakota College Archives). The whole group is represented by a long curved staff resembling those of certain warrior societies, while each runner actually carries a shorter straight staff holding four eagle feathers. Though the particular significance of each feather varies from year to year, the feathers generally stand for spiritual and physical defense. In 1991 the four feathers represented a person dying of cancer, a former runner in prison, a victim of a fatal automobile accident, and the general safety of the team (*The Lakota Times* 10 July 1990).

The local television coverage of the event and its filming by Oglala Lakota College helped to establish the impact on the Lakota community that warrior society meetings more directly achieved in the cohesive space of the camp circle. Electronic media even served to infuse the energy of a coup-talk into the young runners. Although the talk was not actually delivered by the winner, Billy Mills, holder of the gold medal for the 10,000-meter run the 1964 Tokyo Olympics, Mills still supplied a vocal reenactment that induced any kill-talk's intended result:

> Dave Brings Plenty introduced him as "the greatest Lakota runner."
>
> "Maybe one of these young boys will dethrone him, but now he is the greatest," Brings Plenty said.
>
> The runners gathered around Mills' rental car, listening to the radio broadcast of his gold medal victory.
>
> ". . . they're off the curve about to finish the race. 100 meters left. Clark in front. Now DeMuti is staving off the challenge. Clark is sprinting. DeMuti is out in front. Here comes Mills of the USA! Mills of the USA! He won! He won!"
>
> The runners were caught up in the excitement of the announcer's account, and then they circled up to listen to Mills with a quiet respect. (*The Lakota Times* 10 July 1990)

The animal spirits in "The Prairie Dogs" have the same purpose, to transfer energy through the medium of words into the legs
and minds of the listeners. As the direct precursors of the modern
wacipi (dance) or powwow, the society dances retain their enliven-
ing effect, as eloquently stated by Ben Black Bear, Sr.: "Waciya kin
le wo'imaġaġa waśte kin heca nahan nakun wicotawacin kin nahan
waśte ḱaġa oḱihi. Lena ṫuwa ecun śni hantaś ṫokeśke maka aḱanl
ni un kin he slolwaye śni" 'Going to dances is good fun, and also,
dancing can make your disposition good. If someone does not do
this, I do not know why he is on this earth' (Black Bear, Sr. and
Theisz 26–27).

The warrior society "whippers" still punish truant dancers but
in another fashion: "Ho hayapi igluze kin hecena coḱaṫa waci, ho
nahan, ṫaḱu un waciśni hecena he oglaḱe" 'In his street clothes, he is
made to dance in the center (of the dancing area) and he is made to
tell the reason he is not dancing' (Black Bear, Sr. and Theisz 42–43).
The kill-talk is still staged after the (usually) intentional dropping of
a feather or other part of a dancer's outfit:

> Ho wokoyaḱe naḱiśpupi kin he coḱaṫa yanḱe, ho na waci kin
> hena wokoyaḱe wan śpuwahan yanḱe gnaḱe. Waci wicaśa kin
> hena ṫoṗ toḱa ktepi na hena waḱṫoglaḱapi na otuḣ'anpi na
> hehanl wokoyaḱe kin he iḱiḱcupi. Ho na inś taspan spiyeki
> he coḱaṫa eglepi na inś inyan wicaśa ṫoṗ he ktepi na hehanl
> kpamninpi ca ṫuweni oṫuya cin wokoyaḱe naḱiśpu śni.

> The person who dropped the piece from his outfit places him-
> self at the center along with the dropped piece. Then the dancers
> "kill" (four) enemy and they recount their deeds and they give
> away gifts and then take the dropped piece of the outfit. Or the
> case of apples is placed at the center. The dancers "kill" four
> stones, then pass the apples to the people, so no one drops his
> outfit without reason. (Black Bear, Sr. and Theisz 44–45)

The kill-talks may recount educational, charitable, or other civil
achievements as well as actual U.S. military service. The effort is
always expended for the same general purpose, to distribute sources
of strength to the people.

One of the Lakota initiators of the particular *wacipi* style called "fancy dancing," Sonny Larvie, national champion for 1960 and 1961, considers the powwow to occupy the same position of importance that dancing occupies in Deloria's story: "A lot of people talk about the need for unity. I don't see how we can unify if we don't stay with the powwow circle" (*Lakota Times powwow special* Spring, 1991). Although the following general observation does not mention the significant revival of Lakota culture, Larvie does express a realistic concern for cultural loss, reminiscent of "The Prairie Dogs": "In the Lakota today, there is an emptiness, there is something missing, and the spirit of singing and dancing draws you in. Even the nonparticipants are a part of the circle. The people are united again" (*Lakota Times powwow special* Spring, 1991). Larvie goes on to recall the characteristic combining of discipline and fun in the dances of his youth, suggesting the endurance and mood of the much earlier dances Makula and his contemporaries remembered:

> When I was a young man there were a drum keeper, a whistle bearer and a whipper who shooed people out to dance if people were slow to get up and dance.
>
> If the song was really good, the whistle blower would blow his whistle and the song would continue one more verse. But there were limitations.
>
> The whistle bearer earned the right to carry that whistle. They were picked by medicine men or societies that selected these men—their families had give-aways to honor them. (Sonny Larvie, qtd. *The Lakota Times powwow special* Spring, 1991)

In Larvie's summation of all serious adult action, disciplined sacrifice culminates in generous distribution. While the Chiefs' and *Miwatani* societies gave their energies to advising the people, the warrior societies implemented their orders in various ways. In addition to their service as warriors, the societies rotated as *akicita* or camp police for annual tours of duty. As mentioned, they supervised the buffalo hunt, punishing hunters who broke from the group by "striking them senseless" and "cutting up their tipi covers and poles" (Wissler, "Societies" 9). But Wissler says they also had license to mete out punishment for the most serious crimes: "If anyone kills another in camp, the braves kill the murderer." Wissler also mentions police actions adjusted to particular problems and times. Among the pre-reservation Oglala, the *akicita* might severely punish a man for going among the white people, because "they were afraid that the smell of coffee and bacon (foreign smells) would scare the buffalo and make them stay away . . . They did not want the *wakpamni*, the government issue, and did not want the white people coming in" ("Societies" 9).

Lesser crimes were settled through the mediation of the chiefs and members of the *Miwatani*: "They prevent the wronged one from retaliating" by offering him a pipe to smoke and presenting him with a horse," and they tell the guilty one to offer a gift in settlement to the one he had wronged. Though the warrior societies did not need to be diplomatic in enforcing civil order, they were as obligated to promote social harmony as to punish its adversaries. Wissler emphasizes that each society originated in a vision, as "The Prairie Dogs" repeatedly states, and that the vision established rituals to ensure prowess in war. Nevertheless, his "informants maintained that the purpose of all these organizations was to enhance social and fraternal relations among their members" ("Societies" 64). He goes on to describe how society members were expected to sponsor frequent feasts for their meetings as well as to give meat, horses, and clothing to the poor.

This pattern of sacrifice and distribution might also be applied to the elaborate ceremonies that the societies performed for the tribe at large, the community that "The Prairie Dogs" describes as "longing to be spectators" (unit 4). Supplying the poor with practical necessities was only part of the societies' social responsibility. Their dances could produce generous feelings in the audience and could perpetuate these feelings by inspiring emulation. Performances were unlikely to provoke competition between societies, since the average male adult belonged to six or seven different groups (Wissler, "Societies" 67). Since each society had distinctive rituals, no particular group could effectively look better than any other. George Bushotter's description of a Wolf (Dog) society dance reveals how much care was expended on appearance, and how important ap-

(*above*) Omaha Society dance recreated 4 July 1898 and 1903, drawn by Amos Bad Heart Bull. From *A Pictographic History of the Oglala Sioux* by Helen H. Blish (Lincoln: University of Nebraska Press, 1967). Print 408.

(*below*) Mounted Warriors honored for rescuing fellow warriors under fire enter the dance ground. Re-creation of society rite on 4 July 1898 and 1903, drawn by Amos Bad Heart Bull. From *A Pictographic History of the Oglala Sioux* by Helen H. Blish (Lincoln: University of Nebraska Press, 1967). Print 407.

pearance must have been for Bushotter to remember so much detail from his childhood. Ella Deloria translates Bushotter's admiration:

> They held this ceremony amid all manner of splendor . . . Orna-
> mented strips of stiff hide fastened at the temples and allowed
> to hang in a loose bunch; ornaments imitative of the cactus;
> earrings; long thin shells (*wasu,* hail; *huhu,* bones) in a tight
> wide piece worn close about the neck, and a solid piece worn as
> a breastplate; and ties for the braids, of otterskin, and leggings
> with the wide beading up the outer seam; (or quill work); and
> extra fine moccasins they wore. And on some of the leggins of
> the members, tiny closed bells were sewn in a row all the way
> up the outer seam, on that extra piece that extends past the
> seam like a flap; and they had the trailing piece of the breech
> cloth all covered with quill work or sometimes beaded. This
> item all the members had.
>
> They wore ornamental ties for the hair; and the pieces worn
> over one shoulder, and the opposite hip, in bandolier style,
> were especially handsome. It just seemed as though they wore
> the finest finery there was. (Bushotter 120:11)

The effect of the elaborate costuming, as well as the other elements of drama in these rituals, may be compared to Western dramatic theory, both ancient and modern. Longinus (Roman, first century A.D.) believed that the best drama produced an intangible and beneficent "effluence" that transferred virtue to the audience (Longinus 80). Schiller's definition of dramatic value corresponds closely to the intent of the animal spirits in "The Prairie Dogs." The "dwellers in permanent houses," like Schiller's eighteenth-century urbanites, long to be roused from their "torpid" routines: "when we are dis-gusted with the world, and a thousand worries oppress us . . . the stage revives us, we dream of another sphere, we recover ourselves, our torpid nature is roused by noble passions, our blood circulates more healthily" (Schiller 445). Beyond restoring vitality through en-joyment, the more "serious occupation" of drama is nothing less than the power to "recreate us."

This ideal of transformation informs much of Lakota religious thought, and the society rituals were no exception. Everyone in

Dance Garters or Anklets. From *Vestiges of a Proud Nation: The Odgen B. Read Northern Plains Indian Collection*, ed. Glenn B. Markoe. Courtesy of the Robert Hull Fleming Museum (1881.3.154 LA).

attendance knew that each dancer had a spirit helper who super-naturally transformed the dancer's natural effectiveness in war. The audience also knew that the dancing itself would culminate in formal acts of generosity that would reflect day-to-day habits of giving. Such spiritual effects of the theater are a major concern of Jerzy Grotowsky, the twentieth-century Polish director, who feels that plays should not conceal difficult and frightening issues. Lakota

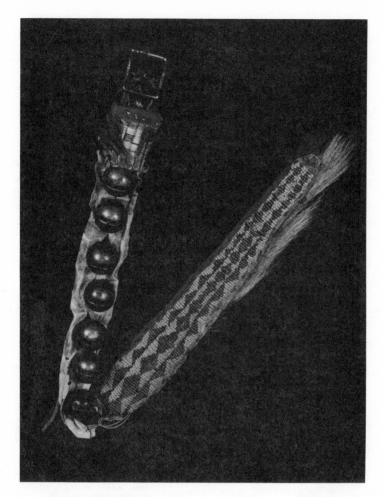

Dance Garter or Anklet. From *Vestiges of a Proud Nation: The Odgen B. Read Northern Plains Indian Collection*, ed. Glenn B. Markoe. Courtesy of the Robert Hull Fleming Museum (1881.3.155 LA).

Society dances always implied the possibility of war or deprivation by celebrating the strength to resist suffering.

Grotowsky's ideal cast of performers is not above or otherwise removed from the audience. The distance between actor and audience that he wishes to close never existed in Lakota society: "Stanislavsky . . . maintained that the successive stages of awakening and renewal in the theatre had found their beginnings amongst ama-

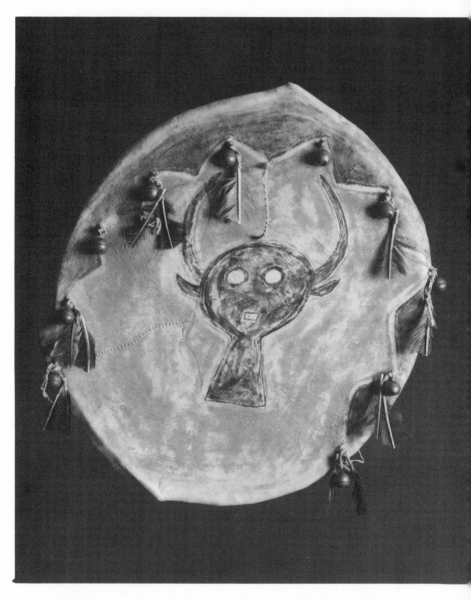

Dance Shield. From *Vestiges of a Proud Nation: The Odgen B. Read Northern Plains Indian Collection*, ed. Glenn B. Markoe. Courtesy of the Robert Hull Fleming Museum (1881.3.72).

Dance Bustle. From *Vestiges of a Proud Nation: The Odgen B. Read Northern Plains Indian Collection*, ed. Glenn B. Markoe. Courtesy of the Robert Hull Fleming Museum (1881.3.45).

Dance Sash. From *Vestiges of a Proud Nation: The Odgen B. Read Northern Plains Indian Collection*, ed. Glenn B. Markoe. Courtesy of the Robert Hull Fleming Museum (1881.3.126).

teurs and not in the circles of hardened, demoralized professionals" (Grotowsky 993). Grotowsky also advocated a return to the spirit, if not the letter of religious theater. Grotowsky's "holy actor" has much in common with a society dancer: "a person who through his art, climbs upon the stake and performs an act of self-sacrifice" (Grotowsky 989). The dancer "represented" his own self-sacrifice in war, but he also demonstrated the power to feed, clothe, and cheer the people through expenditures of energy, concentration, and material wealth in the ceremony itself.

To understand the degree of deprivation suffered by the people at the beginning of "The Prairie Dogs," it is necessary to remember how much non-utilitarian time these dances occupied. If by 1937 the people were dancing rarely, if at all, as Deloria seems to imply, then only elders of Makula's generation would have fully realized the extent of cultural impoverishment during the first fifty years of reservation life. Each society had several ceremonies and each one involved varying dramatizations of social themes. Wissler describes the installation of *Tokala* (Fox) society lance bearers, who were expected to "take the lead in battle and seldom retreat" (Wissler, "Societies" 15). After the society officers selected the lance bearer in a closed meeting, the public drama began when the two society whip bearers searched the camp for the candidate. The "search" acted out the process of careful choice since everyone knew where everyone else lived.

Though the candidate was not immediately informed if he was to gain the honor, his knowledge of tradition rehearsed him for the customary response when the honor was announced: "He usually hesitates." This gesture then cued the society herald to "sing songs referring to the glory and fate of former lance bearers" (Wissler, "Societies" 15), and additional, similarly *enacted* encouragement came from women gathered outside the tipi, who cheered and gave the screech owl cry. Since there was little likelihood that the candidate would actually refuse the lance, his gesture of reluctance and the responsive songs of encouragement were elements in a dramatized affirmation of kinship.

Further enactures of individual sacrifice leading to social distribution then followed. First the society pipe bearer lectured the candidate on the "obligations of his office" (even though he must already have known them), and then the relatives of the candidate (who, in this agreed upon fiction, would seemingly not know of his investiture until this moment) "gave presents to the poor and needy but not to the society or its officers" (Wissler, "Societies" 15).

In an entirely different ceremony, the lance itself, along with other ceremonial objects of the Fox society, was imbued with power. Every spring the society's pipe, whips, lances, and other implements were sacralized in a drama dominated by a series of coup-talks, the *waktoglaka* that forms the first half of "The Prairie Dogs." (units 5–34). An experienced lance carrier presented lances to the new carriers in the previously described ceremony. Then he recited the record of his coups, as if to transfer the energy of victory to his successors. The pipe and whip men did the same, and the cumulative effect, as in "The Prairie Dogs," is for language to actualize deeds. Verbally initiated courage was once again linked to its fundamental purpose: "Then the newly elected men gave away horses and other goods to the public" (Wissler, "Societies" 17–18).

Even the reception of these goods enacted unselfishness. Only old women had license to eagerly appropriate the gifts. By exercising restraint, everyone else showed respect for the giving rather than the gifts. The onlookers contributed to the concluding dance by lending their vocal encouragement. In the feast that followed they represented the sharing of food at the same time as they partook of it.

While some *Tokala* ceremonies took place in the society's own tipi, others like the initial selection of the lance bearers, occurred in various parts of the camp circle. The instructive influence of a warrior society on the larger society was acted out when the members marched from their own tipi to that of one of the chiefs:

> Here they sat in a circle with the drummers and singers in the center. When the appropriate songs were reached, they rose and danced towards the center. The whip bearers usually danced around outside and pretended to whip the dancers into a bunch. The head of the tipi was expected to come out with a pipe and in the name of one of his children or other relatives give a horse to some poor person. (Wissler, "Societies" 18)

The whip bearers "pretended," because the dancers did not need to be motivated to work together, and the chief "pretended" that the dancing had whipped him into an act of charity.

When the reservation Lakota were deprived of these self-defining dances, their depression might well have induced the paralysis suffered by the mythical prairie dogs. Wissler's descriptions give a sense of just how much was lost. The general initiation of *Tokala* members included customary speeches on the virtues, acts, and attitudes that the members should display. The dance that followed visually enacted the infusion of *Tokala* virtues begun by the lectures: "While the custodians of the drum drummed energetically, he danced" (Wissler, "Societies" 20). The immediate result of this ceremonial activity again corresponds to the social result it means to provoke. Because the new member had to learn to put the people's needs before his own, he partook of the concluding feast only after everyone else had been served.

The properties used in these ceremonies take on meaning in additional supplementary dramas. Materials for the wrapping of pipes, lances, and drums were obtained in such a way as to express the society's purposeful relation to the tribe. Members would go to a particular tipi and sing in honor of the child who lived there. Then the society crier would say: "My grandchild, I want to fix something, but haven't the materials (meaning beads, buckskin, sinew) and I have come to ask for them" (Wissler, "Societies" 17). The parents then supply the materials and sometimes have the child give away a horse.

Even before they were made, the ceremonial objects were understood to derive much of their strength from the cooperative will of the community. The objects projected the visible discipline and care that went into making them upon the character-shaping intent of the dance. All the materials were first smudged in the smoke of sweetgrass. Then they were assembled before the ceremony in the society tipi, which had been sanctified by spreading sage and placing a mellowed earth altar in the rear opposite the door. The *Tokala* drum was made from a hollow tree and covered with a skin from a black tail deer. Its sides were decorated with porcupine quills, eagle plumes, and bells. The pipe was also quill wrapped, with green mallard feathers decorating the end of the stem. An eagle feather was attached to each lance, while from the whip handles whole kit fox skins were suspended. The decorated objects implied kinship and familial respect in that the quill work and wrapping were done by women. The ceremony also taught loyalty by exemplifying it in birds and animals noted for that virtue.

When the investing ceremony in the society tipi ended, its influence was again extended to the community. After the whole group of about sixty members had danced around the whole camp circle, the pipe bearer passed from the back to the front of the line to lead a brief run before the members stopped and formed a circle around him. The choreography accents spiritual and social harmony. Nothing and no one comes before the pipe, the source of all relationships that make life worth living. With this priority established, the particular contribution of the warrior society was conclusively celebrated. The bearers of the ceremonial objects held them up, everyone danced, and the women trilled during a special song commemorating a warrior's ultimate sacrifice: "Herald, have you heard why a comrade returns not?" (Wissler, "Societies" 22).

In "The Prairie Dogs" the willingness to endure suffering is embodied in the prairie chicken, the guardian of the *Cante T'inza* (Brave Hearts' Society). His *waktoglaka* recounts how he lay painfully wounded by a large arrowhead embedded in his backbone. His suffering ended only after the bone had wasted away enough for the arrowhead to fall out (unit 27). The prairie chicken's *waktoglaka* associates the expectation of having to endure pain with society membership. Several societies, including the Black Chins, an offshoot of the *Cante T'inza,* and the screech owl's *Miwatani,* enacted the principle of sacrifice by directly experiencing pain. The holders of ceremonial objects demonstrated their worthiness to place them in their hands by carrying hot coals. Although they rubbed calamus root, tallow, and earth paint in their palms before picking up the coals and placing them in the center of the ceremonial tipi, the distinction between reality and representation was unusually fine, even for a societal rite (see Wissler, "Societies" 29).

"The Prairie Dogs" describes the *Miwatani* as a non-military, advisory group of older men, but at an earlier time it was a typical warrior society (see Wissler, "Societies" 73). A man selected to be a "sash wearer" for this society was expected to attach the sash to a stake when under attack by enemies. He could only retreat when a fellow warrior released the sash (see Introduction and "Stake Carriers" text). Those who wore the society's distinctive war bonnets were expected to be equally firm in battle. Their initiations both prepared them for danger and sent confidence into the hearts of beholders who had such men to defend them:

> The maker of the bonnets tells one of the men to bring some coals in his hand. He does this slowly without showing signs of pain. The grass is burnt as a smudge. The bonnet maker, holding his hands in the smoke and taking the things he is making, holds them over the smoke to make them *wakan*. He is the only one who performs this ceremony. The next morning he will probably call on the other candidates to bring the coals. (Wissler, "Societies" 46)

The forms of sacralizing war bonnet materials reinforce the ability to withstand pain by giving the sacrifice a purpose greater than the making of individual reputations. The pain is willingly accepted, because the warrior's body, like the bonnets themselves, acquires sacred power for a sacred purpose. Again, as in the Fox society rites, chosen society members "pretend" to look for those who will take on this profound responsibility. The previous bonnet wearers bring in coals while "a large crowd looks on" (Wissler "Societies" 46; for more on carrying hot coals by the *Miwatani* society, see Beckwith 423, Densmore 327; for a contemporary drawing, see Blish 107; for the dramatized choice of a bonnet wearer of the *Cante T'inza,* see Buechel, *Lakota Tales and Texts* 321–24 where the narrator mentions that the society's tipi had its sides rolled up for the onlookers).

In "The Prairie Dogs" each animal spirit reiterates that society dances cannot simply be instituted because they are good for the people: "Lena lecetukta tka nahanhcike lo. Tohanl kola nagi woslolye icupi na un oiyokipiya unpikte ca hehantukte lo" 'These things shall be; but not yet. What time my friends (human beings) receive knowledge through the spirit, and thereby can live more happily, then it shall be' (unit 45). Wissler's informant, Thunder Bear told how a visionary experience, rather than a ritually sought vision, came to four warriors who then instituted the first societies: *Tokala* (Fox), *Canie T'inza* (Brave Hearts), *Kangi Yuha* (Crow Owners), and *Miwatani* (Owl Feather Headdress). The men were on a war expedition near the Black Hills, when they saw a wolf that turned into a man. As they pursued him, he stopped four times to hold up what was to become the lance of each society and to sing its songs. Then, turning back into a wolf, he stopped and told them that each would lead a society.

On the fourth night after that, as they journeyed homeward, the wolf told them to have their people move to a new camp and to set up four special tipis. Then he presented each warrior with the ceremonial implements of the society:

> For decorations on the lances, the chief birds shall be the eagle, spotted eagle, osprey, owl, crow, magpie, and large hawk. *Canie t'inza*, you shall tan otterskin well and wrap your lance with it. *Tokala*, you paint your lance red and arrange four bunches of feathers with four different kinds in each bunch. *Miwatani*, you paint your lance red and decorate at one place with owl feathers. *Kangi yuha*, you shall have a lance as long as a man and decorate it with crow and magpie feathers continuously from top to bottom, an eagle tail feather at the top and a spotted eagle tail feather at each of two intermediate points. (Wissler, "Societies" 72)

The other implements were decorated in equally distinctive detail.

While everyone else was away at a buffalo hunt, the four men were brought into the special tipis where they were instructed by four more spirit helpers in human form: "Each said, 'The one who gave you these things sent us here to teach you the songs. You have been given long life and great power.'" Then for eight more days the men made the lances and other regalia. Supernatural confirmations of the newly received power then occurred. On the day after the lances, rattles, whips, and whistles were distributed, just as the four instructors had predicted, the founding warriors encountered and killed four enemies. The symbolic number suggests that working together, the societies were invincible. To kill four enemies is the same as to defeat all enemies. Since such a victory rate was literally impossible, the societies created an unshakable sense of mutual trust rather than actual triumph.

The society dances imparted confidence without minimizing the imminent danger that they always implied. Still, the dances did not emphasize threats arising from weaknesses in the dancers themselves. In this respect the implicit "theory" of the dance differed from much Western dramatic theory. While Longinus, Schiller, and Grotowsky look toward the positive transformation that drama effects in its audience, much Western drama follows Aristotle in purifying the audience by exposing "fatal flaws" in human nature. Goethe felt that drama implied an imperfect world because art was meant to present an ideal reality (481), while Hegel felt that art was neither superior nor inferior to nature and had no transforming impact on the audience at all (525–26).

Modern theorists like Artaud work under the psychoanalytic assumption that the theater should make spectators aware of the worst side of their nature, so that they will be able to withdraw from an impulse to "war, riot, and blatant murder" ("No More Masterpieces" 766). He compares his concept of therapeutic drama to "tribal music cures" that make people aware of destructive "forces," so that they will not be controlled by them (766). Lakota ceremonies, in contrast, actualize benevolent forces—forces that are trusted to control those they protect in the course of a ceremony or in combat, because they, like the human beings who temporarily contain them, are inherently good.

Even in Grotowsky's advocacy of "sacred theater," the effects of a negative view of human nature differentiate his purpose from that of a Lakota performance. His argument extends the confessional vein that links saints' lives to case histories:

> The theatre must attack what might be called the complexes of society . . . the myths which are not an invention of the mind but are, so to speak, inherited through one's blood, religion, culture and climate. . . . If we start working on a theatre performance or a role by violating our innermost selves, searching for the things which can hurt us most deeply, but which at the same time give us a total feeling of purifying truth that finally

brings peace, then we will inevitably end up with *representations collectives*. ("The Theatre's New Testament" 988)

The collective representations are meant to cure whole societies of their sins or complexes.

Lakota society's image of itself has always been more favorable, from the Fox society's initiations to the Sacred Hoop Run. The most profound contemporary version of Lakota ritual drama has been The Bigfoot Memorial Ride commemorating the massacre of three hundred members of Chief Bigfoot's band at Wounded Knee, South Dakota on December 29, 1890. More than three hundred riders participated in the 1990 ride that began at Fort Yates, North Dakota, and ended at Wounded Knee, tracing the route of the Hunkpapa and Minneconju Lakota as they tried to find shelter from the subzero weather and the U.S. army. Their ordeal and its tragic culmination is not simply recalled but relived. The Bigfoot riders suffered the cold for the some of the same reasons the *Miwatani* members carried hot coals.

Besides the commemorative purpose, the riders thought of themselves as contributing to the future of Lakota culture. Like the warrior society members, the Bigfoot riders have a distinguishing staff and insignia, and as in war parties of the past, they left their filled pipes in their sweat lodges at home and smoked them in prayer only after their return. One rider, Cedric Goodhouse, revealed the characteristic attitude toward personal sacrifice when he observed: "The people were using old values and wisdom to make decisions, a lot of bravery was shown, fortitude in enduring the hardships of the ride. They showed unseen strength for the good of all. Above all, the spirituality of the ride was visible" (*The Lakota Times* 8 January, 1991).

Before each day's ride began, the mounted riders formed a ceremonial circle to pray, sing, and eat sacred food. As the circle broke, "the women trilled the tremolo," the *unhnagicala* (screech owl cry). In 1937 Makula and Deloria implied that a return to Lakota custom, represented by the warrior society dances, would restore spiritual and social identity to the reservation Lakota. In 1990 the Bigfoot Memorial Ride, with its direct experience of sacrifice, its prayers,

Arvol Looking Horse, keeper of the Sacred Pipe holds the staff of the Big Foot
Memorial Ride as he prays to give thanks for the safe completion of the seventy-
five-mile journey on 29 December 1988. Courtesy of *Indian Country Today*
3 January 1989.

and its ceremonial staffs and eagle feathers, powerfully fulfilled the
hope foretold in "The Prairie Dogs."

One of the ride's leaders, Alex White Plume, spoke of restricting
membership for the same reasons that the societies made admission
a special honor: "Only people who have it in their hearts to rebuild
a nation should come" (*The Lakota Times* 19 June 1990). The father
of one young man was reluctant to let his son undergo the ride's
hardships, but after White Plume spoke to him, the man agreed,
saying in White Plume's recollection:

> You know son, fifty years ago the Bureau of Indian Affairs told
> me to do what they told me and I'd be happy. I'm still living in
> the same house I built with my own hands fifty years ago and
> I'm not happy. I've lost my traditions and my way to pray and

so I'm sending you on this ride, son, and you are going to lead this family back to our Lakota way of life. (*The Lakota Times* 19 June 1990)

The man's reference to the expectation that a house would bring happiness echoes the despair of the dwellers in permanent houses in Deloria's story. The government's suppression of Lakota dancing accompanied the policy of dispersing the traditional camp circles into isolated houses on individually allotted lands: "In spreading along the creeks of the reservation, the Indian families built log cabins and established themselves on the land much like rural white families" (Macgregor 37). Without the camp circle as its theater, the dances could not have immediately flourished in the same way, even if the government had not banned them outright.

Federal policy intended to reduce the psychological as well as the physical focus from the tribe to the smaller, Euro-american concept of family: "The extended family group which formerly erected its lodges together now stretched in a line of separated homes" (Macgregor 66). The government effort to transform hunters into farmers was partly ideological and partly political. The agricultural way of life in early twentieth-century America was considered morally superior and part of the civilizing process. But the break-up of the *tiyošpaye* also took governing power away from the chiefs, so that it could be wielded by the Indian agents and superintendents. When the Lakota first came on the reservation, the government strategically removed the most important chiefs from central positions of influence by giving each one the equivalent of a state house. The chiefs lived in frame houses of two stories, as compared with the log cabins in which the people lived. It is no wonder that Deloria and Makula associate "blok-yankala" 'permanent dwellings' with immobility of spirit and a low point in Lakota history. The sense of being trapped was compounded by a general deprivation of movement, both in the dance and in the seasonal migrations that had expressed sacred as well as practical concerns (see Goodman 11–14).

The sense of being penned in also affected political identity. In "The Prairie Dogs," the Chiefs' and *Miwatani* societies represent the participatory form of traditional Lakota government in which large groups of elders came to consensual decisions for the group. For the first half-century of the reservation period, this thoroughly democratic system was replaced by the dictatorial rule of the Indian agent. After 1934 the Collier Act brought a Western style of democracy that has since been criticized for not being representative. Many Lakota have felt that the representation of thousands of people by a few elected officials does not truly express or provide for the will of the majority. At Pine Ridge, community leader Cecilia Fire Thunder has recently urged the institution of regularly scheduled community meetings in each district, so that office holders can attend to priorities determined by their constituents. Otherwise, she says, twenty-one "haves" on the tribal council will continue to act without direct knowledge of the wants and needs of twenty thousand "have-nots" on a 1.5 million-acre reservation (speech to the Oglala Women's Society, 7 September 1988, videotape, Oglala Lakota College).

In the nineteenth century the council of leading elders, the Buffalo society or Big Bellies in "The Prairie Dogs," governed the camp by agreement rather than by vote. If one of the chiefs disagreed with an important decision, he might leave the circle and form his own camp with other families that agreed to join him (Walker, *Lakota Society* 24). Legal decisions and their enforcement were sometimes enacted instantly by the *akicita* (camp police), who were usually members of the warrior society taking its turn for annual duty. Because they had to maintain laws that most people agreed to support, the *akicita* were chosen for their "knowledge of the traditions of the Sioux" (Walker, *Lakota Society* 59), revealing again that warriors sustained the mental life of the people as a priority equal to physically protecting them.

The chiefs too were as responsible for stimulating thought and feeling as prosperity and order. Wissler describes the Chiefs' society as comprised of the majority of "efficient" men over forty. From their number the society "elected seven chiefs (*wicaśa itancan*) to govern the people. Once elected, the chiefs served for life, but they based their actions on open discussions in the council tipi (Wissler, "Societies" 8). The chiefs delegated responsibility for matters of immediate importance, particularly in war or hunting, to four "shirt wearers," while four *wakiconze,* or magistrates, regulated domestic order. The selection of these officers was ritualized in additional forms of public theater:

> The society of chiefs announced the election of a *wakicun* through the head *akicita.* A stick is prepared to represent the candidate's achievements. Thus, if he has been a victorious *blotaunka* [leader of a war party], a striped stick is used; if wounded in battle, a red stick; if he killed an enemy, a black stick. The *akicita* go to his wife's tipi and thrust the stick into the ground. The woman prepares food and sends it with the stick to the executive tipi. If her husband has been re-elected, he is already there, but, if newly elected, he hunts up a fine pouch, a pipe, a generous supply of tobacco and takes his place in the tent. (Wissler, "Societies" 8)

The ceremony of installation included "instructing" leaders through a form of public oratory that defined Lakota values: The chiefs have "the entire tribe in their keeping"; they must see that everyone has a horse to keep up with group movements and that no "orphan goes unnoticed"; they must control their tempers if someone steals their horses or even their wives, and in mourning even a close family member, they must exemplify a calm, courageous acceptance of death. In addition to these virtues, they must assume responsibility for teaching and entertaining the tribe by giving feasts and by performing their own distinctive dance. Lakota leaders did not sit removed from the people in the equivalent of a royal box but frequently danced to show that kinship was as important to their existence as authority. In their dance they wore buffalo robes with the hair side out and "hooked each other" like fighting bulls (Walker, *Lakota Society* 35) Representing the buffalo as the supreme symbol of loyalty and generosity, they enacted their willingness to risk individual safety in defending the tribe.

In "The Prairie Dogs" the buffalo foretells the Chiefs' society, after defining himself as one willing to endure great pain in order to bring the people the wisdom and forms of ceremonial practice they most need. Undaunted by a back full of arrows, the buffalo bull makes his way to the prairie dogs to deliver the message. He transforms an experience of suffering into the strength to teach by example:

anpetu ataya okagamayanhanpi na wanhinkpe glusotapi yunkan nakeś hehanl amayuśtanpe lo; Ca hena apśunpśunweheya wahpayin na omakizi ca iyuha kic'in le wahinawazin ye lo.

all day they pinned me with arrows, and only when they had exhausted their supply did they leave me alone. So there I lay with arrows toppling about me, and when I was healed, I put them all on my back and carrying my load so, I come to stand here. (units 33–34)

The buffalo has similar significance in the healing ceremony performed by the buffalo dreamer described by Blish. In the ritual drama of the ceremony, the dreamer, wearing a robe retaining the head and horns, is shot twice with arrows while making a complete circuit of the camp. Then he lies down, seemingly weakened from the arrows, and is shot once as if to finish him off. He immediately jumps up "with a roar" and runs to a special medicine tipi, where in the presence of several holy men he coughs up the bullet (Blish 278). The ceremony, like the society dances, may impress some viewers as a literal embodiment of supernatural protection. Taking the performance as a whole, however, mature observers might have recognized the enabling of spiritual growth through dramatic portrayal. Lakota ritual drama can restore the prairie dogs because it makes their lives whole and authentic. The prairie dog who daringly runs from hole to hole at the end affirms the value of danger (units 87–88). In the preface to his play, *Miss Julie* (1888) August Strindberg put it this way: "I find the joy of living in the fierce and ruthless battles of life, and my pleasure comes from learning something, from being taught something" (565).

Missionaries and Indian agents did not understand the teaching purpose of non-sacred dances. Though the missionaries directed their initial fire at the "pagan" Sun Dance and Ghost Dance, all Indian dancing was thought to be dangerous. In 1889 the Indian agents, overseeing a puppet court at Pine Ridge, punished dancing with fines, imprisonment, hard labor, or withholding of rations (Utley 31). The harshness arose from an ideology that determined early reservation management:

> These feasts or dances are not social gatherings for the amusement of these people, but, on the contrary, are intended and calculated to stimulate the warlike passions of the young warriors of the tribe. At such feasts the warrior recounts his deeds of daring, boasts of his inhumanity in the destruction of his enemies, and his treatment of the female captives, in language that ought to shock even a savage ear. The audience assents approvingly to his boasts of falsehood, deceit, theft, murder, and rape, and the young listener is informed that this and this only is the road to fame and renown. (From a speech by Henry M. Teller, Secretary of the Interior, in 1882 Qtd. in Prucha 296)

Apart from such nearly psychotic moral fervor, most government officials forbade society rituals in the belief that assimilation would eventually free the government from its treaty obligations. As early as 1882 dancing required the official approval of the agent (Laubin 81). Permission was rarely granted, and then only as an inducement or reward, as in 1889 when the Lakota were being pressured into providing the necessary three-quarters vote to pass the allotment legislation, and again immediately after World War I as a reward for military service. Otherwise only Indians thought to be uneducable (those over forty years of age) were permitted to dance for tourists at fairs and rodeos (Laubin 81). Henry Standing Bear described how the official prohibitions attempted to ensure the government's investment in boarding schools like Carlisle:

> On the commissary door and in the trader's store there one day appeared a printed notice, by order of the agent, that no returned student would thereafter be permitted to attend any tribal dance. This was done in an effort to make young people turn away from things traditional. In a short while there came another order which allowed the old people to hold but one dance a week, and no more. Soon another rule followed, stating

that whenever a horse or present was given away, it must be done silently. (Standing Bear, *Land of the Spotted Eagle* 237)

After 1934, however, freedom of expression returned to the dwellers in permanent houses. The joy missing in the mythical prairie dog village must have accompanied realistic hopes in men of Makula's age when Deloria interviewed them in the mid 1930s. A Standing Rock Hunkpapa woman told Reginald Laubin in 1934: "When they stopped dancing, we died. We stopped living. We felt there was nothing left to live for. Now we can dance again, and it brings sunshine into our hearts" (Laubin 81).

A Sinte Gleśka University publication, *Songs and Dances of the Lakota* (1976) by Ben Black Bear, Sr. and R.D. Theisz, expresses the adaptation of warrior society drama to the modern *wacipi* or pow-wow. At the time of transcription, Black Bear, Sr. was an elder who had lived through the ban on dancing long enough to realize its emotional and spiritual impact. Now, in the revival of traditional dancing in the modern powwow, people once again like to "look good" to give others enjoyment:

Owang waśtepi kin he oyate kin taku wanlakapi yacinpi kin he le e. Woawaśtelake. Tohanl wayaci kin awaśteyela kin kte. Ecela el ewacanin kte. Waceyakiye na wowaśi ecanun kin hena ninglustan kin wowaci kin le ake yeksuyin kte. Imaġaġa nic'inyin kte kin na taku śice kin hena el awacanin kte śni. Ayablezab hantaś waci wicaśa kin hena tanyan opici'iyapi. Ho hecetu.

How good they look is something to enjoy. When you dance, you will like it. You will like only it. After you finish praying and helping others, you will always remember the dance next. You will enjoy yourself and you will think of nothing bad. If you would notice, those dancers treat each other well. So be it. (Black Bear, Sr. and Theisz 36–37)

The creation of an atmosphere of mutual admiration brings mutual good will.

The warrior identity of the society dancers solidified cooperative benevolence by reminding the onlookers of the potential threat of a common enemy. Modern powwows celebrate the military tradition in songs alluding to Lakota service in recent wars, and they also include representations of inner threats to disciplined strength of mind:

> Tokala kin iye tuwa ohitike kin he slolyapi. Ho heca un Tokala glahapapi eyapi kin he ecunpi. Ozuye wan ecetkiya yapi kin he iyecel ecunpi. Tuwa ohitike kin hena eca wicakahapapi. Wowaci kin le ecunpi hantaś Tokala itancan kin hena nunp Tokala glahapapi. Wacipi kin hena iyuha kacoka iyewicapi. Wanji wicala śni hantaś apapi na hena tuweni śiglaśni. Tuwa cante kin ikipi hantaś okihi. Ho hecetu.

The warriors themselves know who is brave. Therefore, what is called "choosing (driving) warriors" is done. It is done in the same manner as going to actual battle. Those who are brave are the ones chosen. At this dance, the two chief warriors do the choosing. All the dancers are herded to the center of the dance floor. If one refuses, he is struck and he cannot get angry (no one does). If one has the heart, it (being a warrior) befits him. So be it. (Black Bear, Sr. and Theisz 56–57)

Dancing has been culturally prominent among the Lakota for centuries. In 1832 George Catlin wrote:

> I saw so many of their different varieties of dances amongst the Sioux that I should almost be disposed to denominate them the "dancing Indians." It would actually seem as if they had dances for everything. And in so large a village, there was scarcely an hour in any day or night, but what the beat of the drum could somewhere be heard. These dances are almost as various . . . as they are numerous—some of them . . . keep the bystanders in an irresistible roar of laughter—others . . . excite his pity . . . others disgust, and yet others terrify. (*North American Indians* 274–77; qtd. Laubin 43)

The use of dramatic representation at Lakota gatherings persisted even into the period when dancing was generally banned. At a fourth of July celebration in Kyle in 1926, reported to Beckwith (426–27), only older people danced while young boys did the singing and drumming. Nevertheless, men of various ages reenacted the return of a scouting party:

> Two old men sit before the shelter at the entrance to the danc-
> ing circle with leaves before them to represent the enemy. The
> musicians drum and sing scout songs. A procession on horse-
> back approaches. The leader howls four times like a wolf before
> he gets to the old men and when he meets them he says, "Down
> on the Cheyenne River the enemy camps." The old man lights
> his pipe and gives it to the leader, telling him to smoke it and
> tell the truth about what he has seen. The leader smokes it and
> returns it to the other old man. When the three have smoked it,
> each member of the party gives a present, often to some orphan
> or poor person. While this distribution of presents is going on,
> the scouting party is within the dance circle. (Beckwith 427)

Another performance in 1926 represented the return of a war party. A mock battle was staged, and the winners then paraded through the camp singing a war song. The word for this custom, *ucitapi* (they shoot their guns for them) suggests the purpose of pro- viding emotional energy in addition to efficient defense. Amos Bad Heart Bull depicts the practice of *ucitapi* by specific societies in Blish: Badger (292), Crow Owners (294), Brave Hearts (295), Fox (297). He also draws the reenactment of the *ucitapi* (without guns) at the fourth of July celebration in Pine Ridge in 1903 (Blish 482, 490–91).

In all these dances, parades, and other performances, the people's delight in courage is intensified by the attending women through their *unhnaǧicala* (screech owl cry). But at the end of "The Prairie Dogs" the valorous runner is praised by a male crier's trill rather than by women. The crier is literally one of the burrowing owls (not technically a screech owl) who live among the prairie dogs in their abandoned holes. The story's last line therefore emphasizes how individuals make their particular contributions to the community's state of mind.

The prairie dogs make a home for the owls, and the owls repay them by praising their courage. Warriors dance out their unending resolve to defend the camp. Women sing out their solidarity with the men, and the performance in its totality, like the story Deloria writes, "un . . . wayawiyuśkin, wayables" 'lives . . . for the purpose of making people happy and energetic' (unit 89). As the women praise the warriors, so this story praises the expected revival of Lakota culture in the mid 1930s and demonstrates one form of its future in the written words themselves.

Planting the Seeds of Respect

Social Origins in "The Buffalo People"

Most published Lakota oral narratives are similar in length to "The Prairie Dogs" or shorter. They usually follow a traditional story line and combine episodes, characters, and symbols drawn from the whole narrative reservoir to communicate an idea of particular value for the audience and occasion. Some stories were obviously directed toward small children, while others were addressed separately to young men and young women (see Rice, *Deer Women* 21–46). "The Prairie Dogs," like the other stories discussed here, speaks primarily to an adult audience faced with pressing social problems. In theme and purpose it resembles the Iktomi (trickster) tales printed in Deloria's *Dakota Texts* (1–46). Variations of these humorous stories still bolster confidence and relieve tension, when speakers at community gatherings expose the U.S. government or the Bureau of Indian Affairs as deceptive, wasteful, or incompetent. They are retold in Lakota, English, or a combination of the two with many original twists to suit the moment, but the basic story lines remain to supply a long range perspective on immediate threats as both inevitable and transient.

Although "The Prairie Dogs" is not an Iktomi story *per se,* the initial mention of its occurence at the time when Iktomi walked the earth evokes the immediate social purpose of its telling. The dancing has stopped and the culture has become moribund, because Iktomi is present. The story does not focus on the reasons the prairie dogs are depressed. Instead it concentrates on the solution to the problem, the revival of community energy once inspired by the warrior societies. But the single reference to Iktomi at the beginning evokes the duplicity of the federal government and the American individualism that has weakened the Lakota ideal of interdependence. The narrator suggests that as it was in the beginning, so it will be now. Society dances helped to banish the Iktomi spirit from the camp circle. At the story's outset the people no longer lift each other's spirits in traditional forms of expression. In story after story Iktomi's bragging and incompetence depress the village he invades until he is banished by a culture hero embodying the virtues of courage and generosity (see Deloria, *Dakota Texts* 111). The narrator of "The Prairie Dogs" makes that generosity include public efforts to inspire and enlighten, in addition to providing food, clothing, shelter, and defense.

While "The Prairie Dogs" initially describes Lakota society in a depression that suggests a specific historical situation, Deloria's "The Buffalo People" presents challenges that face every generation even in times of peace and prosperity. The story's published analogues, however, have comparatively specialized messages. A Cheyenne version emphasizes the hunter's virtue of persistence in the hero's pursuit of his buffalo wife, and concludes with the man's overcoming his human fear of a large dangerous animal in order to provide his tribe with meat (Grinnell 87–104). Several Arapaho and Lakota versions mention that the man who follows his buffalo wife to her camp falls asleep during a buffalo dance, so that the buffalo trample him (Dorsey and Kroeber 388–418, Beckwith 399–400, McLaughlin 170–78). The lesson for younger listeners recommends attentiveness during stories and ceremonies. A Lakota version in Deloria's *Dakota Texts* (184–90) highlights the punishment of the conniving mother-in-law and the deserting wife. The mother-in-law is struck by lightning, while the daughter is consumed by wolves. Like so many of the stories Deloria wrote down and wrote about, "The Man who Married a Buffalo Woman" upholds kinship loyalty by representing the whole system in particular relations.

In "The Buffalo People" Deloria addresses the idea of kinship on a much larger scale. Makula told the same story to Walker, and Walker wrote two slightly different versions that are both longer than most published folklore (see *Lakota Myth* 109–18 and *Sun Dance* 183–90). Walker could not speak or write Lakota, and even in their relative elaboration his translations are mere summaries compared to Deloria's bilingual version. It cannot be known whether Deloria produced the longer version because she preserved more of what Makula said than Walker or his interpreters, or because she herself embellished the story according to her own narrative vision. In Deloria's retelling Makula's story concerns creation—not the formation of the spiritual entities, the universe, and its different forms of life—but the origin of tribal identity and social structures. Ideal patterns of relationship are introduced to human society in the camp of Waziya in the first and last episodes, while the hero's encounter with his evil mother-in-law shows the threat to physical and spiritual life in a society where egotism overwhelms respect.

Deloria differs initially from Walker in the favorable identity she gives to Waziya and Wakanka. As she says in her notes (see chapter 2) derived from Bushotter (17:3), Waziya was either a nasty spirit often associated with cold weather, or the first person on earth. Walker, basing his characters on a narrative by George Sword, involves Waziya and Wakanka in an Iktomi-inspired scheme to have their daughter, Ite, replace Hanwi (the Moon) as the wife of Wi (the Sun) (see Walker, *Lakota Myth* 52–57, 289–95). All three suffer a fall through pride and are punished by having to live in isolation on the earth. The negative connotations of the name "Waziya" supply an unspoken dimension to Deloria's first man. They suggest that human beings can overcome natural limitations by directing their energies toward maintaining domestic peace and nurturing children. Waziya's devotion to his grandchildren is carried on by his son's pursuit of his son and sharply contrasted to the buffalo mother-in-law's abuse of her daughters and son-in-law. In the last episode the corn wife provides an ideal of personal sacrifice and wisdom. She teaches her relatives how to regard death, and to bring the best life they can imagine into abundant fruition.

In "The Buffalo People" human beings learn to see themselves in the source of their food. The strength and generosity of the buffalo, the resiliency and grace of the corn objectify human possibility. The ideal male behavior, regardless of individual temperament, is represented by the husband and father who endures physical hardship and the temptation to forget his family and his tribe. The corn wife upholds the woman's obligation to promote peace and harmony in her *tiyośpaye* (community) and to remind her relatives to regard the gathering of food as a sacred duty. But the end of the story also indicates that individual relationships must be emotionally satisfying. In the buffalo camp the identity tests suggest that forgetting one's own wife and child can bring suffering and death. Devotion to the group does not supersede special concentration on immediate relatives. Throughout the story Deloria alludes to those aspects of Lakota thought that disprove notions of a group mind or "tribal mass." (In 1900 Indian "advocate," Merrill E. Gates, paraphrasing Teddy Roosevelt, referred to the Allotment Act of 1887 as "a mighty pulverizing engine for breaking up the tribal mass," in Prucha 342).

At the outset Waziya and Wakanka personify some basic assumptions about innate male and female qualities. While Waziya thinks only of enjoyment, Wakanka has an adult's concern for the future and a "longing for children." But once the first child is born, Waziya abandons adolescence and becomes intensely parental. His natural instincts then grow into social disciplines. Initially, parents gave each child a sense of special worth and self-esteem by spacing births no less than three years apart. The average family did not exceed four children, and a man who fathered more was often criticized for lacking self-control ("Camp Circle Society" 83). Bushotter reports the belief that a child supplanted too soon by a sibling would be weakened from not getting enough milk and from a lack of self-esteem.

> In some cases, babies have died . . . or even when they do not die, their bodies appear like skeletons, and at last such a child refuses all food and grows more and more like a ghost until it dies. . . . But a woman who loves her children never allows this to happen to any one of them . . . [and] when a man allows

a full time of nursing to all of his children . . . then he is admired as a real man who puts his children and their welfare
first. (Bushotter 257:1)

The five children of Waziya and Wakanka are properly spaced,
and the story highlights the excitement surrounding each birth
by describing the less eventful intervals and then intensifying the
passages that delineate the physical characteristics of each child.
Walker condenses Deloria's first fourteen units into "Long ago a
man's woman bore to him two daughters and then a son and then
two more daughters" (*Lakota Myth* 109). Deloria's longer exposition
establishes her version's preoccupation with individual and tribal
differences. The light-haired and black-haired sisters later dote on
their like-complected nephews and eventually marry husbands who
resemble themselves. Deloria may also be implying racial relations
through the color metaphor. All peoples have their own types of
beauty, and individuals from every group can serve other peoples
as well as their own. The corn woman completes what Wakanka
begins with her family. Fecundity as a traditional female virtue depends on the social education of men and women before and after
children are born. Although the narrator comments that Wakanka
"completed her work of creation" (unit 15) by giving birth to her
youngest yellow-haired daughter, the care given to growing and later
to converting harvested corn into food (units 281–303) reveals that
creation is the lifelong work of every human being.

Human individuality served the common purpose that shorter
oral narratives repeatedly defined. When a male culture hero becomes old enough to prove his courage and seek a wife, he makes
four conventional requests to his father. By refusing the first time and
acceding only on the fourth, the father determines that his son is suf-
ficiently resolute. The son's subsequent adventures may then follow
a general outline containing many variations (see Jahner, "Cognitive
Style" 44). "The Buffalo People" is not a culture hero story, though it
is as widely told and as varied. Sometimes the buffalo woman is only
testing her husband; sometimes the good yellow woman is an elk
rather than a corn spirit; sometimes the trouble starts when the two

women insult each other. Deloria polarizes the relationship so that the buffalo woman is entirely self-indulgent, and the corn woman thinks only of her community.

Just as storytelling thrives on variation, the group flourishes if individuals within it are fulfilled in personal relationships based on accepted differences. The delight of each pair of sisters in their special nephew points toward the common priority of renewal. Deloria's version, however, gives special attention to the distinctive role an individual must play in the process. When Waziya sees each woman leaving camp to give birth, he instructs his son to check on her safety (units 39, 46). In Walker's version the unnamed grandfather goes to witness the birth himself (*Lakota Myth* 109–10), a highly inappropriate act in light of the absolute respect-avoidance that fathers and daughters-in-law, like mothers and sons-in-law, are supposed to observe. The whole third episode of the story portrays the danger to social and psychological integrity that disregarding this rule can cause. We can measure Deloria's contribution and the authenticity of her version in details such as this. By peering at his daughter-in-law giving birth, Walker's elder would be an Iktomi to a Lakota audience.

In "The Buffalo People" Waziya evolves from adolescent hedonism to the grandfatherly responsibility of containing and imparting wisdom. He teaches each grandson a lesson that all Lakota take to heart, that the earth is sacred and must be walked with reverence. Within this circumference, however, each child may move according to his own pace and rhythm. The buffalo grandson is given a clear blue day that "rouses men to action" (unit 55), while the corn grandson is given a hazy day, "easy on the eyes" when "a gentle calm prevails" (unit 63). The second grandson's gift of gentleness resembles a statement Deloria recorded from one of Makula's contemporaries:

> Contrary to the common notion that every "Sioux" was *per se* a cutthroat who was never so happy as when he was killing someone, as many outsiders regarded them, there were actually men who chose life-occupations far removed from the warpath because they refused to "spill human blood." When asking about some detail of warfare, I sometimes got the answer, "I cannot

say, for I do not know from experience. . . . I have always been a
man of peace. Ask my cousin (naming him). He was a fighting
man." ("Camp Circle Society" 59).

Walker's version has neither the grandfather teaching the boys to
walk nor their culminating performances before the other adults.
Deloria includes (or adds) the scene to define Lakota priorities
and to introduce the important metaphor of walking-as-living, used
throughout the story and throughout Lakota culture. Most readers
will immediately remember the arrival of the White Buffalo Calf
Woman in several versions of her story: "with visible breath I am
walking" (see Black Elk, *The Sixth Grandfather* 284 and Densmore
68). The song expresses appreciation for spiritual awareness in this
life. The walking metaphor appears frequently in contemporary
Lakota prayer and oratory. In "The Buffalo People" it lends spiritual
depth to the hero's long pursuit of his buffalo son and to the extraordinary speech of respect for women and new life performed at
the end of the episode in the buffalo camp (units 253–55).

Since Deloria intends to convey a comprehensive view of *tiyospaye*
values and of the traditional Lakota "walk" through and beyond
deprivation, she is careful not to truncate the scene of the boys' education. Walker mentions only that the grandfather made the hoop
and stick game for the boys. Deloria portrays the grandfather's role
as she explained it in "Camp Circle Society":

> By day the old man sat around, making useful little things,
> such as toys, arrows, bowls of wood, pipes of red catlinite, for
> the family because it pleased him to keep busy in that way. In
> good weather he sat outdoors, always off to one side, out of the
> way. He needed peace as the active younger folk needed a clear
> runway. ("Camp Circle Society" 80)

Waziya too watches unobtusively over the children as they play,
fostering their independence and teaching trust by example: " 'Take
care, *takoza*, [grandchild] or you may hurt yourself.' Or he said, 'Do
not quarrel with your playmates . . . nobody does so,' meaning, it
is not proper" ("Camp Circle Society" 80; see also Deloria, *Waterlily* 34–36). After letting the children discover their independent

strengths, he imparts a confidence based on communal solidarity when he summons everyone in camp to witness the boys' first great deed. To walk the earth, the boys learn, is to do so for and with the relatives who surround them at the beginning. It is their presence that impels the courage and energy to live:

"Hecetu we lo, takoža!" eya canke ake ihanpi na hankeya ohitika ayapila kin ecel kaoh'ankoya s'e ca eglepi, na hankeya, tankapi kin, "Hinun" eyeye wanwicayakapi canke hecena ihat'at'a inyank iyayapi ke'.
Hecenahcin manipila. . . .

"That is right, my grandsons!" he encouraged them, so they took another step; and gradually they grew braver, and advanced by stepping out more rapidly; and at last, because their elders admired them, saying, "*Hinun!*" as they watched, they immediately started off, running and laughing.
Immediately from that time, they walked. (units 71–72)

Deloria augments the educational message with a detailed description of the hoop and stick game beginning with its manufacture. Because the grandmother produces the *tehmiso* (hard border of a tanned hide) from which the grandfather cuts strips for the webbing, the hoop (unit 73) demonstrates that everyone helps to strengthen the young directly or peripherally. In its fashioning the grandfather presents an additional lesson in concentration and patience even before the boys discover what the hoop is for. When they have learned to play, and the whole community assembles to praise the skills that guarantee their common future, the hoop's lesson is complete.

Deloria adds that the game taught the boys to count as well as to aim (unit 80). (In the nineteenth century the hoop and stick game also created awareness of the Lakota bands, represented by different marks on the hoop, and geography, beginning with the four directions denoted by the colors. As a ritual the game could heal or summon buffalo (Culin 504). Bushotter (123: 1–5) describes its recreational use: Players threw different colored sticks at the rolling hoop. They scored points when one of their colored sticks matched a band of the same color on the fallen hoop. Played by individuals or teams, a game could involve heavy gambling, have many spectators, and could sometimes last all day.) As an adjunct to reckoning their scores, the grandfather taught the boys how to regard loss. Within the "day" metaphor used earlier, he tells each boy to endure the days that are not his, foreshadowing their father's escalating adversity in part 2.

The first pain that befalls any of the characters occurs when the buffalo boy trips over his stick and hurts himself. Because they are children, they do not assign blame to each other but proceed to play when the pain is gone. A child spontaneously puts trouble in perspective. When one of his aunts inquires worriedly about him, the grandfather affirms the same ideal but from the vantage point of reflection rather than instinct: "Nitośkala wanun-hicahela k'eyaś lilahcin ksuyeyeśni ye lo . . . inaźin yo, takoś, heca wica canmakicapśa icaġe lo!" 'Your little nephew tripped accidentally, but he was not really hurt . . . stand up, grandson, it must be so that if one is man, he must grow up, crashing against the earth now and then' (unit 84). The children's accident represents the introduction of all potential unhappiness. Personal frustration, the sense of thwarted will, circumstances that challenge the illusion of control, become focused in the intentionally unexplained response of the buffalo woman to the accident. As one who excessively magnifies her sense of personal insult, she psychologically abandons the community. The buffalo woman's displeasure is specifically unvoiced (unit 89), so that her physical departure can represent the general effects of obsession with personal wrongs. For such people kinship lacks its pull toward the center, and when her sisters-in-law seek to soothe her and bring her back, she runs so fast in her buffalo form that "no human being could ever catch up with her" (unit 96).

Walker's version gives the buffalo woman a more direct motivation. First she sulks after her son is hurt. Then she exchanges insults with the rush (corn, in Deloria) wife before she leaves (Walker, *Lakota Myth* 110). By attributing anger to the buffalo wife alone, Deloria makes the corn woman's emergence as the feminine ideal more credible. Like the White Buffalo Calf Woman she will come to grant spiritual power, physical sustenance, and social order. Both the corn and buffalo wives have to undergo the usual ordeal of Lakota wives by having to adjust to complex relationships with their husband's people (see Deloria, *Waterlily* 175–78). Some women probably looked for reasons to return to their own homes, but the society could not have cohered unless most wives patterned themselves after the model of the corn woman. Instead of being jealous of her husband's intent to pursue his buffalo wife and son, she proceeds to empower him. (The Lakota have had medicine women as well as men, but their presence and practice has diminished in the cultural adversity of the twentieth century, see M. Powers 87, 96–98 and Bushotter 178).

While the buffalo elders and the corn woman reveal advanced wisdom to adults at the end of parts 3 and 4 (units 235–54, 268–326), Waziya makes it possible for children to permanently embody his message. His fashioning of the hoop parallels the corn woman's expert arrow making (units 99–100). Deloria makes the arrows reveal virtues the man will later manifest: Their shafts are from "the best and straightest sticks" and they are fletched with crow feathers, because "kaṅgi kin iśnala owotanlaḣcin kiyin nanśna tehanlhanl ihunni kin he un hecun" 'the crow of all birds flies straightest and goes farthest' (unit 101). The Kaṅgi Yuha (Crow Owners' Society) used crow feathers for the same reason (see Densmore 319).

The arrows derive their accuracy and impact not only from the hunter's skill and concentration but from love of family. Hunters and warriors carried their wives and children in their minds and hearts where their presence strengthened the will to survive when danger threatened. The yellow feather ornament the corn woman gives to protect her husband expresses her never absent love: "ośteka ca yuḣaḣaya peslete kin el eca-unḱa yunkan he e ca gluźun" 'she extracted it from her head, as if it were planted there' (unit 103). The plume is also connected to the food metaphors at the end. Like the ears on a corn stalk that the tassel "surmounts," the plume nourishes to give life (unit 104). Deloria's sense of the plume's sacredness corresponds to Black Elk's, as he describes implements of the *Hunka* ceremony: "The tassel which grows upon the top of the ear of corn, and which we have represented here by the eagle plume, represents the presence of the Great Spirit, for, as the pollen from the tassel spreads all over, giving life, so it is with *Wakan-Tanka,* who gives life to all things" (Black Elk, *The Sacred Pipe* 109).

In Deloria's version only, the first arrow the man tries heads straight toward a hillside and then "incredibly" lifts over it and disappears (unit 106). Its "magic" suggests the creative attitude: Continue on as best you can, remember your power and your loved ones, and then wait to see what happens. Miracles can occur only for those who are careful in technique and constant in purpose. Reversals of expectation must never deter an adult man from his lifelong responsibility to the next generation. The hero's strength comes primarily from loving his son. The boy promises that if his father continues to track and trust him, both will have all that they need (the water that wells up in his little hoofprint, unit 115).

Deloria's vivid description of the thirsty man's arrival at a wooded break on the open plains, a place where trees can live because water is present, intensifies the challenge he faces both sensorily and symbolically: "Ho yunkan wana el ihunni na wanyake c'eyaś atayaś mni wanice . . . ee tuktel mni tka kin ecel maka kin wana nakśakśa nan opapun kin hena wi-kata u nakas'-inś'inya ececa" 'Now then when he got there, there was no water at all . . . instead where it had once been water, there the earth was now cracked into cakes, whose edges were curled upward in the sun's heat' (unit 123). First the hopeless dry cakes become loam. Things get still better when he finds his son's single track filled with cold water, but fear returns when it seems impossible that the small imprint could hold enough to restore him. The bubbling up of all he needs including enough to rub on his head and chest, implies that love for one's relatives, even apart from supernatural help, can carry a person to improbably favorable results.

When he reaches his wife's camp for the second time, the detail that night is about to fall (unit 129) accentuates the idea of following one's quarry to the limits of strength and circumstance. The woman's apparent love and concern create another obstacle. So potentially does his careful attempt to prevent a recurrence of her desertion, when he ties his belt to hers and wraps her hair around his arm (unit 138). After creating this seeming certainty, he might well be crushed when he awakes the next morning to find that his precautions were of no avail. But recognizing that his buffalo wife is now his enemy, he relies on remembering those he loves to prevent himself from being weakened by anger or despair.

Following the arrow once again, he calls upon the physically absent corn wife to bring him the small whirlwind that lifts him across the muddy river that no human being could cross (units 235– 37). Deloria has him stopping to rest on the far bank against an oak tree so "giant-like, as in a vision" that "it seemed never to have had a beginning" (unit 239). Again the man gathers strength from his sense of living in order to continue a collective existence that stretches far into the past and future. By absorbing the tree's power to endure, he readies himself for the tests his buffalo wife says that he will surely fail in her camp (units 154–55).

Whereas the pursuit suggests the physical hardships that threaten to break a man's nerve, the buffalo camp contains domestic temptations that can also destroy a man. The story shows that a man must focus on his own wife and not commit adultery, and that he must focus on his own children to preserve their sense of special significance and self-esteem. While the whole kinship system reinforces each relationship, the narrator also shows that neglecting to properly observe any single relation threatens the whole system. The danger is immediately present in the behavior of the buffalo mother-in-law, the story's major adversary. Her first utterance is a shriek. The soft-spoken manner of traditional Lakota people expresses the absolute necessity of peace within the group (see Bunge 116–22). Nerves and emotions suffer as little strain as possible from the restrained tone and volume of everyday speech. When the woman first appears and loudly abuses her daughters in public (unit 160), the audience knows that little good can be expected from her. No one should be criticized this way, and Lakota children should be especially reinforced in their self-esteem, since self-confidence can prevent internal competition from shattering a small community.

The buffalo mother-in-law represents people who use standards of good conduct to gain power for themselves by criticizing others. In the first instance the hospitality she demands of her daughters is a traditional feminine virtue meant to create loving bonds in the community. Here the mother-in-law uses the ideal to condemn others for being inhospitable and lazy. The same misuse of social discipline occurs in her hope that her new son-in-law will disgrace himself by choosing a woman other than his wife. Then she can "kill" his reputation and influence. Like the temptation to abandon his journey to the camp, the "confusion" (unit 166) of natural attraction to others is overcome when the man thinks of his son. Deloria makes this harder than the transitory challenge of exhaustion he had endured outside the circle. In Walker's version the man simply follows his son's directions and picks up the signal to identify his wife (*Lakota Myth* 113–14). Here the buffalo sisters are so alike that the man is too baffled to think until "he happened casually" to see his son shooting play arrows into the air (unit 167). The agreed upon signal is not intentionally remembered. The man is lucky (or perhaps guided) to survive sexual diversion. When his gaze embraces his son shooting arrows as he had done, he sees the image of his mature purpose.

Still, the grown man must remember his relationship to his wife, even if the wife does not behave as a wife, in order to maintain the community. Aside from incest or physical abuse, the worst violation of kinship respect occurs when the mother-in-law ignores the strict avoidance that should exist between her and her son-in-law. First the "aggressive" woman opens the stone door to her son-in-law, intending the door to crush him when it swings back (unit 170). This suggests the psychological distraction that the breakdown of kinship can cause. Again this "kills" the person's Lakota identity, and eventually the community, because people who do not respect each other will not work together to survive. Mother and son-in-law, like father and daughter-in-law were never supposed to speak directly to each other (except in emergencies), to look directly at each other, nor even to pass near each other (Bushotter 253:2). Walker mentions that the mother-in-law repeatedly speaks to the young man (*Lakota Myth* 114–15), but Deloria preserves the full oral impact by putting her first address in the form of a direct quotation: "Ho, takoś, lecel le untipila ye" 'Now, Son-in-law this is how we manage to live, such as it is" (unit 172). Ironically, this is how the Lakota would *not* manage to live, using kinship only to condemn others for failing to use it, or using the rules selectively and ignoring them whenever it suits one's purpose. Such people live only to isolate themselves above the group. The cultural emphasis on *wahwala* (gentle speech and action), especially in social situations, is again reflected when the woman who thinks only of herself, rather than of her part, walks across the camp circle "anacan s'e" 'shaking and jarring with each step' (unit 179).

Once she has made her temporary exit, the man and his sisters-in-law exhibit an ideal relation. Since a man often married sisters-in-law together as plural wives, or married one later after she had been widowed, his arranging their hair (unit 180) is socially appropriate and narratively conventional. Although it usually expresses special esteem for a wife (see Deloria, *Waterlily* 172–73), it also reminds the man of a possible future responsibility, and the women that they will never be left without someone to hunt for them. Into this scene of comfort and reassurance comes the enraged mother-in-law, ranting about being slighted by another woman, who refused to give her a tipi pin because she has her own son-in-law to get tipi pins for her (units 181–82). As with the buffalo wife's pouting departure, the scene reveals that kinship obligations can evoke destructive pride in some people, and a debilitating anxiety to please in others who are less aggressive. The gnarled chokecherry stick, jokingly given her by the other woman and thrown down in rage by the mother-in-law, stands in contrast to the arrows made by the corn wife and then made again by the hero for his son. The stick is also like the mother-in-law herself. Though it comes from a chokecherry bush that bears fruit to nourish, and though as a tipi pin it represents the will to secure a home, it is not connected to any source or purpose and is therefore "warted," a fragment unlike the gigantic oak that gave the hero strength (unit 148).

The husband, however, plays the proper role of a man living with his wife's people (less common than the reverse, see "Camp Circle Society" 156) by immediately seeking to please his mother-in-law, to show her the special respect that she of all respect-relations should receive (unit 183). Once again the "whirlwind," generated by the affection of his corn wife, saves him from the physical danger of the snakes that guard the chokecherries and from the rejection of his gift by the mother-in-law as soon as he returns (units 185–90).

Although she throws the chokecherry sticks away, ostensibly because she fears the snakes' revenge, the man resists resentment with the same thought that has always aided him in the past. In transforming the sticks to arrows for his son, he redirects the energy of anger at injustice, an anger that would be as self-indulgent as that of his mother-in-law, into constructive provision for his people's future. As supernatural figures like the White Buffalo Calf Woman or wise elders of each generation have taught, so the man learns not only what he should do but how he should do it. The benevolent inspiration is from elsewhere, the loving act and the number four are ceremonial: "Hecena wagmeza winyan kin wanhinkpe-wakan kaġe c'un kiksuya canke ecehcin iś-eya wahinkpe-wakan top cinca-hokśila kin kicaġin na kal pusya otkeya ke'" 'So the corn woman's method of making magic arrows being fresh in his memory, he made some exactly like them, four magic arrows for his boy; and hung them up to dry' (unit 192).

The necessity for human beings to complete the protective intent of supernatural powers is also suggested when the thunder birds try to kill the man on his second quest to please his mother-in-law. Just as a human community cannot thrive if it is dominated by individuals, even spiritual entities must treat human beings as relatives rather than subjects in a cosmic kingdom. The "Great Spirit Judge" calms the thunder beings with the *tiyośpaye* (kinship-community) concept, just as potential rage in the man had been redirected toward preservation of one's family rather than revenge against one's enemies: "Ayuśtanpo! Tunweni he yaktepikteśni ye lo! He iś-eya wakanyan un we lo. Ituya le can wan el hokśi-icah-yakiyapi k'un niye iyunkala ihank-yakiyape lo!" 'Let be! Never can you kill him! He too has magic power. In vain do you with your own hands destroy the very tree where your young are reared!' (unit 202). In "The Buffalo People" Deloria describes how the Ree (Arikara) and the Lakota were branches of a common tribe. She may mean their relation to represent a general interrelation among different peoples. Like individuals within a tribe, different tribes and races are asked to remember their original unity and to appreciate their separate ways of being human (see also Black Elk, *The Sixth Grandfather* 307–14). In the thunder bird episode even powerful spirits must respect other beings that possess less dramatic means of expression but share an equal power to live according to their unique natures.

The message, like the coup talks of the small animals in "The Prairie Dogs" (see chapter 3), lends strength to the man's final encounter. Neither size, strength, nor an enemy's accurate assessment of personal vulnerability can daunt a man who remembers the children he loves more than himself. In the last identity test the man's strength has clearly grown. Shortly after arriving at the buffalo camp, he had been confused by the resemblance of the three sisters to his wife. He only happened to remember to look at his son for strength and inspiration. In the last test at the dance of the buffalo boys, it is the son who becomes anxious while the father shrewdly delays his selection in order to pique the mother-in-law and, as it turns out, to find a way to destroy her (units 215–18). The boy frantically wiggles his ears for his father to see, but the father now has ears to outwit the enemy in the same way that stories help listeners to sense threats to their personal and social integrity long before they come near.

In killing the mother-in-law and her ally, Crazy Bull, the man quells an individualism that only satisfies itself. As long as particular abilities serve the group, competitive individualism is a cultural strength. The hoop and stick game, therefore, forms an appropriate background for the culminating scene of violent action. It represents the good forms of competition that provide a contrastive background for the destructive competition that cannot be tolerated. Crowds of people surround and enjoy the game. In contrast the "solitary tipi" of Crazy Bull stands "in the wilder parts" away from the tribal camp, objectifying the inhumanity of the isolated self (units 220–21). The mother-in-law's tactic once again is to use an attitude intended to preserve social harmony as a weapon against it: "Leceya le wicaśa akantula kin ḣtayel cunkinta nitawin-hakakta kin okiya keyapi nan oyate kin iḱikoṗ kin" 'They are saying that this man-of-earth was seen courting your youngest wife at the wood-gathering last evening; and all the people are in an uproar over it!' (unit 223). Crazy Bull's immediate fury is inappropriate. It recalls the ceremonial admonition of a new chief—even if someone steals his wife, he must never take revenge against a Lakota (see Black Elk, *The Sixth Grandfather* 390).

The "uproar" the mother-in-law mentions corresponds to the distraction and feuding that real or rumored adultery might cause. Small details in Deloria's language image the idea of social threat as the mother-in-law "wawanyanka kin p̆azazan" 'worms her way into the crowds' (unit 224). This is followed by a thematically reiterated danger to the binding power of respect: "T̆uweniś hecunkeśni, isto el yunini" 'Quite improperly, she nudged him on the arm,' immediately preceding the outrage of direct address, "Takoś, iyaya!" 'Son-in-law, go off!' (unit 225). Once again the mother-in-law uses a benevolent admonition, against gossip, in a malevolent way: "Heceya, oyate waaiyap̆ s'a ke cin, wana ake t̆uwa tatanka-gnaśkinyan ki tawicu-hakakta wan oyakiya keye-okiyaka" 'Right now, true to the habit of gossiping, which people have, somebody has again told the crazy bull that you courted his youngest wife' (unit 225). Deloria repeatedly expresses the idea that strictures against adultery and malicious gossip, like other seriously regarded customs, only work if they are observed by loving people. Otherwise malicious people can twist them to condemn others and gain power for themselves.

In response to this ambition, as to any attack by physical enemies, the storyteller counsels unsentimental retaliation. Vicious people may target individuals, but they undermine communities. The hero does not run but "nazin" 'stands' against the invading enemy (unit 226). The single word *nazin* provides one of the strongest metaphors of courage in Lakota storytelling and oratory. The hero kills the crazy bull and the mother-in-law ceremonially with four arrows, as if to suggest a ritual of purification: One arrow strikes Crazy Bull between the eyes, one in the eye, one finishes him off, and then a split second later, one kills the mother-in-law as she charges from the opposite direction (units 228–30). The man tells his son that he had to kill them because they "makipazinpi" 'they bore me ill will' (unit 233).

While the arrows find their culminating use in striking evil, the healing that follows employs only metaphors of peace. Deloria's buffalo ceremony is culturally comprehensive, much like Black Elk's

Great Vision (*The Sixth Grandfather* 111–42). The placement of the buffalo elders evokes ritual practice (and therefore continual renewal), though it does not consistently resemble any specific sacred rite. In this case the generalizing of metaphor and gesture by the narrator suggests the effect of all rituals on the people's minds and wills and conveys, without attempting to appropriate, the meaning of "power." The twelve elders sit facing east in a new "pte owaci," the bare spot cleared by the buffalo in their dance. In the Buffalo Woman ceremony, about to be instituted, a similar space represents a buffalo wallow (see Black Elk, *The Sacred Pipe* 124). In the absence of the mother-in-law the location narratively symbolizes the purification of all pollutants, societal and spiritual. The Sun Dance circle is prepared by a grass treading dance (see Deloria, "Sun Dance" 39), and the grass is cleared on a much smaller scale but with the same meaning for the mellowed earth altars on which pipes are placed for varying purposes and occasions (see Dorsey 451).

The elders draw the hero into the center of the cleared space where they sit and call upon him to make the personal sacrifice demanded of ceremonial participants: "wicaśa maka akanl un kin e, na unkiye iyotahena yaun na iyeniśkakta ce" 'between the men-on-earth and ourselves you are to be forever the interpreter' (unit 241). Holy men who communicate regularly with spirits travel further from the circle of daily life than men who leave the circle only to hunt and fight. In these activities the male role mediates between predictable domestic routines and unpredictable quests. To be "of use," as the man says, means accepting the hard realization that one must often explore a strange place for the sake of those in a familiar one. In never being permitted to return to his original home the man represents an irreversible entrance into responsibilities borne only by the most spiritually advanced individuals.

Deloria's portrayal of holiness in human form in the four "ancient buffalo men" creates a sense of wonder far beyond the visual image, much like Black Elk's description of the six grandfathers (*The Sixth Grandfather* 115–19). The red paint on their hands and faces is a sign of official entitlement in several ceremonies (see Rice, *Black Elk's Story* 127–28, 134–36 and *Ella Deloria's Iron Hawk* 167–68), but the narrator identifies the abalone disks in their ears as "wakan-tawoyuha" 'supernatural properties,' and the prairie plants that each separately wears in his hair are special signs of the buffalo spirit (the burrs), the power to purify (the sage), the power to make grow (the buffalo plant), and the power to enlighten (the sunflower stalk) (see Bushotter 234: 1). Bushotter comments that since buffalo heads were covered with burrs after the hunt, men deferred to the buffalo spirit by wearing the burrs themselves, acknowledging, as the Great Spirit Judge earlier told the thunders (unit 202), that all forms of life live in a mysterious way and that no particular species can live without respectful acknowledgment of the others.

Close observation of all animals and direct communication with their spirits, especially that of the buffalo, is central to Lakota spiritual thought and practice (see Densmore 172–76). After the four most sacred buffalo men are seated, the spokesman for the buffalo elders presents his striking oration on their "relentless errand" to establish the sacredness of young women (units 253–55). It extends the story's emphasis on the hero's devotion to his son and its equal emphasis on women who exploit the respect due to them as mothers. In her notes accompanying an alternate translation of "The Buffalo People" (Deloria Family Collection, Dakota Indian Foundation, Chamberlain, South Dakota 298: 35), Deloria states that Makula recited the speech for her on several occasions as the oration that began "the buffalo ceremony for young girls in their purity." He repeated it word for word on each occasion, so that she understood it to be "a set form."

Walker's description of the Buffalo Woman ceremony contains similar ritual elements. The longevity promised for the woman in the speech's last line, her "hinaste-ska" 'locks of white at evening tide' (unit 255, line s).corresponds to a prayer for Lakota continuance in Walker: "She will live to be old./ Her tribe will live" (Walker, *Sun Dance* 147). The tribe must therefore take special care to properly shape, through ceremony and daily example, the women who are to contain that life. A girl's first menstruation is therefore celebrated as a momentous occasion, the equivalent of a young man's vision. The "mni wan luta" 'scarlet water' in Makula's speech is the ceremony's chokecherry juice, symbolizing both the girl's entrance into fertility and the heightened consciousness of respect for the Lakota customs that make her life sacred. In Walker's description the girl bends and drinks from the bowl as a buffalo would. Then the girl, the people, and the generative power of the buffalo come together: "My friends, this young woman gives you this red water so that you may drink of it and be her friends. Let all who are her friends drink of it" (*Sun Dance* 149).

In "Standing Holy," another unpublished manuscript, Deloria explains the reference to "hokśicalkiyapi" 'children beloved' (unit 253) in a song about a different ceremony. Children whose parents could afford all the accoutrements of giving their children "beloved" status —a special tipi, special clothes, frequent giveaways in the child's name—had their daughters initiated into the Hunka group: "Whoever is beloved must first be sung over in a Hunka ceremony, and then at her first flow's end, she must have a buffalo ceremony, also known as the singing over one having her flow" ("Standing Holy" 33: 62). [Menstruating women lived off by themselves in a special menstruation lodge during this period (see M. Powers 70), so that the occasion was known to everyone. The word for menstruation was "iśnati" 'living alone.' In "Standing Holy" (33: 59) Deloria adds that by the 1930s the word had become shameful, so that a euphemism, "Tokeca—something is the matter" was used instead: "But the people of the past spoke very plainly, so they didn't think anything of that word, and they even went so far as to celebrate it with a ceremony in a way to honor it, and that great rite that the people had was brought to them by Standing Holy."]

The steady rhythm of Makula's speech (to be discussed in more detail later in the chapter) is also conventionally associated with the buffalo's virtue of endurance and with the endurance of the people. The life-as-walking metaphor forms the whole second episode of the story when the man pursues his son and his future. The fecundity and vitality of the buffalo and their continual movement provides the energy of the speech that Deloria calls "beautifully worded" (Deloria Family Collection 288: 35). Several songs recorded by Frances Densmore contextualize Makula's unique elaboration. The following song expresses fortitude:

waziyatakiya	in the north
tate	the wind
manipi	they are walking
wasu	the hail
obobduya	beats
manipi	they are walking
	(Densmore 288)

Another song expresses the importance of manifesting consciousness as one lives rather than simply living:

oyate wan	a tribe
ho	their voices
taninyan	could be heard
manipi	(as) they walk
eyanpaha	the heralds (leaders of the herd)
ho	their voices
taninyan	could be heard
manipi	(as) they walk
	(Densmore 289)

And Densmore's version of the White Buffalo Calf Woman's song suggests the connection between her ideal womanhood and the tribe's ritual shaping of their daughters in unselfishness and self-respect. The steady walking toward something scarlet, the renewal of life, resembles the rhythm and dedication of the buffalo in Makula's speech (see also Black Elk's much shorter speech in *The Sacred Pipe* 122).

It is at the end of the ceremonial speech and in the story's last episode that two of Makula's tellings, the first to Walker, the second to Deloria, most dramatically diverge. In "The Buffalo Woman" (*Lakota Myth* 109) the man remains with the buffalo, while his son returns to the original family, who are the Lakota. In "The Buffalo People" the man and his son remain with the buffalo, where "the Lakota people sprang from the buffalo boy" (unit 257), while the original family of Waziya and Wakanka, their daughters, and the corn wife become the Ree people. The apparent concentration on the Ree in the last episode has a particular Lakota resonance, both in its continuing portrayal of the ideal woman through the corn wife, and in the difficult historical transition of the Lakota from hunting to farming or other forms of sustenance. If the Lakota at one time were united with a corn growing people, perhaps farming is not foreign to them in any fundamental sense (on Lakota resistance to farming see Hyde, *Spotted Tail's Folk* 9, 43, 80, 147, 171, 181–82, 202, 222, 380). The story suggests that corn provides spiritual nutrition (lessons in living well), just as the buffalo always had.

The corn wife's leadership in the last episode directly counters the insults to feminine identity and responsibility enacted by the buffalo mother-in-law and her daughter. She is the "older sister" of her *tiyośpaye,* much as the White Buffalo Calf Woman was the older sister of the nation (Densmore 66). She teaches her relatives how to bear the loss of their son and brother, grandson and nephew, as if she were responding to mortality. First she teaches by example. She goes off by herself to mourn long enough to gather her strength but not so long as to weaken those who depend on her. When she returns to the group, she infuses a new will to continue and new customs to re-inforce mutual respect. In direct response to her father-in-law's need to be comforted, she responds that her desire to honor him centers her love for the community: "Hetanhan ca tunkanku nan takośku ohowicakilapi kin le wicoḣ'an kin u we lo" 'From that day forth it is said, the precedent was made for children-in-law and parents-in-law to love and defer to and avoid each other out of courtesy' (unit 269).

The woman's subsequent words and actions suggest that ob-served kinship is the first principle of survival. The overtness of the avoidance relation stands for the less demonstrated but equally valued attitudes of the whole system. All behavior must be con-ducive to keeping the camp circle harmonious. It was "sacred" and only "mutual good will belonged there" ("Camp Circle Society" 18). When the corn woman suggests moving in space after an experience of loss to a "sheltering bend" of the Missouri river, she also moves the people ahead in time from a "place" where sorrow has shadowed their life to another perspective where order and momentum return. The family's loss of the man and his son may also represent the tribe's loss of the buffalo and of their former lands. The woman then directs them toward the utilizing of new resources to serve their long-standing love for each other. Although corn is a new food, it is regarded reverently and planted ceremonially. Makula implies that a different diet need not lessen one's appreciation for the gifts that enable life.

The story's acknowledgment of the common source of all food emerges in a parallel between the sacred walking of the buffalo in the Buffalo Woman ceremony and the ritualized walking down the rows in the act of planting. When the corn woman leads the family back to the field for the four formal visits, they learn to appreciate the corn's lesson long before the harvest. Through the cycle of its life the corn teaches the sacredness and beauty of all life. The people celebrate each stage much as they had earlier gathered to praise the buffalo and corn boys' first walking and again their first hoop and stick game. (The Buffalo Woman ceremony similarly praises female puberty as it represents both a unique phase and the cycle as a whole.) The final description of the ripened corn reflects an ideal maturity. The image conveys the importance of every young and old person, the relation of the individual to the group, and the ability to recognize and use a supernatural guardian:

> Iciyamni-ipi yunkan wana oblaye-tanka kin el santuhu eca-hanskaska can inkpa kin ekta wagmeza-winyan kin wacinhe wan eca-un k'eyaś hingnaku kin kaeyaye c'un heca icaġa ke'. Oblaye kin ataya cankuyetuntunyan hena hin na tate-hiyu ca akiyecel kawinś iyayin na akeśna iyuha-kaska ecel kigla can oiyokipi ke'.

> The third visit showed the stalks well formed and tall, with a plume surmounting the top like the ornament the corn woman used to wear which her husband had taken with him.
> These all stood evenly in rows over the whole level land, and with every breeze they all swayed and bent together and then all together righted themselves again, creating a beautiful motion. (units 292–93)

In its last stage the corn presents an image that corresponds to the heavy "burden" of the man who remains with the buffalo: "Miye kin tokaśni . . . . mitaoyate nipikte cin he e iyotan ye lo" 'What am I? That my people should live, that is of supreme importance' (unit 256). A leader is both nourisher and nourishment. Chiefs belong to the buffalo society (see chapter 3). Here the appearance of the corn provides a similar model for adult identity:

Icitopa-ipi yunkan wana wagmeza wahuwapa-hanskaska wašteste suntun ca tonana hu kin iyohi tkeya ikoyak hin.

The fourth visit showed corn, long beautiful ears, all ripened, several borne on each stalk making a heavy burden for it. (unit 295)

Deloria's image of the corn swaying in the field evokes the ritual use of cornstalks in the Hunka ceremony:

The swinging of the cornstalks in this manner is very *wakan*, for its represents the corn when the breath of the Great Spirit is upon it, since, when the wind blows, the pollen drops from the tassel upon the silk surrounding the ear, through which the fruit becomes mature and fertile. (Black Elk, *The Sacred Pipe* 110)

As a gift from a supernatural source that initiates the mysterious power to grow, corn, like babies or game animals, must be preserved and transformed by human hands. Each person has a particular task. Waziya moves more slowly and so has the sedentary job of cutting the pumpkins into strips (unit 299), but still, as a man, apparently has the strongest back and so digs the pit for the first food cache (unit 302). (On food caches, see Deloria, "Camp Circle Society" 127–29 and *Waterlily* 178–79). Others help to guarantee the future by making the first corn drying rack and the first corn *wasna* (dried corn mixed with berries and fat, like pemmican) (units 298, 300).

All of these preparations get the people through the winter, as the corn woman has gotten them through the shock and sorrow of mortality. The joy of being privileged to partake of creation enters into the series of marriages at the end. Once again individuality is taken into account, in that the black-haired girls and their yellow-haired sisters find compatible mates, while the corn woman herself eventually marries by mutual agreement without needing to consult her relatives (on the independence accorded to a mature woman in choosing a husband, see Deloria, "Camp Circle Society" 153–54 and *Waterlily* 224). Nevertheless, the corn woman does not neglect to use her marriage as an opportunity to express another lesson in respect. She tells her sisters-in-law that although her brother left them, she "was bound to you" and could not leave, because "your nephew is yours as well as mine, and for me to take him away never entered my thoughts" (unit 325).

The story ends as it had begun, with marriage and the promise of children. Its narrative fullness promises cultural renewal as well. Makula apparently believed that human beings could independently transmit teachings that spirits originally gave:

> He told me he can officiate at a buffalo ceremony; right now he could sing over anyone ready for it, he says. I asked him, "Did he dream of the buffalo?" He says, "No." But he liked the teaching so well that he had both his daughters sung over, and two other close relatives. And each time, he used the same official. And then this man who acted the part of the go-between for the buffalo people and the humans, said to him that if he liked, he would teach him the secret and cause him to be a qualified official. He did so. He is going to tell me about it next time. It is the very first intimation I have had of the transfer of a vision, without the person actually experiencing it. (Deloria Family Collection 288:35)

Nevertheless, Makula and Deloria have not diminished respect for the ceremonial tradition through their narrative adaptation. "The Buffalo People" develops the major themes of continuity and kinship more vividly and in more metaphorical detail than any written version of this widely told tale.

Deloria's narrative and linguistic technique deepens the story's meaning. She reinforces the establishment of social harmony in the first episode with a balanced doubling of key phrases. When the hero tells Waziya of his desire to travel, his request is put into a nearly identical formula on each occasion:

Ate, leceya lila omani-wakinica ye lo . . . Ito ka wi mahel iyaye cin hecetkiya mninkte.

Father, over this way, I have an uncontrollable wish to go on a journey. . . . I want to go where the sun goes down. (unit 18)

Ate, leceya omani-wakinica ye lo. Hehanl wi hinape cin hecetkiya mnikteňicin.

Father, right now I have the urge to go on a journey. . . . Next I want very much to go where the sun comes up. (unit 29)

The doubling calls attention to the request as part of the culture hero convention and foreshadows the immediate outcome of marriage and the ultimate outcome of tribal generation. In the same way the father's conventional reluctance to agree accentuates the ritual of a young man's need to demonstrate his resolve and prove himself through actions:

"Hehehe, cinkś, nakun tuwa iňanhan mninkte ecin k'eyaś ta-kunl ikusekta yunke lo," eyaya k'eyaś hecenaś wanň'unśni kakena icimani-iyaya ke'.

"Alas, alas, my son, for even though one might say, 'I go but for a little while,' there might be something to prevent his return." But the son, disregarding him, went off yonder on a journey. (unit 19)

"Hehehe, cinkś. . . . nakun tuwa iňanhan-mninkte ecin k'eyaś takunl ikusekta yunke lo," eyaya k'eyaś hecenaś ake kakena iyaya ke'.

"Alas, alas, my son. . . . For even though one might say, 'I go but for a little while,' there might be something to prevent his return," he said, but disregarding it again he went off in yonder direction. (unit 30)

The doubling also creates confidence in the story's and the tribe's eventual state. Young people determined to overcome all obstructions will come to know and tell a full range of experience.

Doubling is next used to describe how each set of sisters greets the buffalo wife and the corn wife as she enters camp. In both instances providing all members of a *tiyoṡpaye* with special relatives eliminates resentment between haves and have-nots. The image of the sisters-in-law linking arms contributes to the overall sense of kinship harmony being established in the tribe: "Isto anunkatanhan koyakyapi na aḱupi" 'They hooked arms with her on each side and brought her' (unit 26); "isto-koyakyaḱ . . . aḱupi" 'linking arms with her . . . they escorted her' (unit 33).

After this doubled celebration of new life, the two boys grow to add a sense of balanced opposition to the pattern. While Waziya tells each child of his separate gifts, he emphasizes their common obligation to reverence the earth in nearly identical words:

Ho, takoża, anpetu kin le tanyan wanyaḱa yo . . . . towanzica na waṡte ye lo, iwicaḱibleze cin heca ye lo . . . . Le nitaanpetu ce . . . . anpetu-lececa ca el maka ayalikta ce . . . . Maka kin le awali tka wakan ye lo . . . . canke heun ohinni wakan-laya amawani ye lo . . . .

Now, Grandson, observe this day well . . . . See it is continuously blue and beautiful . . . . intense, rousing men to action, such a day is this . . . . this is your day . . . . on such a day shall you step upon this earth. I walk upon this earth, but it is a holy earth . . . . therefore always I walk upon it reverently . . . . (units 56–57)

Ho, takoża, anpetu kin le tanyan wanyaḱa yo . . . . ahanziya, iṡtiyowicaṡniżeṡni . . . . asasyela wanḱe lo . . . . le nitaanpetu ce . . . . anpetu-lececa ca el maka ayalikta ce . . . . Takoża wanmayaḱa yo. Maka kin le awali ye lo . . . . Ho, tka wakan, kin he un ohinni oholaya amawani ye lo . . . .

Now, Grandson, mark well this day . . . . hazy, easy on the eyes; a gentle calm prevails; this is your day . . . . on such a day you are to step on the earth . . . . Consider me, my grandson. I tread this earth . . . . but it is a holy earth, and so always I tread it with awe. (units 63–64)

In the second episode, the man's pursuit of his wife and son, doubling is less pronounced, since the mood of harmony and balance has been interrupted. It is used only to express the man's intensifying effort. On the first leg of his journey he walked half a day, "anpetu okise ataya mani" (unit 108), and on the second he and his quarry ran half a day, "anpetu okise inyankapi" (unit 122). Once he reaches the buffalo camp in part 3, balanced repetition occurs only when he risks his life to try to please his mother-in-law and establish harmony, and when he later makes the best possible use of his failure to do so. Before departing to retrieve the chokecherry branches and the birdlings, his sisters-in-law offer nearly identical warnings: "K'eyaś tunweni tuweni heciyatanhan ni gliśni k'un" 'But nobody ever returns alive from there, alas!' (unit 184); "Śice, akśaka tunweni tuweni heciyatanhan gliśni k'un" 'brother-in-law, what is so bad about it is that nobody has ever returned from there alive!' (unit 196).

Then after the mother-in-law rejects the gift because she fears retribution from the snakes and the thunders (ironically, since she is the one to fear), the man twice indicates the proper way to regard enemies. By making arrows out of the discarded sticks and feathers, he transforms the potentially wasted energy of his own anger into the overriding effort to create the future. Later when the time is right, he will have his chance for revenge. Such enemies always return in each individual life and in each generation. They can be defeated only if one's aim is not deflected by impatience, and if one's will to fight is not weakened by forgetting to love:

> kośkalaka k'un tawicu kin ki na heya ke: "Iyayin nan canpahu kin etan waśteśtehca wanhinkpe-waśte ece aku wo," eya canke agli ke'.
>
> Hecena wagmeza winyan kin wanhinkpe-wakan kage c'un kiksuya canke ecehcin iś-eya wanhinkpe-wakan tob cincahokśila kin kicagin nan kal pusya otkeya ke'.

> the man told his wife to go and bring him four of the very best ones, and she did so.
>
> So the corn woman's method of making magic arrows being fresh in his memory, he made some exactly like them, four magic arrows for his boy; and hung them up to dry. (units 191–92)

wicaśa kin tawicu hupahu wanźi kin hiyoyeśi ke'. Agli ca etan
wiyaka icu nan cinċa tawanhinkpe k'un iyaktun ke'.

the man sent his wife after one of the wings. When she brought
it, he took out a feather and winged his son's arrows with them.
(unit 207)

Perhaps the narrative technique of doubling, as it may have come
down to Deloria through Makula, reflects a Lakota saying, "When
there are two of something, then it is true" (Pete Catches, lecture,
Loxahatchee Historical Society, Jupiter, Florida, 20 April 1990). In
an interview (American Indian Research Project, South Dakota Oral
History Center, tape no. 383, 26, 27 March 1969) Wallace Eagle
Shield told Deloria a similar version of the proverb related to him
by his father. He added that from the beginning everything was created in pairs and that even adversities would usually come together.
Though Deloria cautioned Eagle Shield about taking this literally,
she had used the idea metaphorically to express the universality
of particular events, and the undeniable virtue of a hero who has
repeatedly proved himself.

Apart from doubling, Deloria includes another significant repetition in the third episode. She communicates the appropriate impact
of the buffalo mother-in-law's disrespect by having her address the
hero as "takoś" 'son-in-law.' Direct address is not present in Walker's
versions. By putting this forbidden form of communication into dialogue, Deloria personifies the mother-in-law as the ultimate threat
to peace and order. Her unconventionality is both laughable and
horrible. Her first words to him, "Ho, takoś" (unit 172) immediately
follow her attempt to crush him with the stone door. Next she calls
him to sit next to his wife in order to find an excuse for killing
him if he cannot determine which of the four sisters she is: "Ho,
takoś, micunkśi kici iyotaka" 'Now then, Son-in-law, sit down by my
daughter' (unit 174). On the third occasion Deloria again associates
the abuse of respect with death, when the woman calls upon the
man to select his son from the thousands of buffalo dancers: "Ma
takoś nicinca kin ikikcu" 'Well, Son-in-law, take out my grandson'
(unit 214)

The woman seems to seal her fate by using the term, "takoś" as direct address exactly four times in a kind of inverted ceremonial completion. On the last occasion she literally tries to get rid of him, as she annihilates respect by actually touching him: "Tuweniś he-cunkeśni, isto el yunini na, 'Takoś, iyaya!'" 'Quite improperly, she nudged him on the arm, and said, "Son-in-law, go off!"' (unit 225). Just as she is the primary force of social destruction in the story, so the young man represents the counterforce that must always win if Lakota culture is to survive. Her behavior represents the Lakota sense of obscenity. While the avoidance custom is no longer prac-ticed by all Lakota people, its message of respect for the sources of life and the ongoing will to protect the community through an atti-tude of mutual regard permeates the whole of Deloria's story. Lakota life today retains the basic values upheld by "The Buffalo People" in various adaptive forms.

Some of the older storytelling techniques, though less in evidence today, may yet be revived. In a Lakota translation of Paul Goble's *The Buffalo Woman,* one of that artist's superbly illustrated books for children derived from the Lakota oral tradition, Albert White Hat, Sr. uses the storytelling forms of *keyapi* and *ke* (they say, or he or she said) in rendering Goble's English text into a richly detailed Lakota version (not yet published as a bilingual edition by Goble and White Hat, Sr.). Deloria's practice of using *śke'* as a variation of *ke'* and *keyapi'* to indicate stronger emphasis was a consistent prac-tice in her Lakota language work (see Rice, *Deer Women* 52–55 and "Narrative Styles" 284–90).

Based on the evidence of *Dakota Texts,* some narrators used *śke'* several times at the beginning and end of a story. Otherwise they ended units of thought sometimes in *keyapi',* but usually in *ke',* except for rare moments of dramatic intensity or editorial empha-sis when they used *śke'.* In "The Buffalo People" Deloria alternates *keyapi'* and *śke'* four times at the beginning up to the birth of the first child (units 1, 2, 4, and 6). Thereafter she uses *śke'* to indicate very unusual events, such as the birth of the boy after those of his two older sisters (unit 11), and the birth of the first yellow-haired girl whose coloring is so unusual that at first she appears inhuman (unit 12).

Ške' intensifies the growing power after the corn woman's head plume is identified as a corn tassel (unit 104). It emphasizes her supernatural identity when she immediately knows that her husband has decided to remain with the buffalo (unit 261). Finally, *ške'* reinforces the conclusion's image of social unity. The summary of marriages is followed by *ške'* (unit 327) as is the affirming reference to the strength and health of future generations (unit 328).

Ške' also lends force to the corn woman's arrows after they are completed with crow feathers, underlining the statement that the crow flies straight and fast (unit 101) and suggesting that the man will manifest the same virtue. *Ške'* here expresses power to effect one's will. In another instance it emphasizes the limits of that power, when the Great Spirit Judge tells the thunders to refrain from killing the hero, since the different forms of life have an equal right to live (unit 203).

In a story that begins and ends by promising new life, it is not surprising that the concept of origination receives the most systematic use of *ske'*. The word follows the introduction of the first hoop and stick game (unit 76), the clearing of the first buffalo wallow and dance circle (unit 210), the performance of the first Buffalo Woman ceremony (unit 257), the making of the first corn drying rack (300), and the digging of the first food cache (303). The repetition of firsts, marked by *ske'*, emphasizes renewal and adaptation rather than invention, and while the technology can vary, strong individuals must transmit the best of the human spirit. The two corn husbands and two buffalo husbands are different and yet the same. Each promises the arrival of a new member of the community in nearly identical words: "Kila iš-eya ukta keye c'un" 'A friend of mine says he too is coming here' (unit 307; see also units 309 and 311). Since each generation must live out their own creation story, "The Buffalo People" ends in a new beginning.

In the last episode orderly sequence consistently enables this renewal. After the corn woman goes off to mourn her husband's loss by herself, her family asks her to come home in four visits: first by her youngest sisters-in-law, then by her oldest sisters-in-law, then by her mother-in-law, and finally by her father-in-law. In agreeing to follow but not to accompany him back, she institutes the custom of avoidance (units 268–69). Though her self-imposed isolation cannot bring her husband back, it does result in the significant emergence of a relationship that will strengthen the tribe's self-respect and its will to live.

The same emphasis on directing the tribe away from irretrievable loss influences the lessons in planting, as an orderly procedure that represents endurance, transformation, and fulfillment: "Yunkan iyuha paogla-yeya wiyohinyanpatakiya etunwan inaźin-wicaśi canke oko-tuntunyan inaźinpi ke'" 'She told them all to take places, side by side, facing eastward in a straight line; they did this, leaving spaces between each one' (unit 282 and continuing through unit 287). The rite begins facing eastward to indicate its life-generating purpose. Then each person moving in concert with the others sows seeds, learning to appreciate every stage of preparation as well as its result: "Oblaye kin ohanskeya k'eyaś ohangleya ataya hecel ecun yapi" 'The ground was long, in its stretch ahead, but they went its entire length in this way' (unit 285). The four subsequent visits to the corn field serve the same purpose (units 289, 291, 292, and 295). Each time the corn and pumpkins are beautiful in a different way. Patience becomes a virtue bringing present fulfillment rather than a means to an end.

Although her translations are for the most part effective and assured, Deloria apparently did not feel that a free translation could do justice to Makula's recitation of the oration that accompanied the Buffalo Woman ceremony (units 253–55). She supplies only a word-by-word translation. In Makula's experience the speech was always spoken in the same way, and the beautiful language that Deloria noted (Deloria Family Collection 288:35) was therefore generally traditional rather than a product of her own or Makula's art. Coming into the story after the social and spiritual disruptions caused by the buffalo mother-in-law, the speech blends the virtues of persistence and harmony through its exact verbal repetition.

The last word of each line ends in a future tense verb, so that in Lakota the final sound is *kta,* the particle for the future or conditional, followed by *ce,* a particle for emphasis. In the first stanza (unit 253) the last sound in English cannot be so consistent, varying between "walk" and "make," so that the movement of the buffalo does not sound as steady, or as the hero later calls it, "relentless" (unit 256). In addition to the common ending, the whole last word of each line of the first stanza is the same for six of the eight lines, "manipikta ce" 'they shall walk,' and is broken only by "kaġapikta ce" 'they shall make,' in lines c and d (unit 253). The consistency convey-ing endurance is supplemented by rhythmic balance for harmony: lines a and b have approximately the same number of syllables, as do lines e and f, while the somewhat shorter lines c and d, and g and h, also match each other in length. Lines c and d supplement the effect of unity by differing only in one word: the altar is "waśte" 'good' in line c and "wakan" 'sacred' in line d. "Waśte" and "wakan" contrib-ute alliteration to the overall effect. The first stanza also balances the opposites of age and youth in the ridged hoof nails of the buffalo men moving toward the children-beloved (lines b and e) through extremes of heat and cold (lines g and h). The indication of cold, "Niya taninyan manipikta ce" 'with breath showing they shall walk' (unit 253, line h), suggests the manifestation of wisdom by evoking the song of the White Buffalo Calf Woman (see Densmore 68).

In stanza 2 the "manipikta ce" to express the movement of the buffalo men changes significantly to "imanipikta ce" for all six lines. The prefix adds the sense of purpose, meaning "on account of" (see Deloria, *Dakota Grammar* 42). The buffalo nation moves not only to protect the girl but to maintain the values suggested by the symbolic objects that begin each line. In her other translation of the story, Deloria notes that "ognake" (line i) means "container," and in sacred contexts refers to the pipe (Deloria Family Collection 290:37); "mni wan luta" (line k) is the red water in the Buffalo Cere-mony; "kanṗeśka" (line m) refers to the abalone, cowry, or porcelain disks worn as earrings in ceremonies; and "wanbli-sun" are the eagle feathers that denote courage and wisdom in both secular and spiri-tual leaders. The addition of *i* to "imanipikta ce" causes the gram-matical objects—container (pipe), red water, abalone, eagle feathers —to represent the goals of adult effort and the term, "Ikce wicaśa" 'Indians' or "common people," at the head of the remaining line (b) defines the tribe as the collective recipient of the honor bestowed on any member.

The woman in the speech, as in any given Buffalo Ceremony, therefore represents the whole Lakota nation. The lines of the last stanza are longer and the rhythm less intense, as if to soothe, after the determined forcefulness of the first two stanzas. It begins with the young woman who contains the future and praises her unpolluted potentiality with alliteration: "wicinċala wotiyemnaśni," (unit 255, line o), literally a girl unmarred by inner corruption or outward assault; *mna* means swelling, and *mnahan* means rip or tear. Despite her youth she is a life-carrier and is accorded the highest respect. Men carry her to drink water with the buffalo elders and give her a red cane like those held by the four holy grandfathers, who sit before the twelve men of eminence (unit 251; on the red cane as a gift from the buffalo spirits to buffalo dreamers, see Densmore 174 and Walker, *Sun Dance* 147–48, 150–51). The number of holy men corresponds to the number of buffalo men in the speech. According to Deloria, they walk eight roads (line b), because "there are eight feet going" (Deloria Family Collection 37). She also notes that the red cane represents longevity and is received mystically at the time of the ceremony from the buffalo people (Deloria Family Collection 290:37).

The next to last line is the longest and softest, as if to express the gentle manner in which ceremonies guide children into the responsibilities of adult life: "Tatiye wan iye tawapi ca iyopteya maka nakiptanyeśni yuhomnipikta ce" 'In the wind-direction that is their own on the earth, and without oversetting hers, they will turn her' (unit 255, line r). Childish inclinations are not harshly halted but made to circle naturally from a stasis of passive reception to a steady motion of giving. The four buffalo travel east toward the sunrise to achieve renewal, personified in the girl. The Lakota term for the east is suitably metaphorical "wohinape" (unit 253, line a), literally "where it comes out." Then at the end of the speech they turn to the west, the direction of difficulty, where responsibilities must be endured.

The east-west movement of the speech does not refer to absolute divisions of consciousness. Rather, the balance of movements toward and away from the source reflects the simultaneous concentration on renewing the group (the east) and the transience of individual protectors (the west). Although the girl's initiation to adulthood is gentle, it will strengthen her to endure all the ordeals that westward movement implies. The hero of the story also traveled west to overcome threats to kinship and survival. The speech's last line is the story's promised end: "Na hinaśte-ska ohtayetu ekta wakicunzapikta ce" 'And for her, locks of white at evening-tide they shall decree' (unit 255, line s). The "decree" cannot be guaranteed for every individual but is demonstrably present for the tribe in every generation that survives to practice the Buffalo Woman ceremony. The last line speaks of a manifested mystery that transcends personal fate, a fullness of experience rather than of years.

Deloria maintains the story's devotion to children and harmonious kinship relations through a sensitive use of the diminutive. The suffix *la* (see Deloria, *Dakota Grammar* 57) is used with nouns, verbs, adjectives, and adverbs to express nuances of endearment and softness from childish speech to mild weather. The frequency and range of its usage in "The Buffalo People" helps to create the protective tenderness that culminates in the ceremonies for the buffalo woman and for sowing the corn.

The hero's unflagging dedication to his son, that of the buffalo elders to their daughter, and of the corn woman to her *tiyośpaye* stems from a sense of their vulnerability. When Deloria refers to the "wicaśa-akantu*la*," the first 'men-on-earth' (unit 2), she adds *la* to "akantu," 'on' or 'upon,' to suggest that human beings are small, that they do not dominate their environment, and that they will need the social structure the story introduces. Waziya is actually childish, thinking only of present pleasures and of sleep (unit 3), until he begins to assume responsibility for his children.

Their appealing qualities evoke protectiveness. The "iśta-kin sapyela" 'black eyes' of his first daughter are not small eyes but the eyes of a little one, connoting their charm. And when the little one smiles, the *la* qualifies her smiling, "iha ece-un*la*" rather than the girl herself. When *la* is applied to verbs describing a child's action, the English usually reads, "the little one did this or that," but in Lakota the verb receives the *la*, describing the immaturity of the action rather than the actor, and conveying the sense of childish activity rather than a fixed convention or image. When Waziya begins to admire his first child, he speaks of her being "miciwaśtela" 'pretty for me' (unit 7) rather than of simply being pretty, a process rather than a state of being childlike. Later the growth of all his children is referred to as "icaḣ-ayapila" 'they grew up' (unit 16), just as the emergence of the corn baby, in his father's first view, receives the la, as does the adjective: "yunkan wagmeza sanṫuhu wan. . . . na isakiṗ wanźi iś-eya ula k'eyaś nakeś hinapela ca nunuźela" 'there stood a corn stalk. . . . and close by it a little one was also coming, but it had only just sprung up, and it was tender' (unit 47).

Deloria uses la repeatedly in the opening section to describe the children. The boy is "t'insyela" 'solid' (unit 11) or "hanskela" 'tall' (unit 13). She also uses la for their actions: "oiyankela" 'she ran about of her own accord' (unit 8) or "napaṫakiciyuzapila" 'the two little boys took hands' (unit 70). La is also used to describe the words or actions of adults directed toward children. Here la communicates tenderness of attitude in the subject rather than simply smallness in the object. When Waziya pets his first daughter, the verb is "kignala" (unit 7) from kigna (to soothe) plus the diminutive. When the corn woman's sisters-in-law carry their newborn nephew back to camp, the carrying is "ayapila" (unit 51), connoting their tenderness toward the little one rather than their own size.

Other uses of la in the first section indicate its ability to evoke sympathy. When Waziya asks his daughter to bring his grandson so that he can teach him to walk sacredly, he is referred to not simply as "wicaḣca" 'the old man' but "wicaḣcala" (unit 53), perhaps because the lessons he is to impart reveal loving purpose. In a similar sense he tells his second grandson that his day is to be "asasyela" 'gentle and calm' (unit 63), and later when they play at hoop and stick, the second son prevails when the day is "ablakela" 'overcast and calm' (unit 81).

In addition to size, mood, or atmosphere, la describes surfaces. When Waziya selects wood to fashion the hoop, it is "kcakcala na laṗlaṗela" 'smooth and supple' (unit 74), linking the game's implements to its small players and its maker's mood. La also expresses brevity of duration. Waziya begins to instruct his grandson "kiglapilaka" 'the minute his daughters were out of sight' (unit 55).

Or it expresses a gradual inner process, as when the children take their first steps: "ohitika ayapi*la*" 'the little ones [steadily] grew braver' (unit 71).

The diminutive is not used to refer to the girl in the Buffalo Woman ceremony (units 253–55) and is generally not used for deeply serious matters or dangerous situations. Its use and non-use, however, heightens the dramatic effect in parts 2 and 3 of the story. When the hero sees his son after the first day of travel, the boy "śkate*la* k'un ayuśtan" 'left his play' (unit 110). The *la* attached to "śkate" 'play' accents the boy's abrupt transition to the adult responsibility of protecting his father's life. When he waves to his father "ohiteye*la*" 'energetically' (unit 111), *la* maintains the idea that he moves like a child and preserves the lovable element that inspired his father's pursuit. The tension between his childish limitations and his life-preserving task continues in references to his speech, "ie*la*" 'he said' (unit 112), when he warns his father for the first time of his mother's destructive intent, and "eye*la*" 'he said' (unit 115), when he instructs his father to find water in his left footprint.

Once they have entered the buffalo camp, the son's actions and his words take the diminutive less often as the danger to his father grows. When he tells his father to look for him shooting arrows during the initial test of choosing his wife rather than her sisters, the boy's words are followed by "eyin" 'he said,' not "eye*la*" (unit 158), and when he departs to rejoin his mother, he is said to "inyanka" 'run' (unit 158), not to inyanke*la*." The boy's size has not changed, but his words are urgent and he is not playing. When the confused father later happens to glance in his direction, the boy who appears to be an innocent child gives the crucial signal as a "hokśila*la*" 'small boy' playing with "wanhinkpe*la*" 'play arrows' (unit 167). In these uses the diminutive accents the effectiveness of the trick.

As the father's confidence develops, the son's childishness returns. Before the last identity test when he becomes impatient of his father's ability to find him among the dancers, the boy is called "hokśila*la*" as he "nahma-wokiyake*la*" 'communicated something secretly to him' (unit 208). The boy's ear-wiggling signal, however, does not take the verbal or adverbial diminutive, probably because they would lessen the life-or-death intensity of the scene (unit 215). When the boy later complains that his father did not recognize him sooner, the tone of his words causes them to be followed by "eya" 'he said' (unit 218) rather than "eyela."

This is the end of the boy's active role in the story, but the father himself is called "wicaśa akantula" 'man-on-earth' to indicate his relative size as he stands among much larger beings in the crowd of buffalo watching the hoop and stick game (unit 219). The *la* also magnifies the bravery of his heroic deeds: the killing of the implicitly gigantic crazy bull and the buffalo mother-in-law in her animal form (units 226–30). The mother-in-law had been introduced as "winunhcala wicaśaśni" 'a tricky old woman' (unit 154), so that in the case of her obvious lack of innocence, the *la* can only be ironic. It is used with even more irony just before the buffalo dance, because she violates the most strictly observed custom of respect by ignoring the avoidance rule: "winunhcala k'un ake takosku kin na, 'Ma takoś, nicinća kin ikikcu'" 'the old woman came to her son-in-law, saying, "Well, son-in-law, take out my grandson"' (unit 214). For the final confrontation when her malice is completely undisguised, the irony of "winunhcala" is no longer necessary. First the "winunhca" (unit 240) becomes a buffalo cow and charges the hero. After he kills her, he learns that the "winunhca," (unit 232) and Crazy Bull had persecuted the buffalo people for a long time.

The diminutive is used sparingly from this point on. The "wicaśa akantula" 'man-of-earth' is again made small in the center of the buffalo circle (unit 239), but the human species is not diminished when the man is assigned his crucial role: "wicaśa maka akanl un kin e, na unkiye. . . .iyeniśkakta ce" 'Between the men-on-earth and ourselves you are to be forever the interpreter' (unit 241). Here the man is simply "akanl" 'upon' the earth, not "akantula" 'small upon' the earth.

The story's remaining diminutives typify narrative practice. Waziya, as a beloved and bereaved elder, who is honored by the corn woman's introduction of the avoidance taboo, is referred to as "wicahcala," not simply 'the old man,' as the translation says, but the little or dear old man (unit 266). The narrator also applies *la* to a non-human protector, the "oblula" or 'sheltering bend' of the Missouri river where the people move (unit 280). The first crops that grow there, like the children at the outset, are clearly in need of careful nurture, since they emerge as both "toye*la*" 'small and green-ish,' and "nunuże*la*" 'tender and yielding' (unit 289). In a conclusive use *la* connotes the general thematic reverence for the life cycle and the overriding adult responsibility of protecting all embodied spirit as long and as resourcefully as possible. In the following passage "kanpi" means literally 'they are old': "Tanyan oko wanilya, osni hiyukteśni iyacinyan kaḣ-wicakiyin na yuśtanpi yunkan hel kunku, tunkanku kici, wana kanpi*la* ca tiwicakiya ke'" 'Carefully, without open spaces, planned to keep the cold out, she had them make it [the first earth lodge], and when it was done she placed her parents-in-law there, now so old' (unit 317).

The careful making of the earth lodge reflects the storytelling technique of Makula and Deloria. Together they worked to shelter the ancient stories they loved on the written page. Like the Ree moving to earth lodges, or the reservation Lakota moving to permanent dwellings (see chapter 3), the stories may find other homes, perhaps theatrical or cinematic. Whatever the form, it will need to find ways to say *la*, the syllable that gives "The Buffalo People" so much of its feeling and purpose.

Appendix

The Deloria Family Collection at the Dakota Indian Foundation in Chamberlain, South Dakota contains an English language version of "The Prairie Dogs," unaccompanied by a Lakota text. It is not dated, and it differs slightly from the English translation given here. At the end of the narrative portion of this alternate version, however, Makula provides a series of historical and descriptive comments on the warrior societies. Makula's concluding reminiscences found only in the holdings of the Ella C. Deloria Research Project at the Foundation, are reproduced here as Deloria remembered and wrote them.

Now these societies were thus instituted long ago by the animal spirits, and laid aside, foreordained, for the men-on-earth. In time one of them was revealed to a man who sought a spiritual message while fasting; and strangely, they say it was the *Tokala* Society first. Then others discovered the other societies and soon the Dakotas had all six of them. They were the oldest. Such later ones as *Sotka-yuha, Wicinska* [White-Marked] (which they say was derived from the wolves, but in later times certainly), *Kak'ega* [Scrapers], and [*Ska Śunkakanyanka*] the White Horse Riders—all these were very much later. They were diffused in their organization and did not have such established forms or rules as the others. When these came into being, people were introducing all sorts of things at will. The White Horse Riders especially is of very recent origin—since the Wounded Knee and Messiah religious difficulties.

Kak'ega societies didn't use drums. Instead they took the flat part of an elk's horn, and on one edge they cut deep grooves, like the edge of a long-toothed saw. These they held in their hands, and keeping time with the singing, they played on the saw edge by striking it with a single downward stroke away from the person. There was no return stroke with the direction reversal, i.e. towards the person, but always away from it. *Ka*—with the striking motion away from the actor; *k'ega*—grating on something with a hard surface. That is where they got their name.

Several beautiful songs of the oldest societies are still remembered. Here is a Crow Keeper's [*Kangi-yuha*] song:

1. Kola, akicita waun na
   He un aiyapi waun we lo!

   Friend, as a soldier (police) I am,
   And therefore I lead a life of criticism!

2. Kola, akicita waun na
   He wanapeya waun we lo!

   Friend, as a soldier I live,
   And that (means) I live to be avoided! (to be feared; to
   cause them to dodge or run from me.)

3. Kola, akicita waun na
   He wana henamala ye lo!

   Friend, as a soldier I live,
   And that means that I am now as good as non-existent!

4. Kola, akicita waun na
   He wanagi ca waun we lo!

   Friend, as a soldier I live,
   And that means it is as a ghost that I live! (Meaning he is
   virtually dead; being exposed to danger constantly.)

In later times various Dakotas conceived the societies in dreams through *wakanpi* [animal spirits] and then instituted them in the various bands. After the *wakan-ḣaġapi* [sanctifying rite] in which the founder related his vision and then proved his right by supernatural acts, then the members feasted and sang at their meetings. Later they added the dance to their activities.

The *Tokala* was founded perhaps several hundred years ago. My grandfather told me the story of its founding when I was a very small boy. The man's name is not remembered; it is too long ago. This is the story:

A man had a vision; and he dreamed about a society in which the *Tokala* was to be the guardian spirit. He therefore proceeded to reveal it to the people. His dream was identified with the Thunder.

So one afternoon, when the Thunders were returning *maka-mani* (travelling on foot, that is, so low that they seemed to be touching the ground), he had four new tipis erected facing the west. Then he had a large tipi of preparation facing those four, i.e. facing east, at a short distance from them.

In the tipi he had his singers whom he had trained to sing his newly composed songs.

Also he had his special officers in the tipi. There were four lances borne by four specially picked men; and four leaders, the founder being one of these, and he carried the pipe. Then there were two whips of special make carried by two picked men; and there were two "Praisers," chaste young women picked to give the screech owl cry at the correct instances.

All the singers and the four leaders, the four lance bearers, the two whip bearers, and the two chaste young women, sat in the tipi of preparation, while the thunder rumbled threateningly behind them, as if assenting to the undertaking. The people, forming a great semi-circle, stood facing the west, behind the four smaller tipis. In front of them were great quantities of food ready for the feast.

Soon the singers began singing softly the song the founder had taught them, which he in turn was taught by the *wakan* [spirit] who instructed him to do this:

1. He wakanyan inapa nunwe,
   He wakanyan inapa nunwe,

Mitacannunpa he tokeya inapa nunwe—
Kola heyape lo!

May that emerge, go out from here, in a sacred manner,
May that emerge, go out from here, in a sacred manner,
May my pipe go out from here first—

Thus have my friends spoken! (Friends are the Thunders.)

2. Repeat first stanza.
3. He wakanyan inapa nunwe,
   He wakanyan inapa nunwe,
   Sungila waste he tokeya inapa nunwe— .
   Kola heyape lo!

May that one go out from here in a sacred manner,
May that one go out from here in a sacred manner,
May a good red fox first go out from here—
Thus have my friends spoken!

4. Repeat third stanza.

With that song, the founder first emerged from the tipi of preparation holding a beautiful new pipe with the handle wrapped in a red fox skin and extended out so that for a moment all the people saw was a pipe coming out.

Following him came the three other leaders, and then the lance bearers and the two whip bearers, and then the two beautiful girls, and lastly the singers. They were very formidable in their paint and their haircut (not the women), and as a body they spun around until they faced the west, and the four lance bearers held their lances extended toward the west in the face of the storm, while the singers sang and the pipe was held to the Thunders:

1. He wakan ca kinyan ye waye,
   He wakan ca kinyan ye waye,
   He wahukeza wakan ca kinyan u waye!

That is a sacred object which I send flying (to you),
That is a sacred object which I send flying (to you),
That is a sacred lance which I send flying (to you)!

2. Repeat first stanza.

3. He wakan ca kinyan u waye,
   He wakan ca kinyan u waye,
   He wahukeza wakan ca kinyan u waye!

   That is a sacred object which I cause to come flying,
   That is a sacred object which I cause to come flying,
   That is a sacred lance which I cause to come flying!

4. He wakan ca kinyan ye waye
   He wakan ca kinyan ye waye
   He wahukeza wakan ca kinyan ye waye!

   That is a sacred object which I cause to go flying,
   That is a sacred lance which I cause to go flying!

Then the singers sang again:

   Kola lena aglinazin ye,
   Wanyaka yo!

   Our friends returning have come to a stand nearby,
   See them! (meaning the lances.)

   Then the four lance bearers went and each planted his lance before one of the four tipis and stood holding them, facing the west
while the singers sang another song:

   He wakinyan oaku kin wanzikzi mitawa ye,
   Wakinyan oyate kin heyape!

   It is that an occasional one of the thunder-returnings
      is mine,
   The Thunder people have said so! (meaning he can
      influence an occasional thunderstorm.)

   Then the pipe bearer and the three other leaders entered one of
the tipis, and the singers sang:

1. Mitacannunpa kin,
   Howokawinh hiyaya nunwe,
   Wanlaka nunwe!

My pipe,
May it circle about the camp;
May you witness it!

Then the lance bearers all entered the second tipi, and the singers sang:

2. Mitawapaha kin,
Howokawinh hiyaya nunwe,
Wanlaka nunwe!

My lance,
May it circle about the camp;
May you witness it!

Then the two whip bearers entered the third tipi, and the singers sang the third stanza:

3. Mitaicahape kin,
Howokawinh hiyaya nunwe,
Wanlaka nunwe!

My whip,
May it circle about the camp;
May you witness it!
(The whip was symbolical not only of war and the chase, but also of the police duty of the members. The common name for whip is *icapsinte*.)

Then the two chaste women entered the last tipi and the singers sang the last stanza:

4. Mitawicaaglata kin,
Howokawawinh hiyaya nunwe,
Wanlaka nunwe!

My cheerer (screech owl crier),
May she circle about the camp;
May you witness her!

Then they came out of the tipi after a little while, and the leader stepped out in the center where everyone could see him, and he silently pointed the pipe mouthpiece towards the Thunders, offering it for them to smoke. And whereas when the ceremony began, the storm was so nearly on the camp that an occasional rain drop struck the eye of a spectator sharply, causing him to be blinded for a moment, the Thunders changed their minds, the clouds split in two in the very center, and one half moved to the south around them, and the other half moved to the north around them, only to reunite in the east behind them and to travel eastward with more fury and force than before.

That was a miracle which made the people believe that the founder had supernatural power, for he was leagued with the Thunders which promised him supremacy over at least an occasional storm. The man now led his group around the camp, and everyone looked on with awe.

Afterwards the food was eaten, and the ceremony was at an end. Then several men asked for membership, and those whose records merited their acceptance were taken on; but after that, the new members only entered on invitation.

I, [Makula], joined the *Tokala*.

There was a man of the *Hunkpapaya*, a member of the *Wakpokiya* sub-band. And he was said to *Wakantanka ihanbla* (He dreamed God, i.e. saw the Great Spirit himself in his vision.) His name was Hitunkasan-mato (Weasel Bear).

Four of us were invited at the same time, because there were four men out. That group generally had about forty members. Kinyan-hiyaya (He Goes by Flying), Mato-hlo-inyanka (Bear Runs Growling), Paunka (He causes to fall by pushing against), and myself were invited. And the official crier from the *Tokala* tipi went around calling our names one day. Then he would say, "Maconala ca icaśtan mayahinapikte!" 'There are few of me, so you shall meet me face to face!' (as though the society itself, as an animate thing, were talking.)

They didn't ask us first if we would accept. They simply challenged us outright by thus heralding; and one who was brave enough to meet the material obligations and didn't have the prestige among the people to raise from them whatever he lacked at the time, and so dared to refuse the invitation, was regarded as very low in the tribe.

The societies were especially careful whom they picked because they didn't care to be ignored if they issued an invitation. In all our cases it was a fortunate choice. My father was very much elated that I should be picked and set out at once to assemble all the goods required for making a suitable entry.

After this announcement nothing much happened until the next official meeting at which time we were taken into the society. It was kept alive in the tribe for the primary purpose of making its members take on fresh courage from time to time, so as to keep up their standards of manliness.

Orthographic Notes

In *Ella Deloria's The Buffalo People*, as in *Deer Women and Elk Men: The Lakota Narratives of Ella Deloria*, and *Ella Deloria's Iron Hawk*, I have modified her orthography to accord with the current predominance of the Buechel system on the Lakota reservations in schools, colleges, and newspapers.

The following examples occur in "The Buffalo People":

Deloria's Spelling	This Edition
Héc'eš mak'á ak9l nahą́hcį tuwénihcį ų́sni k'ų (unit 1).	Heceś maka akanl nahanhcin tuwenihcin unśni k'un (unit 1). Deloria provides the syllabic accent for eveɪy word. I have removed these accent marks, since they are already known to most speakers and because in most cases Lakota words are accented on the second syllable.
akǫl, nahǫhcį (unit 1).	The subscript hook, nasalizing the preceding vowel, is here written simply as n, in line with current practice, akanl, nahanhcin.

icakiẓeśni (unit 16), *ạpetu* (unit 3).

Deloria does not mark medial c, k, p, t. Since the Lakota sounds do not correspond to the English pronunciations of these letters, I have marked them as Buechel does, *ićakiẓeśni, anṗetu*. When the consonants are juxtaposed, the second receives the medial pronunciation while the first is aspirated: *opta* (unit 3), *hecetkiya* (unit 18).

hec͟eś, mak͟a, t͟awicu (unit 1), *p͟ehị* (unit 6).

Deloria marks the aspirate sounds of c, k, p, and t with a diacritic (͟) taking up a separate space.above and following the preceding letter. Since the aspirates c, k, p, t are more common than the medial pronunciations of these letters, I have left them unmarked, as Buechel does: *heceś, maka, tawicu* (unit 1), *pehin* (unit 6).

kig.nala (unit 7).

Deloria employs a period in "clusters of sonants" to indicate "a very weak articulation of the following vowel" (*Dakota Grammar* 5). The period also marks a slight pause between the consonants. I have removed these periods throughout, since most readers will not recognize their purpose: *kignala* rather than *kig.nala* (unit 7).

The following diacritics mark sounds that may be found in the opening units of "The Buffalo People" and throughout this edition:

When ḣ is gutteralized, it has a dot above it: *nahanḣcin* (unit 1).
When ġ is gutteralized, it has a dot above it: *imaġaġa* (unit 3).
When ċ sounds like g in gentle, it has a dot above it: *ċisċila* (unit 109).

When k̇ sounds like g in give, it has a dot above it:
k̇ici (unit 1).
When ṗ sounds like b in bill, it has a dot above it:
anṗetu (unit 3).
When ṫ sounds like d in day, it has a dot above it:
ṫuweniḣcin (unit 1).
Unmarked c sounds like ch in chair:
heceya (unit 1).
When ś sounds like sh in ship, it has an acute accent mark:
wicaśa (unit 1).
When ż sounds like Russian zh or French j, it has a dot
above it:
wanżi (unit 5).
Unmarked s and z correspond to the same letters in English:
saṗsaṗa (unit 6), *zizi* (unit 12).
The glottal stop, a brief cessation of breath, is marked by ',
occupying a separate space between letters:
k'un (unit 1), *ic'iyin* (unit 3).

Works Cited

Artaud, Antonin. "No More Masterpieces." Trans. Mary Caroline Richards. *Dramatic Theory and Criticism*. Ed. Bernard F. Dukore. New York: Holt, Rinehart, and Winston, 1974. 760–66.

Beckwith, Martha. "Mythology of the Oglala Dakota." *Journal of American Folklore* 43 (1930): 339–439.

Black Bear, Sr., Ben and R. D. Theisz. *Songs and Dances of the Lakota*. Aberdeen, South Dakota: North Plains Press, 1976.

Black Elk. *The Sacred Pipe*. Ed. Joseph Epes Brown. New York: Penguin, 1971.

——. *The Sixth Grandfather*. Ed. Raymond J. DeMallie. Lincoln: U of Nebraska P, 1984.

Blish, Helen. *A Pictographic History of the Oglala Sioux*. Lincoln: U of Nebraska P, 1967.

Buechel, Eugene, S. J. *A Dictionary of the Teton Dakota Sioux Language*. Pine Ridge, South Dakota. Red Cloud Lakota Language and Cultural Center, 1970.

——. *A Grammar of Lakota*. Rosebud, South Dakota: Rosebud Educational Society, 1939.

——. *Lakota Tales and Texts*. Ed. Paul Manhart, S. J. Pine Ridge, South Dakota: Red Cloud Lakota Language and Cultural Center, 1978.

Bunge, Robert. *An American Urphilosophie: An American Philosophy BP (Before Pragmatism)*. Lanham, MD: University P of America, 1984.

Bushotter, George. *Teton Myths*. Ed. and trans. Ella Deloria. ca. 1937; MS 30 (x8c.3), Boas Collection. Philadelphia: American Philosophical Society.

Catches, Pete. Lecture. Loxahatchee Historical Society. Jupiter, Florida, 20 April 1990.

Catlin, George. *Letters and Notes on the North American Indians*. Ed. Michael Macdonald Mooney. New York: Crown, 1975.

Collier, John. *Indians of the Americas.* 1947; rpt. New York: New American Library, 1975.

Culin, Stewart. *Games of the North American Indians.* New York: Dover, 1975.

Deloria, Ella. "The Buffalo People." "Dakota Tales in Colloquial Style." 1937; MS 30 (X8a.16), Boas Collection. Philadelphia: American Philosophical Society.

———. "The Buffalo People" ("Generation Story"). Deloria Family Collection 271:18–295:42. Chamberlain, South Dakota: Dakota Indian Foundation.

———. "Camp Circle Society." Unpublished manuscript. Pierre: South Dakota State Archives.

———. "Colloquial Dakota." "Dakota Ethnographic and Conversational Texts." 1937; MS 30 (X8a.7), Boas Collection. Philadelphia: American Philosophical Society.

———. *Dakota Grammar.* 1941; rpt. Vermillion, South Dakota: Dakota Press, 1982.

———. "Dakota Tales in Colloquial Style." 1937; MS 30 (X8a.16), Boas Collection. Philadelphia: American Philosophical Society.

———. *Dakota Texts.* 1932; rpt. New York: AMS Press, 1974.

———. *Dakota Texts.* Vermillion, South Dakota: Dakota Press, 1978.

———. "Dakota Texts from the Minnesota Manuscript." 1941; MS 30 (X8a.17), Boas Collection. Philadelphia: American Philosophical Society.

———. "Dakota Texts from the Sword Manuscript." 1876–1909, 1938; MS 30 (X8a.18), Boas Collection. Philadelphia: American Philosophical Society.

———. "The Prairie Dogs." "Dakota Tales in Colloquial Style." 1937; MS 30 (X8a.16), Boas Collection. Philadelphia: American Philosophical Society.

———. "A Sioux Captive Rescued by His Wife." "Old Dakota Legends." 1937; MS 30 (X8a.21), Boas Collection. Philadelphia: American Philosophical Society.

———. *Speaking of Indians.* Vermillion, South Dakota: State Publishing, 1983.

———. "Stake Carriers." "Dakota Tales." 1937; MS 30 (X8a.15), Boas Collection. Philadelphia: American Philosophical Society.

———. "Standing Holy." "Old Dakota Legends." 1937; MS 30 (X8a.21), Boas Collection. Philadelphia: American Philosophical Society.

———. "Teton Myths" (The George Bushotter collection). MS 30 (X8c.3), Boas Collection. Philadelphia: American Philosophical Society.

———. *Waterlily.* Lincoln: U of Nebraska P, 1988.

———. "A Woman Captive and Her Baby." "Old Dakota Legends." 1937; MS 30 (X8a.21), Boas Collection. Philadelphia: American Philosophical Society.

Deloria, Ella, Wallace Eagle Shield, and Sophie Many Deeds. Discussion on teaching the Lakota language. Audiotape no. 383. 26, 27 March 1969. Vermillion, South Dakota: South Dakota Oral History Center.

DeMallie, Raymond J. Afterword. *Waterlily* by Ella Deloria. Lincoln: U of Nebraska P, 1988. 233–44.

Densmore, Frances. *Teton Sioux Music.* 1918; rpt. New York: Da Capo, 1972.

Dorsey, George A. and Alfred L. Kroeber. *Traditions of the Arapaho.* Chicago: Field Columbian Museum, 1903.

Fire Thunder, Cecilia. Address. Oglala Women's Society. Videocassette. 7 September 1988. Oglala Lakota College Archives.

Goethe, Johann Wofgang von. "On Truth and Probability in Works of Art." Trans. Simon Gray Ward. *Dramatic Theory and Criticism.* Ed. Bernard F. Dukore. New York: Holt, Rinehart, and Winston, 1974. 477–81.

Goodman, Ronald. *Lakota Star Knowledge: Studies in Lakota Stellar Theology.* Rosebud, South Dakota: Sinte Gleska University, 1992.

Grinnell, George Bird. *By Cheyenne Campfires* Lincoln: U of Nebraska Press, 1971.

Grotowski, Jerzy. "The Theatre's New Testament." Interview with Eugene Barba. Trans. Jorgen Andersen and Judy Barba. *Dramatic Theory and Criticism*. Ed. Bernard F. Dukore. New York: Holt Rinehart, and Winston, 1974, 978–95.

Hegel, Georg Wilhelm Friedrich. "The End of Art." Trans. Bernard Bosanquet. *Dramatic Theory and Criticism*. Ed. Bernard F. Dukore. New York: Holt, Rinehart, and Winston, 1974. 522–26.

Hymes, Dell. *"In vain I tried to tell you."* Philadelphia: U of Pennsylvania P, 1981.

Hyde, George E. *Spotted Tail's Folk: A History of the Brule Sioux*. Norman: U of Oklahoma P, 1974.

Jahner, Elaine A. "Cognitive Style in Oral Literature." *Language and Style* 15 (1982): 32–51.

———. Introduction. *Lakota Myth* by James R. Walker. Lincoln: U of Nebraska P, 1983. 1–40.

Laubin, Reginald and Gladys. *Indian Dances of North America: Their Importance to Indian Life*. Norman: U of Oklahoma P, 1977.

Longinus. "On the Sublime." Trans. W. Rhys Roberts. *Dramatic Theory and Criticism*. Ed. Bernard F. Dukore. New York: Holt, Rinehart, and Winston, 1974. 76–82.

Macgregor, Gordon. *Warriors Without Weapons: A Study of the Society and Personality Development of the Pine Ridge Sioux*. Chicago: U of Chicago P, 1946.

McLaughlin, Marie L. *Myths and Legends of the Sioux*. Bismarck, North Dakota: Bismarck Tribune, 1916.

Murray, Jannette K. "Ella Deloria: A Biographical Sketch and Literary Analysis." Unpublished dissertation. University of North Dakota, 1974.

Picotte, Agnes. Biographical Sketch of the Author. *Waterlily* by Ella Deloria. Lincoln: U of Nebraska P, 1988. 229–31.

Picotte, Agnes and Paul N. Pavich. Introduction. *Dakota Texts* by Ella Deloria. Vermillion, South Dakota: Dakota Press, 1978. ix–xi.

———. Introduction. *Speaking of Indians* by Ella Deloria. Vermillion, South Dakota: State Publishing, 1983, xi–xix.

Powers, Marla N. *Oglala Women: Myth, Ritual, and Reality*. Chicago: U of Chicago P, 1986.

Prucha, Francis Paul, ed. *Americanizing the American Indians: Writings by "The Friends of the Indian" 1880–1900*. Lincoln: U of Nebraska P, 1978.

Rice, Julian. *Black Elk's Story: Distinguishing its Lakota Purpose*. Albuquerque: U of New Mexico P, 1991.

———. *Deer Women and Elk Men: The Lakota Narratives of Ella Deloria*. Albuquerque: U of New Mexico P, 1992.

———. *Ella Deloria's Iron Hawk*. Albuquerque: U of New Mexico P, 1993.

———. "Narrative Styles in *Dakota Texts*." *On the Translation of Native American Oral Literatures*. Ed. Brian Swann. Washington: Smithsonian Institution Press, 1992. 276–92.

Schiller, Friedrich. "The Stage as a Moral Institution." Trans. anonymous. *Dramatic Theory and Criticism*. Ed. Bernard F. Dukore. New York: Holt, Rinehart, and Winston, 1974. 440–45.

Standing Bear, Luther. *Land of the Spotted Eagle*. Lincoln: U of Nebraska P, 1978.

Strindberg, August. "Preface to *Miss Julie*." Trans. E. M. Sprinchorn. *Dramatic Theory and Criticism*. Ed. Bernard F. Dukore. New York: Holt, Rinehart, and Winston, 1974. 564–74.

Sword, George. "Dakota Texts from the Sword manuscript." 1876–1909. MS 30 (X8a.18), Boas Collection. Philadelphia: American Philosophical Society.

Tedlock, Dennis. *The Spoken Word and the Work of Interpretation.* Philadelphia: U of Pennsylvania P, 1983.

Utley, Robert M. *The Last Days of the Sioux Nation.* New Haven: Yale U P, 1963.

Walker, James R. *Lakota Myth.* Ed. Elaine A. Jahner. Lincoln: U of Nebraska P, 1983.

——. *Lakota Society.* Ed. Raymond J. DeMallie. Lincoln: U of Nebraska P, 1982.

——. *The Sun Dance and Other Ceremonies of the Oglala Division of the Teton Dakota.* 1917; rpt. New York: AMS Press, 1979.

Wissler, Clark. "Societies and Ceremonial Associations in the Oglala Division of the Teton Dakota." *Anthropological Papers of the American Museum of Natural History* 11.2 (1912): 1–99.

Index